To Maliol

SPARROWS IN THE HALL

ENQUIRIES INTO THE PAST FAMILIES OF
BRIAN DOUGLAS HAMMOND AND SHEILA ISOBEL AFFLECK

Best wishes

from

Sheila + Brian

First published in the United Kingdom in 2015 by

The Cloister House Press

ISBN 978-1-909465-26-8

SPARROWS IN THE HALL

ENQUIRIES INTO THE PAST FAMILIES OF
BRIAN DOUGLAS HAMMOND AND SHEILA ISOBEL AFFLECK

Brian Douglas Hammond

Quotation from *Ecclesiastical History* (2,13) - completed 731AD
The Venerable Bede (c673AD-735AD)

'Talis,'[inquiens,] 'mihi videtur, rex, vita hominum praesens in terris, ad comparationem eius quod nobis incertum est temporis, quale cum te residente ad coenam cum ducibus ac ministris tuis tempore brumali, accenso quidem foco in medio et calido effecto coenaculo, furentibus autem foris per omnia turbinibus hiemalium pluviarum vel nivium, adveniensque unus passerum domum citissime pervolaverit qui cum per unum ostium ingrediens, mox per aliud exierit. Ipso quidem tempore quo intus est, hiemis tempestate non tangitur, sed tamen parvissimo spatio serenitatis ad momentum excurso, mox de hieme in hiemem regrediens, tuis oculis elabitur. Ita haec vita hominum ad modicum apparet; quid autem sequatur, quidve praecesserit, prorsus ignoramus.'

The present life of men on earth, O King, as compared with the whole length of time which is unknowable to us, seems to me to be like this: as if, when you are sitting at dinner with your chiefs and ministers in wintertime...one of the sparrows from outside flew very quickly through the hall; as if it came in one door and soon went out through another. In that actual time it is indoors it is not touched by the winter's storm; but yet the tiny period of calm is over in a moment, and having come out of the winter it soon returns to the winter and slips out of your sight. Man's life appears to be more or less like this; and of what may follow it or what preceded it we are absolutely ignorant.

Hence the title of this document: *Sparrows in the Hall.*

Contents

Front cover: Brian Hammond and Sheila Affleck on their wedding day, St Mary's Church, Bridgwater, Somerset, 30th March 1963

Back cover: Brian and Sheila at their Golden Wedding Anniversary, Carlyon Bay Hotel, St Austell, Cornwall, 13th April 2013

Book I

The Ancestors of Brian Douglas Hammond

Introduction

My four grandparents came from widely differing areas of the United Kingdom but they met in the last few years of the nineteenth century in London

Harry Charles Hammond was born in Andover, Hampshire, in 1857. His ancestors had lived in the area, which is famous for its prehistoric and Roman settlements, for at least two centuries, but his parents brought the family of two brothers to Canning Town, East London, in the 1860s. A few years later, a third and then a fourth son were born

Laura Hitchin, who became Harry's wife in 1900, was born in Stourbridge, Worcestershire. She retained to the end of her life a strong West Midlands accent. But her grandfather, Francis, was born in Shropshire and the family appear to have lived in the shadow of the Wrekin, and near the ruined Roman town of *Viroconium Cornoviorum* (Wroxeter), since at least the beginning of the 18th century.

Coulson Douglas Defty came from Sunderland and he spoke with a strong Geordie accent. His family is well documented back to a certain Robert Deft, born in Gateshead in the middle of the 17th century. It is an unusual surname and is still much restricted to the North-East. Some earlier examples are found in Yorkshire. The reasons for his intriguing first name and equally important middle name will be discussed later.

My fourth grandparent, Catherine Tait Hood, was born in Aberdeen, well and truly in ancient Pictland; but some of her ancestors, the Taits, originated in Shetland and her grandfather, John Hood had journeyed to Nova Scotia in the early 19th century and there married a woman of German descent before returning to Scotland. Amazingly (to me) I never could detect the slightest hint of a Scots accent in my grandmother's speech, although I knew her well until she died in 1950, just before my 21st birthday.

In fact, all four grandparents survived into my early adulthood. I regret very strongly that I did not question them more closely about their very interesting origins. My grandfathers died in 1945 and 1948 but Laura Hitchin survived until 1955. She had been quite forthcoming about her family but unfortunately, because of a foolish family quarrel, I last saw her in 1951.

7

Here they are in a photograph, probably taken at my parents' wedding in 1927. The Hammonds are to the left, the Deftys to the right.

I have spent twenty-five years of research, starting in the year of my mother's death in 1982, to reach my present state of knowledge. I have of course been helped by the efforts of other researchers, but I have only one close relation, my cousin Joyce, surviving my mother's death.

The Hammonds of Andover

The surname is a very common one, found in most English counties. The derivation is German or Frankish, and appears to have been brought to this country at the time of the Norman Conquest. It is related to the German *Heimat* and the Anglo-Saxon *ham* (= 'home'). It was common as a first name in the Middle Ages and appeared in many forms - even as *Hamlet,* the name of Shakespeare's son. A rich Lord Mayor of London, friend of the future Edward III, was known as *Hamo de Chigwell* and in 1201 the name *Hamund de Gosham* is found, relating to Gooseham in Cornwall. As a young boy my nickname was either *Hammie* or *Hammo.* In the 20th century an author named *Hammond Innis* wrote popular adventure novels, but as a first name Hammond is now quite rare.

John Haman the Serge Weaver

The first Hammond I can be reasonably sure of being a direct ancestor is a certain John Haman (this is how his name appears on his will) who died in Andover in 1719. The Andover burial register shows:

'13 June 1719 John Hamond was buried only in woollen.'

The words 'in woollen' refers to a law that was in force at the time, which was intended to protect the English wool trade.

I have conjectured that John was born about 1655, for in 1680 he married Mary Drew, daughter of Thomas and Mary Drew. These latter both made wills in 1698, respectively 19th January and 18th February. Mary describes herself as a widow and made her will soon after her husband's death. Mary, John Haman's wife, inherited a considerable sum.

Mary bore John 11 children but four died in infancy, including twins, Katherine and Ann, who, baptised on the 26th November 1699, were buried a few weeks later.

Below is shown John's family, as revealed from his will, which was composed only four days before his burial.

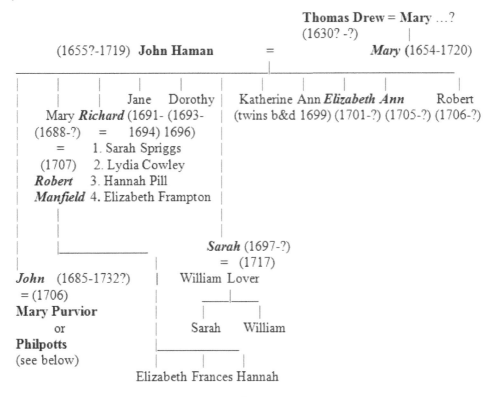

9

Those names shown above in *italics* are mentioned in John Haman's will. It is so unusual that I reproduce it below, exactly as it was written:

June 9th 1719

I John Haman Beqeive to my Son John
Haman y^e Tenement that Richard Butcher

For he and his aires for ever

Lives in and the door place shall be in ye old
place and the outlet that belongs to it
And the out let y^t belongs to this house
Shall be ten foot at each end after the
Petision is up there shall [be] one yard left
Clear for the Passage and he shall come
Up ten foot and I bequeive to my Son
Richard One Shilling and I bequeive
One Shilling to my Daughter Sarah
Lover I bequeive to my Daughter Elizabeth
Haman One Shilling I bequeive to my Daug
=hter Ann Hamman One Shilling and to
Robert Manfeild One Shilling and I
Leave my beloved Wife Mary Haman
Executrix

I declare that
This is my last
Will and Testament

Witness my hand John Barrett   **H**   Senr
Thomas Paine   The mark of John Haman
Mary
Witness the hand of Mary[?] Bran….[?]
The mark of Elias Goodall   **X**

[Reverse of Page]
I give to My Beloved Wife Mary Hamon
The Tenement She now lives in to be att
Her own Disposing
1720 Hamon Johis
        Do
J Hamon
Andover
Loss[?] Arthi[?]
1720
23 May 1720   Jurat Extrix et quod bona et Sutta[?] defuncti non extendunt Ad
Re…[?] ut redit   Coram me R Bridroacke

This document is quite unlike any other will that I have come across.

First of all, in contrast to all other wills of the 17th and 18th centuries that I have seen, it dispenses with the usual assertion that the testator, although weak in body, is of sound mind. Next there are no instructions as to the burial of the body. Then there is the script: the letters are round, almost child-like, unlike the hands of the educated writers of the time, which are often quite difficult for the modern reader to interpret.

But it is the phraseology, the immediateness of the message, which are so striking. Here we can almost hear the voice of the speaker, transcribed by a person who seems only slightly removed from the illiteracy of the testator. Take the spelling: 'bequeive', 'Petision', 'aires'; the grammar: 'for *he*', 'and *he* shall come up'; the repetition: 'and the outlet that belongs to it And the out let y[t] belongs to this house'; and the general confusion in the description of the tenement.
I find myself moved by this close contact with my ancestor.

Yet, despite its almost primitive nature, the document seems to have been proved, judging by the Latin text of an educated person - perhaps a local lawyer or priest - found on the reverse of the will.

It can be assumed that John's eldest daughter, Mary, died some time between 1707, the year of her marriage to Robert Manfield, and the date of the will. Manfield himself died in 1720, leaving a memorandum which was witnessed by among others the same Elias Goodall whose name also appears on John Haman's. As Robert Manfield, John's son-in-law, is described as a serge weaver, it may be that John Haman followed the same trade, which was widespread in Andover at that time.

John Hammond, the Alexanders, the Philpotts and the Purveyors

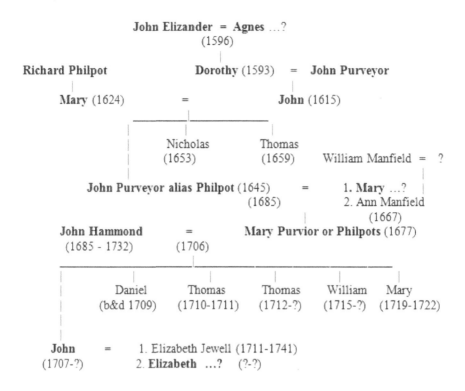

Now the story becomes far more complicated.

The main problem is: why do the children of John and Mary Purveyor bear alternative surnames? The clue seems to be that I have been able to find no marriage date for John Purveyor and Mary. This must surely mean that their children were born out of wedlock, or that there was an irregular marriage. The alias is even carried to the next generation - Mary, John Hammond's wife. This seems strange if the relationship is as I deduce. There is, however, always the possibility that the record has become obscured because of adoption by other members of the family.

It is noticeable that of John Hammond's six recorded children, three died at a young age. Two marriages are recorded for John Purveyor (b 1645). The fact that the second - to Ann Manfield - occurred when he was forty suggests that his first wife died in childbirth. There may indeed have been other children born to the first marriage, whose names are not recorded, or perhaps Mary had a series of miscarriages, culminating in her death.

Finally, it is interesting how over the generations a surname denoting an occupation has become changed: Purveyor > Purvior; and a common first name can be distorted to the point where it is almost unrecognisable: Alexander > Elizander.

The Romsey Connection

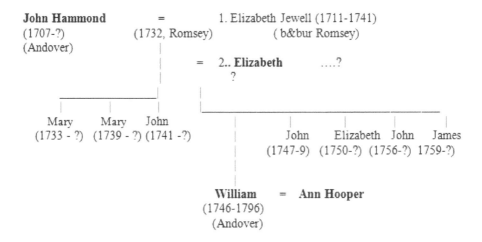

In 1947, in the company of some friends, I was on my way to the West Country on the old Southern Railway line. Just past Salisbury we began to see a series of bill-boards beside the line: 'You are approaching the Strong Country,' 'You are near the Strong Country.' This continued until we arrived at Romsey where the boards announced 'You are in the Strong Country.' It was then that we discovered that the 'Strong' indicated a brand of cider. A later encounter with Romsey was to prove more interesting.

I had great trouble with this section of the story. Having found that the line back to William Hammond (b1746) was secure, I was unable at first to discover his parentage, not helped by the fact that the Andover registers are incomplete for the 18th century. A number of Elizabeths, married to a Hammond, had to be rejected and it was not until there was confirmation from the Romsey register that the John Hammond who married Elizabeth Jewell came from Andover that I could be sure of having the right family. It is not clear how John came to meet Elizabeth, nor why she was buried in Romsey, for their three children were all baptized in Andover, where presumably the family was living.

Their first child, Mary, died and a second girl was also named Mary in 1739. In 1741 a third child, John was born, causing the death of his mother. Shortly after this, John Hammond must have married another Elizabeth, whose surname is unknown, (or perhaps they were unmarried) because William was born in 1746. Then a second John died after two years. Three more children were then born (including a third John) and they appear to have survived.

13

Reaching Back

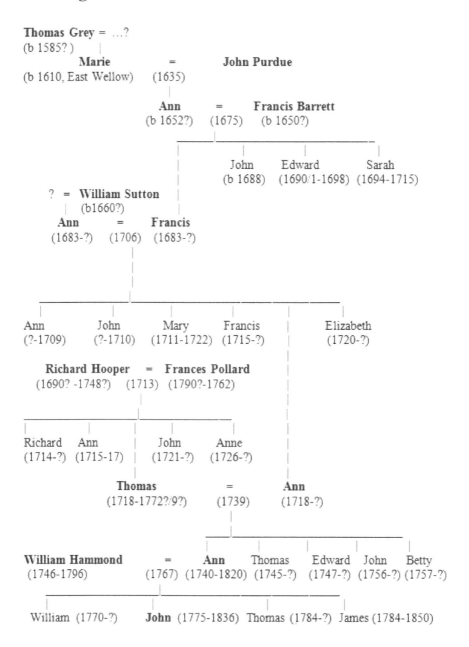

Thomas Grey = ...?
(b 1585?)

Marie = John Purdue
(b 1610, East Wellow) (1635)

Ann = Francis Barrett
(b 1652?) (1675) (b 1650?)

John   Edward   Sarah
(b 1688) (1690/1-1698) (1694-1715)

? = William Sutton
(b1660?)

Ann = Francis
(1683-?) (1706) (1683-?)

Ann   John   Mary   Francis   Elizabeth
(?-1709) (?-1710) (1711-1722) (1715-?)   (1720-?)

Richard Hooper = Frances Pollard
(1690? -1748?) (1713) (1790?-1762)

Richard   Ann   John   Anne
(1714-?) (1715-17)   (1721-?)   (1726-?)

Thomas   =   Ann
(1718-1772?/9?)   (1739)   (1718-?)

William Hammond   =   Ann   Thomas   Edward   John   Betty
(1746-1796)   (1767) (1740-1820) (1745-?)   (1747-?) (1756-?) (1757-?)

William (1770-?)   John (1775-1836) Thomas (1784-?) James (1784-1850)

This trawl back again to the 1590s reveals the usual sad loss of young children but there is unfortunately nothing in the records to reveal the causes of such deaths. Measles is often quoted as the usual suspect but bad sanitary conditions must have played their part.

But there are increasing signs of a more human approach in the registers to the lives of ordinary people and snatches of information break the surface. For example, the recording of the baptisms of the children of Francis Barrett's and Ann Sutton's children is accompanied by the word 'jnr' after Francis' name, indicating that his father was still alive (and presumably still thought capable of fathering children.) Another comment relating to Ann Hammond (née Hooper) states in the Parish Register on her death that she was 'of the Post-house 81 years'. Ages are not always mentioned, even as late as 1820. There is, however, a more interesting development which comes to light in this section of the narrative: the change in the calendar. It is worth digressing for a moment to examine this development.

In mediaeval times dates were usually indicated by the regnal year of the reigning monarch and the nearest church festival. This practice can be seen to have survived in some of the wills to which I shall be referring later. Confusingly, the start of the year could be said to be either on the 25th December or 25th March. At the time of the Reformation in the Book of Common Prayer the start of the year was fixed on the 25th March. This was supposed to be both the time of the beginning of the creation of the world and also the time that Christ was conceived in the womb of the Virgin Mary.

In 1752 two changes were enacted by Parliament: first, England abandoned the Julian calendar and adopted the more accurate Gregorian system of calculation. This had been in use in Roman Catholic countries since 1582. The adoption of the Gregorian system necessitated losing eleven days and the day following 2nd September 1752 was renumbered 14th. This caused an outcry in certain quarters where people imagined they had lost part of their lives. ('Give us back our eleven days!')

Secondly, the beginning of the year was brought forward for 25th March to the preceding 1st January. This meant that January, February and most of March in that year became the first months of the new year. Many parishes, in anticipation of the new system, had begun to use it before the official time and so one occasionally finds entries like '5th February 1626/7'. We shall find several examples of this practice; one such is as follows:

Richard Hooper buried 27th January 1748/9

This means that he was buried 27th January 1749, but officially at that point (ie before the Act of 1752) the year did not end until 25th March.

Finally, before we move on to the next generation, it will be noticed that both Thomas and James seem to have been born in 1784. In fact, they were both *baptized* on 25th December 1784. We do not have their dates of birth. They may therefore have been twins; on the other hand, perhaps Thomas's baptism was delayed for some reason; although this happened in the case of two of my cousin's sons, it was unlikely in earlier times: children were baptized as early as possible to ensure their salvation.

The Knights

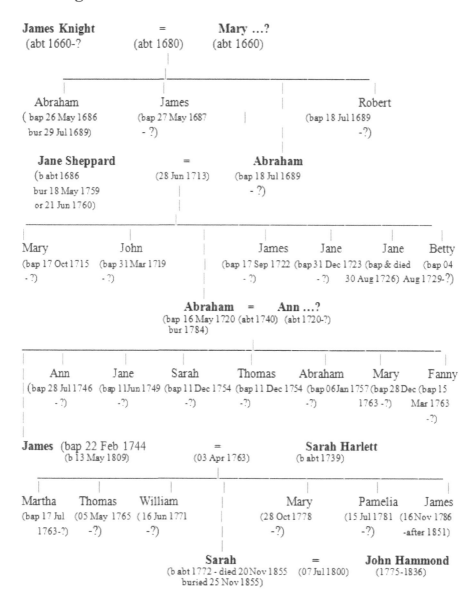

James Knight = **Mary ...?**
(abt 1660-?)   (abt 1680)   (abt 1660)

Abraham   James   Robert
(bap 26 May 1686   (bap 27 May 1687   (bap 18 Jul 1689
bur 29 Jul 1689)   - ?)   -?)

Jane Sheppard = **Abraham**
(b abt 1686   (28 Jun 1713)   (bap 18 Jul 1689
bur 18 May 1759   - ?)
or 21 Jun 1760)

Mary   John   James   Jane   Jane   Betty
(bap 17 Oct 1715   (bap 31 Mar 1719   (bap 17 Sep 1722   (bap 31 Dec 1723   (bap & died   (bap 04
- ?)   - ?)   - ?)   - ?)   30 Aug 1726)   Aug 1729-?)

Abraham = **Ann ...?**
(bap 16 May 1720   (abt 1740)   (abt 1720-?)
bur 1784)

Ann   Jane   Sarah   Thomas   Abraham   Mary   Fanny
(bap 28 Jul 1746   (bap 11 Jun 1749   (bap 11 Dec 1754   (bap 11 Dec 1754   (bap 06 Jan 1757   (bap 28 Dec   (bap 15
- ?)   -?)   -?)   -?)   -?)   1763 -?)   Mar 1763
-?)

James (bap 22 Feb 1744   =   **Sarah Harlett**
(b 13 May 1809)   (03 Apr 1763)   (b abt 1739)

Martha   Thomas   William   Mary   Pamelia   James
(bap 17 Jul   (05 May 1765   (16 Jun 1771   (28 Oct 1778   (15 Jul 1781   (16 Nov 1786
1763-?)   -?)   -?)   -?)   -?)   -after 1851)

Sarah   =   **John Hammond**
(b abt 1772 - died 20 Nov 1855   (07 Jul 1800)   (1775-1836)
buried 25 Nov 1855)

16

Several matters are worthy of mention at his point. In the first place, it will be noted that I have been unable to find the ancestries of several wives of the Knight family; and in two cases, not even their unmarried surnames have come to light.

Next, it will be seen that having lost one baby, Jane, Abraham Knight and Jane Sheppard saw their next, another Jane, die on the very day of her baptism.
Sarah and Thomas Knight, children of Abraham and Ann, were baptized on the same day. As with a previous example of this, we cannot be sure why this is so.
James Knight, the last name shown on the chart, is known to have survived after 1851 because he appears on the Census list for that year.
It is not shown on the chart, but we know that James and Sarah Knight were living at Charlton, a village just north of Andover, but in the same parish, because five of their seven children are noted as having been born there. This information is missing for the entries for Sarah and Pamelia.

The most interesting information to emerge from this portion of the narrative consists of an indenture involving Abraham Knight, born 1620. Here is the document in full. Part of it is a printed form; unnecessary parts have been struck through and essentials added in by hand:

> This Indenture made the twentyfifth Day of January in the fourth
> Year of the Reign of our Sovereign Lord George the second by
> the grace of God, of Great-Britain, France and Ireland, King,
> Defender of the Faith etc Annoq Dom 1730/1 Witnesseth that
> the Bailiff, Approved men & Burgesses of the Borough of
> Andevor [sic] Paying the Master hereinafter named the Sume of
> Six pounds & Cloathing the Apprentice hereinafter named (which
> the said master doth hereby acknowledge) out of the Charity
> money by them recd by vertue of a Bond entered into by them by
> Frances Dowlet Esqr dece'd with the Consent of Abraham
> Knight of Andevor [sic] aforesaid Labourer ffather of the Apprentice
> have put and placed, and by these   Presents do put and place Abraham
> Knight the younger a poor Child of the said Parish of Andevor [sic]
> Apprentice to James Ealls of Longparish in the County of Southton
> Taylor with him to dwell and serve from the Day of the Date of these
> Presents for the Term of Seven years. During all which term the said
> Apprentice his said Master faithfully shall serve in all Lawful Business,
> according to his Power Wit and Ability; and honestly, orderly and
> obediently in all Things demean and behave himself towards his said
> Master and all his during the said term. And the said James Ealls for
> himself, his Executors and Administrators, doth Covenant and Grant
> to and with the Said Bailliff Approved men and Burgesses and their
> Successors for the time being, by these Presents, that the said James
> Ealls the said Apprentice in the Art Trade or Mistery of a Taylor shall
> teach & instruct or cause to be taught and instruct'd And shall and will,

during all the term aforesaid, find, provide and allow the said Apprentice,
meet, competent, and sufficient Meat, Drink, and Apparel,
Lodging, Washing, and all other Things necessary and fit
for an Apprentice. And also shall and will so provide for the
said Apprentice, that he be not any way a Charge to the said
Parish of Andevor [sic] or Parishioners of the same;
but of and from all Charge shall and will save the said Parish
and Parishioners harmless and indemnified during the said term.
And at the end of the said term, shall and will make, provide,
allow, and deliver unto the said Apprentice double Apparel of
all sorts (that is to say) a good new Suit for the Holy-days, and
another for the Working-days. In Witness whereof, the Parties
above said to these present Indentures interchangeably have
put their Hands and Seals the Day and Year above-written.

Two Pence Paid

    Sealed and Delivered
    In the Presence of
    Abrahum Knight   James Ealls
    John Bishop
    John Hacker

This document has so much interest for the modern reader; most is self-evident, but perhaps a few comments may help.

The titles given to George the Second reveal that France was still thought of as being part of his territory, although the loss of Calais in 16th century made it nearly two centuries out of date! The mention of a regnal year is also archaic, although it has survived into modern times.
It is curious that *Andover* is spelled incorrectly (but consistently).
The old word *mistery* (< L *ministerium*) meaning *occupation,* was used in modern times by George Bernard Shaw in his play *St Joan.*
The insistence that the apprenticeship should not be a charge on the parish is consistent with the provisions of the Elizabethan Poor Law, still in operation at the time.
The payment of two pence (stamp duty) was abolished on cheques only towards the end of the 20th century.
It may appear surprising that Abraham Knight senior, although described as a labourer, was able to write, but it seems that uneducated men were quite often taught to sign their names. The writing of Abrahum (as he put it) seems more contrived than that of the other signatories

John Hammond, Ann Dumper and Sarah Knight

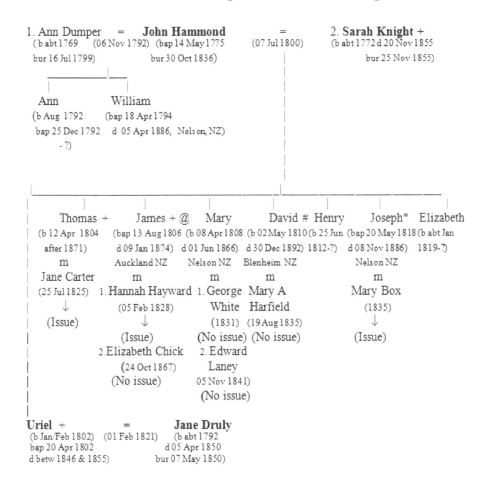

1. Ann Dumper = **John Hammond**   =   2. **Sarah Knight** +
(b abt 1769   (06 Nov 1792) (bap 14 May 1775   (07 Jul 1800)   (b abt 1772 d 20 Nov 1855
bur 16 Jul 1799)   bur 30 Oct 1836)   bur 25 Nov 1855)

Ann   William
(b Aug 1792   (bap 18 Apr 1794
bap 25 Dec 1792   d 05 Apr 1886, Nelson, NZ)
- ?)

Thomas +   James + @   Mary   David # Henry   Joseph* Elizabeth
(b 12 Apr 1804 (bap 13 Aug 1806 (b 08 Apr 1808 (b 02 May 1810 (b 25 Jun (bap 20 May 1818 (b abt Jan
after 1871)   d 09 Jan 1874) d 01 Jun 1866) d 30 Dec 1892) 1812-?) d 08 Nov 1886) 1819-?)
m   Auckland NZ   Nelson NZ Blenheim NZ   Nelson NZ
Jane Carter   m   m   m   m
(25 Jul 1825) 1. Hannah Hayward 1. George Mary A   Mary Box
↓   (05 Feb 1828)   White   Harfield   (1835)
(Issue)   ↓   (1831) (19 Aug 1835)   ↓
          (Issue)   (No issue) (No issue)   (Issue)
     2. Elizabeth Chick 2. Edward
      (24 Oct 1867)   Laney
      (No issue)   05 Nov 1841)
              (No issue)

Uriel +   =   **Jane Druly**
(b Jan/Feb 1802) (01 Feb 1821) (b abt 1792
bap 20 Apr 1802   d 05 Apr 1850
d betw 1846 & 1855)   bur 07 May 1850)

+ Silkweavers
* Ag Lab/Gardener
# Silkweaver/Ag lab
@ also a Brickmaker

We come now to the interesting story of John Hammond, his two wives and his children.

He was the second son of William Hammond and Ann Hooper. William, their first-born had married early, at the age of 17. We do not know if he had a special licence to marry.

Certainly when John came to marry, two and a half years later, a special licence was obtained. It was in fact signed by John on the very day of the marriage, 6 Nov 1792.
In the document John makes an oath that he is a minor, a bachelor and has his father's consent to marry Ann Dumper, who is a spinster, is 'aged upwards of one and twenty years' and has lived in the parish for 'four weeks last past.' The document is signed by John Hammon and countersigned by 'Wm Pedder Clk [in holy orders], Surrogate.' Pedder was in fact a curate in the parish.
The marriage entry in the parish register, dated the same day, reaffirms that John is a minor and that he is marrying Ann Dumper 'of the same Parish Spinster by consent of Parents.' The ceremony was performed 'in this Church by Licence.' The register is signed by William Pedder and John with 'Ann x Dumper - her mark below. The witnesses are Rob. Goddeney and James Holdup, probably the churchwardens.

It is perhaps necessary to remind the modern reader that normally so-called 'banns of marriage' are read on three consecutive Sundays in the parish(es) where the prospective bride and groom are resident so that any objections may be raised. John also had to swear that
'he does not know or believe, that there is any lawful Impediment by Consanguinity, Affinity, or other Cause, to hinder the said intended Marriage.'

In fact, John and Ann had already anticipated events. A child, Ann, had been born in August but was not baptized until 25 Dec1792, ie *after* her parents' marriage. Thus Ann had been conceived about November 1791. At this point, going by his baptism date (14 May 1775), John had been only 16 years old, unless there was a long interval between his birth and baptism.

The question is: why did they leave it so long before getting married? Did John dispute that Ann was his child?

Whatever the reason, a son, William was born to the couple in 1794. Later, he was to emigrate with his half-brothers and half-sisters to New Zealand.

On 16 July 1799, Ann Dumper was buried in Andover churchyard. A year later on 7 July 1800 John was married for the second time - to Sarah Knight. He is described as a 'Widower, 'after 'Bachelor' has been written and struck through, she a Spinster. John again signs the register but Sarah leaves her mark. The same two witnesses as before signed the book and the parson is William Elliot. This time the Banns have been read.

Some years ago one of my correspondents was convinced that John had been 'carrying on' with Sarah whilst Ann was still alive. I see no evidence for this interpretation.

Perhaps it arises from a misunderstanding over John's becoming remarried so soon after his first wife's death. But with two young children what was a widower at that time to do? He needed someone to look after them and Sarah at 25 years old would have been suitable both to fill that role and also perhaps be a mother to more children.

But the real reason may have been the fact both were or had been silk weavers. Contemporary descriptions and pictures of silk weaving frames make it clear that husband and wife needed to work together to carry out the tasks of spinning and weaving the raw silk.

John and Sarah had eight children, five of whom were to emigrate to New Zealand in the 1840s. Only the first two, Uriel and Thomas, and the sixth born, Henry, were to stay in England.

Uriel, my ancestor, bears an extraordinary name and it is a puzzle how John and Sarah came to name him thus.

In biblical terms, Uriel is the name of an archangel - that is to say, he is on a par with Gabriel, Michael and Raphael. His most celebrated appearance in English literature is in Milton's *Paradise Lost,* where, in Book Three, he encounters Satan, who, having been cast out of Heaven, is on his way to corrupt Mankind.

Uriel is described thus:

His back was turned, but not his brightness hid;
Of beaming sunny rays a golden tiar
Circled his head, nor less his locks behind
Illustrious on his shoulders fledge with wings
Lay waving round: on some great charge employed
He seemed, or fixed in cogitation deep.

Now, John's son was baptized about three months after his birth and it is just possible that he had such a crop of fair hair that the parson suggested this rare first name.

But there is another odd twist to the story. A few years earlier, in 1798, Haydn, the Austrian composer, had completed his oratorio *The Creation,* in which the archangels Uriel, Gabriel and Raphael between them relate the story. I have been unable to discover the date of the first performance in England of the *The Creation* but Haydn's music was very popular at this time and it is possible that details of the works had reached the provinces.

Of course, all the above is pure speculation; it is just as likely that the first name, Uriel, was chosen at random and that there is no more to it than that.

But the mystery surrounding Uriel does not end here, as we shall see in the following section.

The Drewleys

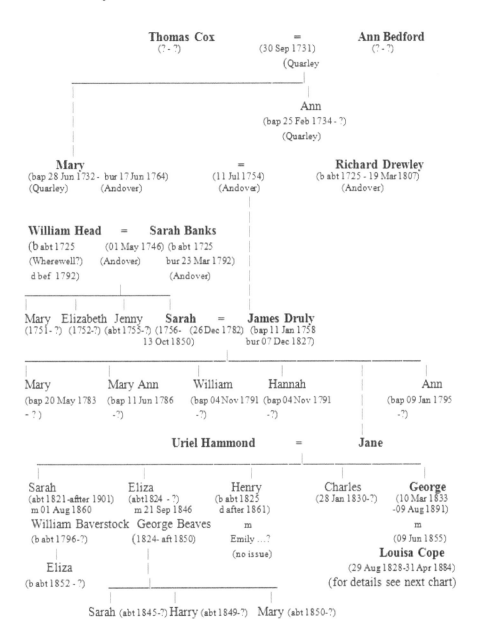

Thomas Cox = Ann Bedford
(? - ?)   (30 Sep 1731)   (? - ?)
(Quarley

Ann
(bap 25 Feb 1734 - ?)
(Quarley)

Mary   =   Richard Drewley
(bap 28 Jun 1732 - bur 17 Jun 1764) (11 Jul 1754) (b abt 1725 - 19 Mar 1807)
(Quarley)   (Andover)   (Andover)   (Andover)

William Head = Sarah Banks
(b abt 1725   (01 May 1746) (b abt 1725
(Wherewell?) (Andover) bur 23 Mar 1792)
d bef 1792)   (Andover)

Mary Elizabeth Jenny   **Sarah**   =   **James Druly**
(1751- ?) (1752-?) (abt 1755-?) (1756- (26 Dec 1782) (bap 11 Jan 1758
                 13 Oct 1850)   bur 07 Dec 1827)

Mary   Mary Ann   William   Hannah   Ann
(bap 20 May 1783 (bap 11 Jun 1786 (bap 04 Nov 1791 (bap 04 Nov 1791   (bap 09 Jan 1795
- ?)   -?)   -?)   -?)   -?)

Uriel Hammond   =   Jane

Sarah   Eliza   Henry   Charles   George
(abt 1821-aftter 1901) (abt 1824 - ?) (b abt 1825 (28 Jan 1830-?) (10 Mar 1833
m 01 Aug 1860   m 21 Sep 1846 d after 1861)   -09 Aug 1891)
William Baverstock George Beaves   m   m
(b abt 1796-?)   (1824- aft 1850) Emily ...?   (09 Jun 1855)
Eliza   (no issue)   **Louisa Cope**
(b abt 1852 - ?)   (29 Aug 1828-31 Apr 1884)
                             (for details see next chart)

Sarah (abt 1845-?) Harry (abt 1849-?) Mary (abt 1850-?)

Information is scanty on many of the persons on the above chart. Nothing is known of the Coxes and the Bedfords except that seem to have come from Quarley, a village a few miles to the west of Andover. The Banks were an Andover family. This is shown not only by Sarah's marriage in Andover but also by two wills which we have: those of an Elizabeth Banks and an Alexander Banks, both dated 1712. Unfortunately there is no evidence connecting them with my ancestors. William Head, who married Sarah, came from Wherewell, just south of Andover. There were, however, Heads in Andover also, for we have the will of John Head, dated 1731. He was a weaver and may have been of a higher status - he speaks of his 'Ten Acres of arable land.'

There is more material on the Drewlys. John Drewly, a weaver, made his will in 1680 and left goods to the value £20-18s-6d, a substantial sum at that time. One item mentions 5 looms so perhaps he employed others.   Yet he was unable to sign his name. He mentions a son, Richard, who may have been the father of my ancestor. Another Druly - that is how it is spelled - Edward, is described in 1707 as a serge weaver and is possibly a son of the previous Drewly (the spelling at this time is far from being stabilised). Finally, there is Richard Druly, perhaps the son of John mentioned above, making his will in 1743. Unfortunately no son Richard appears in the will, so he may not have been the father of my ancestor. There is however a telling observation in the will:

> 'And My Desire is further that if those my two Sons Cant well Agree
> & Live peaceable & Quiatly to geather after my decease that they should
> Gett two honest Neabours who Shall order ones part both of house &
> Land and soe lett Divide as the Men shall order it to be Dun.'

Again we seem to hear the voice of the testator coming across the centuries.

Later, on the same document but in a different hand:

> 'The Eighth day of August 1743
> On which day Edward Drury [sic] Son of Richard Drury [sic] deceased the
> Executor of this Will was duly Sworn before me *etc*'

The confusion Druly/Drury is found even in the nineteenth century.

We return now to Uriel Hammond. And the question is: what became of him?
The latest date we can be sure he was alive is the summer of 1832, because George, his youngest son, was born in March 1833. There is no suggestion on the entry for George's baptism that Uriel was not alive.

Uriel does not appear on the 1841 Andover Census with his family. Because of the nature of this first Census we cannot be sure where he might have been. The relevant entries go like this:

(Mud Town)

Jane Hammond	45	Wid [?]	Y	[born in county]
Sarah do	20	Ag Lab [!]	Y	
Eliza do	17	Silkweaver	Y	
Henry do	16	Ag Lab	Y	
Charles do	11		Y	
George do	8		Y	
Ann Druly	20	Silk Weaver	Y	

The identity of the last person is not clear, but judging by her age, she may have been an illegitimate daughter of Jane, born before the latter was married to Uriel.

The entry 'Wid' is obscured by a line drawn across the page but it seems to be the most likely interpretation. There is a doubt here, however: it was not uncommon for wives whose husbands were absent to say they were widows, in order make things look a bit more respectable.

The next relevant piece of information comes from the marriage of his daughter, Sarah, to George Beaves in 1846. By now Civil Registration had been in operation for nearly ten years and the information is much more specific than on parish registers. The name of Sarah's father is shown as Uriah [sic] Hammond and his occupation as Silkweaver. In the absence of other firm evidence it is perhaps safe to assume that at this point Uriel is still alive.

In 1850 there were two deaths relevant to this story. On 5 April my great-great-grandmother, Jane Hammond, née Druly, died of dropsy. She is described as a charwoman No mention is made of Uriel. A few months later her mother, and my great-great-great-great-grandmother, Sarah Druly, née Head, died at the incredible age of 94. In 1855 came the wedding of George Hammond and Louisa Cope. George's father, Uriel, although not mentioned by name, is now clearly shown on the certificate as deceased.

There is one more death in this section which needs comment and it is that of John Hammond's widow, Sarah Knight. She died at the Union House, Andover of influenza on 20 December 1855, aged 83 years. She is described as a silk weaver and had been shown as a pauper in the 1851 Census.

Now, we know a good deal about the Andover Workhouse. The conditions there were so dreadful in the '40s and '50s that it became the centre of a national scandal. Inmates, who were of course segregated by sex - families being regularly split up - were given bones to crush for fertiliser and it was rumoured that they were so hungry that they chewed on the bones. The building still stands in Andover - a memorial to Victorian self-righteousness and well-meaning heartlessness.

Here is a contemporary account.

And here is a quotation (also contemporary) from a certain Rev H H Milman:

> '*The workhouse should be place of hardship, of coarse fare, of degradation and humility; it should be administered with strictness - with severity; it should be as repulsive as is consistent with humanity…*'

What was my poor ancestor doing at her age in this terrible place? Even as a widow (John had died in 1836) and with her children emigrated to New Zealand, there must have been relatives who could have looked after her, especially her grandchildren, the sons and daughters of the now disappeared Uriel, including George Hammond. It remains a source of anger to me.

Even in my early lifetime the phrase 'in the Workhouse' still retained its aura of shame and hopelessness. This was not helped when, after the system was abandoned in the 20th century, the buildings were sometimes converted into Old Peoples' Homes. One of my most upsetting memories is singing carols to elderly people in one such institution.

Returning briefly to Uriel, there are several possibilities:

- He may have emigrated to another part of the world - not to New Zealand, where there is certainly no trace of him
- He may have died somewhere in the United Kingdom before the beginning of Statutory Registration (1837). Under these circumstances it would be difficult to find him because there is no central record of burials similar to the Mormon Church's documentation of baptisms and marriages.
- He may have died somewhere in the UK after 1837 and have just slipped through the net, so to speak.

In fact, we may never discover what happened to him.

As a postscript to this section, it is interesting that there is no record of any other Uriel Hammond, except one. He was born in the United States in 1781, married in 1807 and died in 1868. He seems never to have left the State of Connecticut.

The Woodmans

Italics = a will or other document exists.

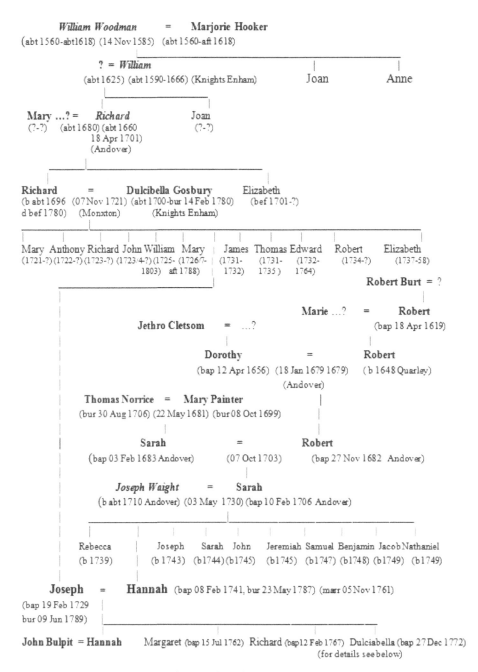

William Woodman = Marjorie Hooker
(abt 1560-abt1618) (14 Nov 1585) (abt 1560-aft 1618)

? = *William* | |
(abt 1625) (abt 1590-1666) (Knights Enham)   Joan   Anne

Mary ...? = *Richard*   Joan
(?-?)   (abt 1680) (abt 1660   (?-?)
         18 Apr 1701)
         (Andover)

Richard   =   Dulcibella Gosbury   Elizabeth
(b abt 1696 (07 Nov 1721) (abt 1700-bur 14 Feb 1780)   (bef 1701-?)
d bef 1780)   (Monxton)   (Knights Enham)

Mary Anthony Richard John William Mary | James Thomas Edward Robert   Elizabeth
(1721-?)(1722-?)(1723-?)(1723/4-?)(1725- (1726/?- | (1731- (1731- (1732- (1734-?)   (1737-58)
              1803) aft 1788) | 1732) 1735) 1764)

                                                    Robert Burt = ?

                                        Marie ...? = Robert
Jethro Cletsom = ...?   (bap 18 Apr 1619)

Dorothy   =   Robert
(bap 12 Apr 1656) (18 Jan 1679 1679) (b 1648 Quarley)
                    (Andover)

Thomas Norrice = Mary Painter
(bur 30 Aug 1706) (22 May 1681) (bur 08 Oct 1699)

Sarah   =   Robert
(bap 03 Feb 1683 Andover) (07 Oct 1703) (bap 27 Nov 1682 Andover)

Joseph Waight = Sarah
(b abt 1710 Andover) (03 May 1730) (bap 10 Feb 1706 Andover)

Rebecca | Joseph Sarah John Jeremiah Samuel Benjamin Jacob Nathaniel
(b 1739) | (b 1743) (b1744)(b1745) (b1745) (b1747) (b1748) (b1749) (b1749)

Joseph = Hannah (bap 08 Feb 1741, bur 23 May 1787) (marr 05 Nov 1761)
(bap 19 Feb 1729
bur 09 Jun 1789)

John Bulpit = Hannah   Margaret (bap 15 Jul 1762) Richard (bap12 Feb 1767) Dulciabella (bap 27 Dec 1772)
                                                              (for details see below)

This is one of the most interesting periods in my family's history.

First of all, although the chart does not reveal it, we know from the details behind the entries that we have the emergence of non-conformism in Andover: for the first time some of the Hammond ancestors are attending the East Street Independent Church. This tiny church, which still exists and is currently used by the United Reform movement, was built some time towards the beginning of the 18th century. It is in the Renaissance style and can be compared to the church built in the expanding dockland area of Sunderland, some distance from the mediaeval church of the old parish of Bishops Wearmouth.

Joseph Waight appears to have been the first head of family among my ancestors to have moved from the Norman-style church of Andover. We do not know why all of his children were baptized in the new church but their names reveal a strong biblical association. Other members of the family continued the practice in the 19th century: the first three children of Thomas, younger brother of Uriel Hammond, were baptized in the Chapel. In 1846, Eliza, second daughter of Uriel, was married there to George Beaves.

The fate of old Andover church is related below:

Andover "old church", demolished in 1842 to make way for the present St. Mary's. Said to have been the largest and finest example in the country of a Saxon church, with Norman accretions, its destruction was in line with the Victorian passion for church rebuilding or modernising, and is now seen to have been, in the words of Mr. Edmund Parsons, the Andover historian, "an act of terrible vandalism".

Had that church been standing today what a tourist attraction Andover would have had! Instigator of its destruction was Dr. William Goddard, who generously paid for the new church, it is said to improve the view from his residence (now the Old Vicarage, Newbury Street).

The old church (naturally!) was claimed to be unsafe, but it needed explosives to demolish it.

Next, the mystery of Dulcibella Gosbury (or Gostney or Cask). The Mormon International Genealogical Index shows the last two as an interpretation of the name when she married Richard Woodman at Monxton in 1721. The bride is shown as being from 'Inham' - which must be a version of '(Knights) Enham'. But I have before me now an enlargement of the parish entry and by no stretch of the imagination can it be interpreted as either 'Gostney' or 'Cask', although these do exist in other records not connected with this one. To me it is clearly 'Gosbury', a name which is found elsewhere, and that is the name I have adopted in my records, although I cannot really explain this puzzle.

As for Dulcibella, the name was apparently quite common in earlier times, appearing in various guises, such as 'Dowsabel'. From the family history point of view, the appearance of the name a generation later indicates that we are on the right lines.

The question of children's baptisms comes up again. The close proximity of years for the Waight children made me at first wonder if two families were involved. But I can find no other Joseph Waight and there is no duplication of names. It will help if we discover Joseph's parents and be clearer about his date of birth. What is most worrying of all, however, is the late birth of Joseph's and Sarah's first child. There may be an error here somewhere but I can find no alternative solution.

I turn now to the most important feature of this section: the survival of wills and property lists. Here is true history, giving us an insight into the way ordinary people lived. The earliest will I have is shown below.

The Will of William Woodman   (HCRO 1618B 59/1)

In the name of God Amen. I William Woodman of the parrish of Knights Enham in the County of *South husbandman, though sick in bodie, yet [-----?] in mynd & of pfect memorie, commend my soule into the handes of my redeemer Christ Jesus, affirming my [----?] & [-------?] to be your [------?] [--------?] & [------?] [---------?] his precious blood, & by noe other meanes to be saved but by his death & passion, soe relying & believing I commend this my bodye to be buryed in the churchyard of Knights   Enham, ther to remain until the coming of my Saviour when my expressed hope is to have a joyfull resurrection & dispose of my temporall goodes in manner & forme following. ffirst I gyve unto the pooer of the parrish xiid. Item I gyve unto my daughter Joan two sheep &   lykewise to my daughter Anne two sheep. Item I gyve unto my god daughter Joan my sonne Willyamm's daughter one sheep. Item my will is yt my wyffe Margerie have the use of all my goodes during her lyfe, & on & att her death, those my goodes equally to be divided & distributed unto my two daughters Joan & Anne Item I gyve unto my sonne Wm one sheep. Item of all other my goodes moveable & immoveable I make my wyffe Margery my onely & sole executrix of   this my will & Testament, &   accordingly all [---------?] be done & pefected [------?]   I make my [---------?] Mr Peter Blake , & my neighbour & go[-----?] to my Tomb. July the 7th. Ano. Regni Jacob. Anglie, ffranc et Hibere. Regib. decimo [----?] et quinquagesimo primo.

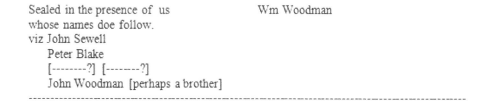

Sealed in the presence of us   Wm Woodman
whose names doe follow.
viz John Sewell
    Peter Blake
    [--------?] [-------?]
    John Woodman [perhaps a brother]

[Reverse of Will]

Probatum fuit --- ?in ---?forma [8 words] =
= ssimi in [7 words] via
[4 words] Anglica [3 words]
[6 words] in [---?]
[5 words] nono die
mensis Septembris Anno [---? ---?] Domini [--]
fuit [--?] et [3 words]
[--?] Marga?ie [4 words]
Execut--? [5 words]
[2 words] ex [3 words]
[3 words]   *'South' = 'Southampton' = 'Hampshire'

An Inventorie of all the goodes & chattels
of Wm Woodman the elder lately deceased

	L s d	[£ p
In primis in the Hall a table board Standing)		
on two posts [?] Item a payer of fyre tongues)	0 - 2 - 8	13
a payer of pott hangers & hooks. Item an)		
---- ? [probably some sort of chair] & two Stooles)		
Item in the Butterie 3 barrells-----------------------------	0 - 3 - 0	15
Item 4 old kettles [?] ------------------------------------	0 - 2 - 6	12½
Item 7 peeices [?] of pewter ---------------------------	0 - 3 - 6	17½
Item 1. pott & 2 bottells with other old stuffe ----------	0 -10 - 0	50
Item in the chamber 4 coffers 1 bedstead)		
made of boarde with Bed clothes) --------	1 - 0 - 0	1-00
Item 1. cow & 1 bullock -----------------------------	2 -13 - 4	2-67
Item 1 horse & 1 pigg ------------------------------	0 -13 - 4	67
Item 30 sheep & lambes ----------------------------	7 -10 - 0	7-50
Item 9 acres of corne & an halfe ----------------------	9 - 0 - 0	9-00
Item his apparell ------------------------------------	0 -16 - 0	80
Sum totale L s d	22 -14- 4	22-72]

p------[?] ------ [?] John James of Charlton
in ye parish of Andover &
John Bullard churchwarden of Knights Enham
Family relationships according to the Will:

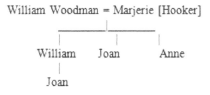

William Woodman = Marjerie [Hooker]
_____|_____
| | |
William   Joan   Anne
|
Joan

I regret that I have been unable to interpret the whole text of this will, including the Latin
details of the proving of it.

As we noted before, the sovereign is deemed to rule over France as well as England and Ireland but not Scotland, which was for another century a separate kingdom. There is also the fulsome commitment to the Christian life and philosophy. This is not just an empty formula but reflects a real fear that if proper regard for doctrine were not observed the result could be eternal damnation. The mediaeval tradition is overlaid by the strictures of the ever-growing cult of Puritanism.

The terms of the document seem uncontroversial. The small legacy to William probably reflects the fact that he may have already accumulated some of the wealth that is apparent in his will of 1667. Joan and Anne, the two daughters, would, on their marriages, have needed property to offer as dowries and if they survived their mother would certainly have had sufficient. His granddaughter is also directly provided for.
It is interesting that William provides 12 pence (= 1 shilling = 5p) for the poor of the parish. This is probably the equivalent in today's money (2007) of about £10.

It so happens that I can conjure up quite a vivid mental image of the small-holding. About 10 years ago, while on a visit to Andover, I drove out to Woodhouse and found one of the old cottages still remaining, surrounded by more modern dwellings. Mr Loveridge, who lived there, invited me in and told me that the other cottages had been pulled down in the 1930s. He said that the cottages had been reckoned to date from the 1600s
Later, I obtained a copy of the 25" map of the area, dated 1873. The cottages are marked, on either side of a road, which ends in a cul-de-sac. Each is shown with a small-holding backing on to open fields. Significantly, a few hundred yards away is Ashley Copse and this must have served the hamlet for a very long time. Also close by is shown what is obviously a substantial manor-house, also called Woodhouse.

I am sure that one of these cottages was where William Woodman and his descendants lived.

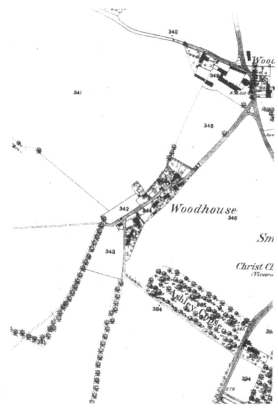

William Woodman Jnr also left a will. It has not survived intact but the following fragment, found in the National Archives, appears to be part of the missing Will:

In the name of God father Sonne and Holy Ghost. Amen. I William Woodman Esq elder of Knights Enham in the County of Southampton husbandman being [....] in body but blessed be God in perfect mind, and memory doe make this my last will and Testament in...........

An Inventory of his goods, has also been found. This is dated 1666, when William Woodman is described as 'deceased' but the will seems to have been proved in August 1667.

Inventory   1666 Ad 110 A True Inventory of all the goods & chattells of William Woodman late Knights Enham in the County of Southton deceased

	L	s	d
In ye hall chamber			
Impr wearing Apparell &			
money in his purse ---------------------------------	3.	00	00
It. one Bed 2 bolsters[?] & bedding----------------------	2.	10.	00
It. one side cuppboard, & table & ioynt stool ---------	0.	6.	8
It. One chest and one coffer -----------------------------	0.	10.	00
It. 3 bushells of malt -----------------------------------	0.	6.	0
It 3 yd [?] of sheet tablecloth & other linnen ----------	2.	0.	0
In ye little chamber			
One bed, bedstead & bedding -------------------------------	1.	10.	0
2 old truncks [?] & an other [?] Coffer ------------------	0.	5.	0
In ye Hall			
One Cupboard ---------------------------------------	13.	4.	0
2 Chaires one ioynt Stoole & form -----	0.	13.	4
One [------] & frame ---------------------------------------	0.	3.	6
In ye Kitchin			
Brasse & pewter ---	2.	10.	0
wooll ---	1.	6.	8
In ye buttery [?] some barrells & other lumber -----------	0.	7.	6
four flickes of bacon -----------------------------------	1.	10.	0

Without doores [= 'outside']

2 browne kine [cows]	3.	10.	0
7 Sheep young [?] & old [?]	11.	00.	00
2 Hogges	1.	10.	00
One Hay ricke	2.	5.	00
A roller six small ladders & some wood	2.	10.	00
About 3 doz. of Hurdles	0.	10.	00
Well bucket & scoop [?] 2 troughs & wheele barrow	0.	10.	00
A grinding [?] stone [?] & trough	0.	4.	00
Six [------] of [------]	2.	00.	00

In ye Barne

Some wheat in straw [?]	3.	00.	00
Barley in ye straw [?]	13.	00.	00
Pease [?] in ye straw [?]	2.	00.	00
fi [-----]s in ye straw [?]	1.	10.	00
Some boards	1.	10	
Wood in ye Malt house	1.	00.	00
A small mill, salt 2 kivers [bowls & tub	1.	10.	00
The lumber [---] ye malt house)			
Table side cupboard & 2 barrells one tub & [?] kiver ----)			
with [?] other lumber in ye kitchen)	0.	12.	00

| | 65. | 09. | 00 |

[Page 2]

Two Bibles & some Other bookes	00.	10.	00
Mattock shovell from barne prongs [?] etc	0.	10.	00
An old [?] , & an old cart [?] [----?]	0.	5.	00
foure bullocks	4.	0.	00

| | 5. | 5. | 00 |
| | 65. | 9. | 00 |

| | 70 . | 14. | 00 |

Peter Blake   The 0 mark of Alexander Barret

Vinssimo [20?] Nono die mensis
Augusti Anno Dmi i667
[---?] Mr [?] Thomas Colmett [---?] in legibus b[-- ?]
Surrogat[-?] [----?] [---?] [--?] Moundford Brampton
militis leg[-?] [----] [----] patris [----?] Georg[-?]
Winton epi[---?] gentis et Admis omniu
bono[--?] [-----?] et p[---?] Wilm[--?] Woodman defuncti
Comissa fuit Andrew Woodman vit eius
[----?] De bono [---?] Dog[---?] [----?] debita e
[----?] Comissis [----?] Jurat? [----?]
Jure [------?]
Obligissa [---?] et   ?

36

The signature of Peter Blake on this document is different from that on the Will of William Woodman senr. They are presumably father and son. The Andrew Woodman mentioned near the end of the Latin section is unknown but is clearly a relative of William

This is a most comprehensive inventory and paints a vivid picture of country life in the 17th century. There are fewer sheep than in the previous will and it is not easy to see where the emphasis has shifted to because there does not seem to be that much more arable produce than previously. The overall picture is of diversity but it would take an expert to make a convincing analysis. The value the goods and chattels seems quite high and I should like to know whether is to some degree the result of inflation or simply an inaccurate assessment. Does possession of bible and other books show that William could read?

The third Woodman will which is preserved is that of Richard, grandson of the first William Woodman. *Italics* indicates a known member of the family

Will of Richard Woodman, died 18 Apr 1701:
In the Name of God Amen *I Richard Woodman* of ye parish of Andover in ye County of Southton Serge Weaver being of Sound & disposing mind & memory (thanks to be [!] God) but Weak & sick in Body & uncertain how soon I may be taken hence make my Last Will & Testament in Manner & form following (that is to say) ffirst I recommend my soul into ye hands of God that made me And I comitt my Body to ye Earth to be Decently buried at ye Discrettion of my Executrix herein after mentioned And of my Temporal estate God has been pleased to Bless me withal after ye payment of my Debts & funerall expenses I dispose of it as follows Imprimis I give & Devise to *my only Sonne & heir Richard Woodman & his heires for ever from ye day whereon he shall attain to ye Age of One & Twenty yeares* All those my four tenemnts with ye appurtences* situate lying & being in ye parish of Whitchurch in ye County of Southton in a Certain Street called Wood Street now or later in the tenures or occupacies* *of Stephen Hall, [see IGI] Edward Brown, Widow Hobgood & Peter Dines* their undertenants or assigne[e]s subject to & chargeable with such legacies & payments as shall hereinafter be by me bequeathed In the mean while my Will & pleasure [is] that *my beloved wife Mary Woodman* shall possess & enjoy all & every ye said tenemnts & premises wth ye appurtences* *until ye sd Richard Woodman my Sonne shall attain to his age of One & twenty yeares* to her own proper use & behoofe but subject and chargeable as aforesaid Item my Will & Pleasure [is] that my *Daughter Elizabeth Woodman Spinster* doe receive out of ye rents & profitts of ye sd tenements ye yearly sume* of thirty [shillings] to be paid her half yearly by even & equall portions at ye most usuall dayes of payment in ye yeare that is to say at or upon ye ffeast of ye Annunciation of ye Blessed Virgin Mary & St Michael ye Archangel *untill her said Brother Richard Woodman shall attain to his age of one & twenty years but no longer* Item I give & bequeath to my said Daughter ye sume* of Twenty pounds to be paid her by her said Brother when he shall attain to ye age of One & Twenty yeares With the Payment of which said severall sumes* Vizt ye yearly sume* of thirty shillings & ye sume of Twenty pounds I Doe hereby charge my said ffour tenemts And whereas by a certain Indenture of Releasse bearing date ye twentieth day of September Anno D#ni One Thousand Seven Hundred I have granted & Sold unto *William Walters of Andover aforesd* Serge weaver ye sd ffour

tenemnts & premisses but in trust for me during my natural life & after b [?] my decease in trust likewise as therein is expressed by which said Indenture of Release I have charged my said estate with ye payment of thirty shillings & with ye payment of Another sume of Twenty pounds to be paid to my said daughter *Elizabeth Woodman* as therein is mentioned Now Be It Known that the said Sumes* (Vist) ye sume* of thirty shillings yearly & ye sume of Twenty pounds in & by ye sd Release to my said Daughter given are ye same two Severall sumes* of Thirty Shillings yearly & Twenty pounds & not Distinct Sumes* from those which to my said Daughter are by this my Will given & bequeathed Item it is my Will & pleasure that if ye sd sumes* of thirty shillings yearly or ye sd sume* of twenty pounds shall be behind or unpaid in part or in all by ye space of Three months after ye same shall be lawfully demanded That then from thenceforth it shall & may be lawfull to [?] & for [?] & I Doe hereby require my said Trustee *William Walter* to enter into ye premisses & out of ye rents & profitts thereof to pay or cause to be paid to my said daughter ye sd sume* of twenty pounds & also what shall be behind or unpaid of ye said yearly sume* of thirty shillings with all loss and charges in ye promising ye payment of ye said sume* or sumes Item if my said *Son shall happen to dye* before he attain to his age of one & twenty yeares I Doe then devise my said four tenements with ye appurtences* to *my said Daughter her heirs & Assignees for ever* Item I give & bequeath to my said Daughter My ffeather Bed feather Bolster fflock Bolster & Bedsteads Lowest [?] Coffer my great Clasp Bible ye Little Table in ye Chamber one Joint Stool & ye Cupboard in ye Chamber ye Chest in ye Shop my brewing Kettle & ye biggest of my other Kettles two Little brass Potts one brass Skellett [= skillet] one pair of Cotterells [= frame for hanging a pot or kettle over a fire] ffive Pewter Dishes ye great new fflaggon one brass Candlestick ye great Keiver [= a shallow wooden vessel or tub] & ye Little Barrell The remainder of my Household goods I Give &
bequeath *to my beloved Wife Mary Woodman* whom I hereby Constitute guardian of my Son & Sole Executrix of this my last Will & Testament desiring to save ye goods for my Son unless urgent necessity compell her to Sell them & I hereby revoke all former Wills by me at any time heretofore made In Witness whereof I have hereunto sett my hand & seale this first day of Aprill in ye twelfth yeare of ye reign or our Sovereign Lord William ye third King of England ect [sic]Annoq [sic]Dni* 1701
Signed sealed published & declared by ye sd   )R *Priest* [?]
Richard Woodman ye testator of his last will   )*Gyles Dowling*   [of Knights
          & Testamnt in the presence of us)   Enham; see IGI]
)*William Walters*

        Richard Woodman'

Notes ( )= part of original text); [ ]= [insertions or comments by BDH];
     * = a special sign in the text over a syllable, indicating abbreviation,
        although most abbreviations have no special sign;
   'ye' always appears with the 'e' in superscript; no punctuation has been added to the text.

Reverse of parchment:

'An Inventory of all and Singular the goods and Chattells of *Richard Woodman* of Woodhouse in the parish of Andover in the County of Southton [Serge] Weaver who departed this life the 18th Day of Aprill in the yeare of our Lord Anno Dom 1701

L   s   d

	L----s----d
Imprimis Wearing Apparell & money in purse	1----5----0
Item one pigg	0----8----0
Item in the Chamber two ffeather beds)	
two ffeather Bolsters one ffeather pillow)	
one fflock bolster three sheets one Rugg)	4----2----0
and one Coverlid [= quilt] three Bedsteads &)	
one fflock bed)___	
Item three Chests three Coffers three)	
Boxes two Trunks one Cupboard)	1----9----0
and one Small Table)___	
Item two pillowtyes [pillowcase?])	
tablecloath & other odd linen)___	0----5----0
Item in the hall & Buttery ffour)	
Kettles three potts three skilletts one)	2---13----0
warming pan one Brass mortar)	
one Brass Candlestick)___	
Item Sixteene Dishes of pewter two)	
fflaggons two Candlesticks two porringers)	1----5----0
two Cupps & one Bason)___	
Item one Iron dripping pan one)	0---10----0
ffrying pan one tin dripping pan two)	
Spitts two dogs three Cottrells [see above])	
one barr one pair of tongs)___	
Item one tallbow [=tallboy?/table?] three)	
joynt stooles ffoure Chayres one fforme)	
two Kivers [= keivers; see above] one tub)	1----8----0
three Barrells one Cupboard one salt box) ___	
Item one Loom & all materials)	1----2----0
Item wood and all other Lumber)	
in & about the house)	0----4----5
Sume total	14---11----5

Giles Dowling, John Allen Appraisers '

I am still astonished by my luck in coming across this last will and inventory, which together give a wonderful picture of rural life in early 18th century Hampshire.

The Bulpits and the Copes

These are the last two families which complete the story of my Hammond ancestors.

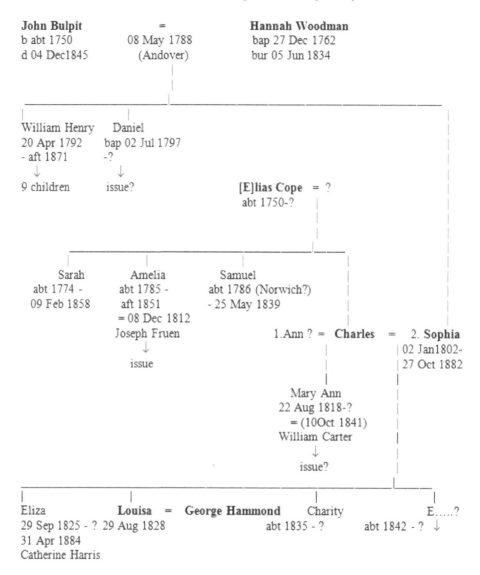

There are a number of points to be raised about the individuals shown above.

First, John Bulpit.

I am almost certain that this is the right ancestor. He appears on the 1841 Census (see below) living next door to, or possibly in the same house as, the Hammonds, including my great-grandfather, George, in Mud Town. He is shown as being 90 years old (which in the 1841 Census could indicate any age between 90 and 100). His household is shown as separate and he appears to be looked after by a Mary Cowdry, aged 14. It turns out that Mary Ann Cowdery (to give her her full name) was the daughter of a George Cowdery and a Martha Bulpit. She was therefore almost certainly related to old John.

John died four years later aged 97. (See below.) This would mean he was born in 1748 but at that time such a date cannot be relied upon. He would have been about 40 when he married Hannah Woodman, and this may have been his second marriage. It is true that the Andover register for 1788 states that he was from Upper Clatford (which lies slightly south of Andover) and that he was a bachelor, but this kind of possible error is not uncommon. At all events, I have no firm information about his parentage. Bulpit was a very common surname in this part of Hampshire.

CERTIFIED COPY of an
Pursuant to the Births and 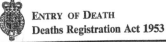 ENTRY OF DEATH
Deaths Registration Act 1953

H

Registration District	Andover	

1845. Death in the Sub-district of Andover **in the** County of Southampton

No.	When and where died	Name and surname	Sex	Age	Occupation	Cause of death	Signature, description, and residence of informant	When registered	Sig re
51	Fourth of December 1845 Mud Town Andover	John BULPITT	Male	97 years	Laborer	Old age Not Certified	Mary Belbin Present at the death Mud Town Andover	Sixth December 1845	Robe R

Certified to be a true copy of an entry in a register in my custody.

.... AC finchr ....Superintende
............................2nd July 1991

I have traced four persons named Cope, living in Andover in the early 19th century and have assumed that they are related. One, Samuel, a silk weaver, who died in 1839, was found in Down Barn at Wild Hern, north of Andover. The Andover Burial register states he was a native of 'the City of Norwich.' This may account for the fact that I can find no Copes in Andover before this time. As for Sarah, the Statutory Death Certificate shows her as a 'Daughter of Lias Cope Labourer Deceased.' I take 'Lias' to mean 'Elias'.
Charles, the youngest of the children was born in Andover. Nothing is known of his first wife, except her first name, and that they had a daughter.

Finally, we have surprisingly little information about Louisa's sisters. With the youngest we do not even have her first name. This is because some Census enumerators in 1851 for Andover entered only initials for all but the head of household, whose full name was given.

George and Louisa

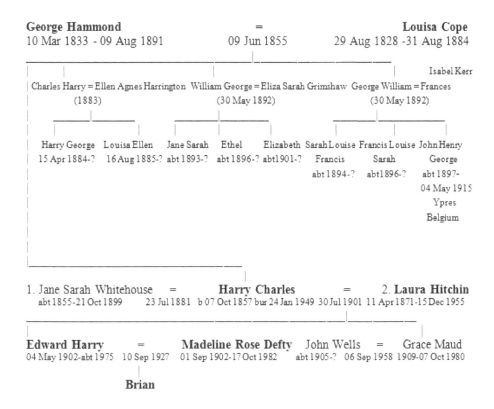

| George Hammond | = | Louisa Cope |
| 10 Mar 1833 - 09 Aug 1891 | 09 Jun 1855 | 29 Aug 1828 -31 Aug 1884 |

Isabel Kerr

Charles Harry = Ellen Agnes Harrington   William George = Eliza Sarah Grimshaw   George William = Frances
(1883)   (30 May 1892)   (30 May 1892)

Harry George   Louisa Ellen   Jane Sarah   Ethel   Elizabeth   Sarah   Louise   Francis   Louise   John Henry
15 Apr 1884-? 16 Aug 1885-? abt 1893-? abt 1896-? abt1901-? Francis   Sarah   George
                                                                  abt 1894-? abt 1896-? abt 1897-
                                                                                          04 May 1915
                                                                                          Ypres
                                                                                          Belgium

| 1. Jane Sarah Whitehouse | = | Harry Charles | = | 2. Laura Hitchin |
| abt 1855-21 Oct 1899 | 23 Jul 1881 | b 07 Oct 1857 bur 24 Jan 1949 | 30 Jul 1901 | 11 Apr 1871-15 Dec 1955 |

| Edward Harry | = | Madeline Rose Defty | John Wells | = | Grace Maud |
| 04 May 1902-abt 1975 | 10 Sep 1927 | 01 Sep 1902-17 Oct 1982 | abt 1905-? | 06 Sep 1958 | 1909-07 Oct 1980 |

Brian

Louisa and George seem to have been singularly lacking in imagination when it came to naming their sons and this was followed in the next generation; except in the case of my grandparents, who, as will be seen later, used names from the Hitchin family.

Ever since I discovered that my grandfather Defty was married before he met my grandmother, and had a son, who was another half brother to my mother, I have wondered whether there were any children from my grandfather Hammond's first marriage to Jane Sarah Whitehouse. So far no issue has come to light. No mention was ever made in the family of Harry's first marriage and I came across it only by accident. Certainly on his marriage certificate to Laura he is shown as a bachelor. They were married in my grandmother's home town and it seems possible that she did not wish her relatives and friends to know that she was marrying a widower aged nearly 44 ('an old maid's last chance; why ever did she want to marry that old man?' was how my mother - admittedly not an unbiased observer - reported Laura's relatives' attitude, though she was in fact only 30).

My father often referred to his cousin, John Henry George, who was killed in the First World War. He said John was over 6 ft, perhaps the tallest in the family. He was killed on my father's 13th birthday, 4 May, which was probably enough to impress a young teenager.

No other of my grandfather's brothers and their children was ever referred to in my hearing, although I met at least three of Laura's siblings. I'm afraid I see here my grandmother's influence. Given her capacity for quarrelling with so many people, I think it possible that by the time I was on the scene she had caused a rift with Harry's relatives.

There remains the question of why George decided to move his family from Andover to Canning Town, at some time between 1861 and 1866.
In Mud Town, Andover George had been a tanner and boot maker, working for his brother-in-law, William Baverstock (husband of his sister Sarah), who seems to have owned a boot-making business there. By the time of the 1861 Census he was a garden labourer and Louisa is shown as a silk-weaver. By then, the silk industry in Andover was on its last legs and perhaps the temptation to move from the town was irresistible. The 1871 Census, as well as showing the Hammonds living at Bell and Anchor Cottages, Canning Town, gives another family from Andover. Perhaps the latter had encouraged a move by the Hammonds.

The dwellings in Mud Town were apparently made of chalk, with probably an earlier frame of wattle and daub. Although they were no doubt lacking in proper sanitation, a study of the next three illustrations will point up the stark contrast between the Hammonds' Andover home and their new surroundings in Canning Town.

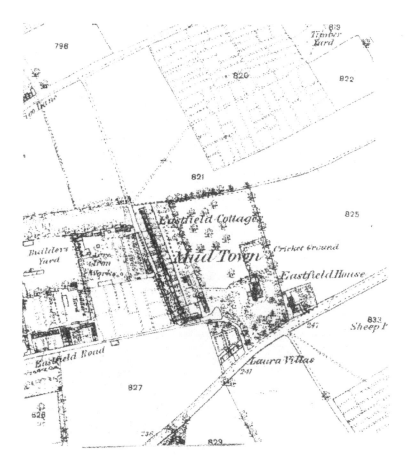

But why Canning Town? All the evidence shows that at the middle of the 19th century it was an insanitary and insalubrious place to live. Lying to the east of the river Lea and on the banks of the Thames, the area was the notorious location of the 'stink' industries which were not permitted to the west of the River Lea. Furthermore, in 1855 a report by Alfred Dickens (the novelist's brother) describes the area as follows:

It was impossible to describe the miserable state Canning Town was in; there was neither drainage nor paving; in Winter the streets were impassable; The cholera raged very much in this district.

Contemporary photographs show open sewers flowing past houses.

45

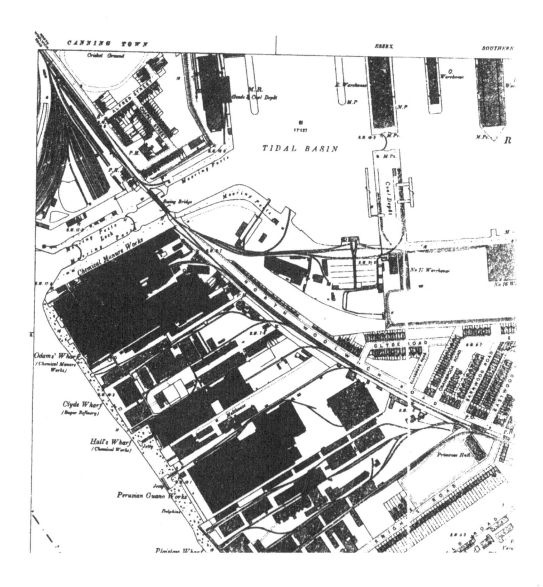

The above print shows the location of the 'stink' industries on the banks of the river. Amongst them is a sugar refinery! Bell and Anchor Cottages (possibly originally called New Model Cottages) are shown slightly below the PH sign (public house).

They are shown again in the following picture, dating from about 1860,

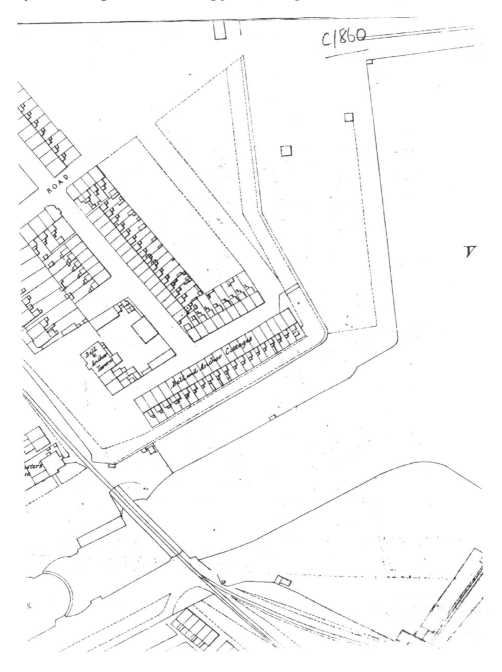

The fact that the Bell and Anchor Cottages may have first been described as Model Cottages may mean that the area immediately surrounding where the Hammonds lived was not so dire.

At all events, that is where my grandfather and his brothers were brought up. Harry lived and worked in the area as a coal porter (like his father) until after his second marriage in 1901.

Louisa died of smallpox in 1884. George died of congestion of the lungs in 1891. It is surprising he survived so long. The life of a coal porter, heaving coal in wicker baskets up from the hold of a ship was dangerous and many serious accidents are known to have occurred. By 1891 Harry had become a foreman and so he stayed until he retired at the age of 70 in 1927. He had unfortunately been injured at some time and could not raise his right arm above shoulder height. He did receive a small pension, but, as my father used to say: if Cory Brothers gave anything away, the first person in the queue would be too late.

My memories of Grandpa Hammond are limited even though I was 19 when he died. He was gruff of speech but a kindly man. He wore a beard and in this regard resembled King George V. He sat for most of the time in the same armchair in front of a french window, smoking a pipe. Within reach was a very old-fashioned wireless (as it was called) which ran on an accumulator, a sort of liquid battery. He read books and newspapers but liked most of all to play at cribbage - my father and I used to take it in turns to play with him. It astounds me now that I did not ask him about his childhood, which began in the third quarter of the 19th century. All I really knew about him was that he was born in Andover and his date of birth. One piece of information that I remember he told me was that his mother insisted always that all the food he was given be eaten up. Any that was not consumed was produced at the next meal - and so on, until it was eaten. My father said that during the General Strike of 1926, Harry insisted, as a foreman, on going in to work, apparently undeterred by the threats he received. He worked until the age of seventy.

He had what I remember as a London accent and his indistinct manner of speaking led to an amusing entry on my parents' 1927 marriage certificate. His Rank or Profession is shown as 'Berth Informer', idiosyncratic, to say the least. I then checked my father's birth certificate of 1902. There Harry Charles Hammond is described as a 'Ship's Berthing Foreman'. Back to the marriage certificate. The vicar was W A Frogley. Now, as a choirboy, I remember Mr Frogley. He retired about 1938 and was by that time very deaf. His deafness must have been incipient ten years earlier and that combined with my grandfather's somewhat incoherent speech had caused the error. But had anyone else noticed?

The Hitchin Family

The Ichins of Shropshire

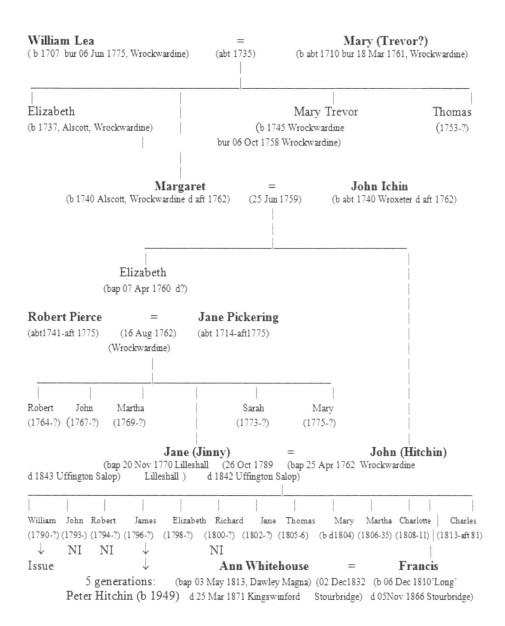

William Lea = **Mary (Trevor?)**
(b 1707 bur 06 Jun 1775, Wrockwardine)   (abt 1735)   (b abt 1710 bur 18 Mar 1761, Wrockwardine)

Elizabeth   Mary Trevor   Thomas
(b 1737, Alscott, Wrockwardine)   (b 1745 Wrockwardine   (1753-?)
                                       bur 06 Oct 1758 Wrockwardine)

Margaret = **John Ichin**
(b 1740 Alscott, Wrockwardine d aft 1762)   (25 Jun 1759)   (b abt 1740 Wroxeter d aft 1762)

Elizabeth
(bap 07 Apr 1760 d?)

Robert Pierce = **Jane Pickering**
(abt1741-aft 1775)   (16 Aug 1762)   (abt 1714-aft1775)
                     (Wrockwardine)

Robert   John   Martha   Sarah   Mary
(1764-?) (1767-?) (1769-?)   (1773-?)   (1775-?)

Jane (Jinny) = **John (Hitchin)**
(bap 20 Nov 1770 Lilleshall   (26 Oct 1789   (bap 25 Apr 1762 Wrockwardine
d 1843 Uffington Salop)   Lilleshall)   d 1842 Uffington Salop)

William John Robert James Elizabeth Richard Jane Thomas Mary Martha Charlotte Charles
(1790-?) (1793-) (1794-?) (1796-?) (1798-?) (1800-?) (1802-?) (1805-6) (b d1804) (1806-35) (1808-11) (1813-aft 81)
↓   NI   NI   ↓   NI
Issue   ↓   **Ann Whitehouse** = **Francis**
       5 generations: (bap 03 May 1813, Dawley Magna) (02 Dec1832 (b 06 Dec 1810'Long'
Peter Hitchin (b 1949) d 25 Mar 1871 Kingswinford   Stourbridge) d 05Nov 1866 Stourbridge)

49

We first meet the Hitchins in rural Shropshire, an area dominated by the Wrekin and very close to Watling Street, the Roman road, now the A5, after it turns westward at Cannock, heading towards Wales. In fact, the first John Ichin we know of came from Wroxeter itself, near the old Roman town of *Viroconium.* This name and Wrockwardine are clearly connected; on the Wrekin there was a British Iron Age settlement.

During the eighteenth century parts of the area must have gradually become more industrialised. Coalbrookdale and Ironbridge are only a few miles away from Wroxeter, on the Severn.

The name Ichin I take to be an illiterate form of Hitchin, a common enough name derived from a diminutive of Richard. In Cornwall the plural Hitchens is frequently found.

The maiden name of Mary, the wife of William Lea, has been deduced from the naming of their third daughter, Mary Trevor. Alscott, where Elizabeth and Margaret Lea were born lies a mile or so to the north-west of Wrockwardine.

The Hitchin family, (or Ichin, Itchen etc) caused me much trouble a few years ago. John Ichin had been born in 1762 in Wrockwardine but his first child appeared to have been born as late as 1802 in Longdon-upon-Tern, where six more children, including my great-great-grandfather, Francis, were also raised. It seemed very late to be starting a family, in the eighteenth century, at the age of forty, and I suspected an earlier marriage. His wife had appeared in the parish register only as Jane and no marriage could be found around 1800 either in Longdon or Wrockwardine.

I wrote to a family historian in Shropshire and she came up with the answer: John Ichin had married Jinny (Jane) Perce in Lilleshall, 26 October 1789 and thereafter from 1790-1800, six children had been born to them and baptized in that same parish. The answer seemed obvious: the family had moved from Lilleshall to Longdon about 1800. But there was more to it than that.

In the Longdon parish register John and Jane are described as being 'of the Waste.' This can only mean that they lived across the Tern in Long Waste, not only a separate village, but in a different parish, Ercall Magna. This in itself is no problem: parents have never been obliged to have their children baptized at their Parish Church; it has always been open to them to have a christening at the nearest church - a sensible provision, given the size of some parishes. So that was all right.

But what about John's move from Wrockwardine to Lilleshall, two parishes away, in 1789? Perhaps his bride was a native of Lilleshall. I looked at the map again. There is a detachment of Wrockwardine parish lying between Wellington and Lilleshall parishes. What did this mean?

A reference book told me that it was common practice in mediaeval times to make woodland areas in one parish available to another in order that the natural resources of a district should be fairly divided between neighbouring communities. I looked at a nineteenth century Ordnance Survey Map and, lying in the sector detached to Wrockwardine parish was 'Wrockwardine Wood.' The area is still so marked on the 1963 1" to 1mile Seventh Series, sheet 119, although by then built upon. (As a matter of interest, a strip of land, marked on the nineteenth century map as 'Wrockwardine Moor,' lay about 1½ miles ENE of Longdon. The strip is still there on the Seventh Series map but it no longer has any name. It lies within the neighbouring parish of Eyton upon the Weald Moors.)

So the answer seems to be that John Ichin was born in the Wrockwardine Wood and was baptized six miles to the west in Wrockwardine parish church. Then he married Jinny Perce in Lilleshall parish church three miles to the NE and lived in Wrockwardine Wood. After their sixth child was born, they moved, about 1800, to Long Waste, about six miles to the NW, where another seven children were born. Mystery solved - perhaps. (Incidentally, Lilleshall means 'Lill's Hill.')

Finally, John and Jinny moved to Uffington, to the east of Shrewsbury. In 2000 I visited the village and found, near the church porch, the headstone commemorating the deaths of John, Jinny and their daughter, Martha. As the last was only 29 when she died there may have been some tragedy, although nothing specific is mentioned.

(Uffington, Salop, 2000.)

Jane Pierce was 19 when she married and it is recorded in the Lilleshall parish register that the marriage was by licence and with the consent of her parents. For the mechanics of marriage by special licence, see the marriage of John Hammond and Ann Dumper.

The Whitehouses and the Walkers

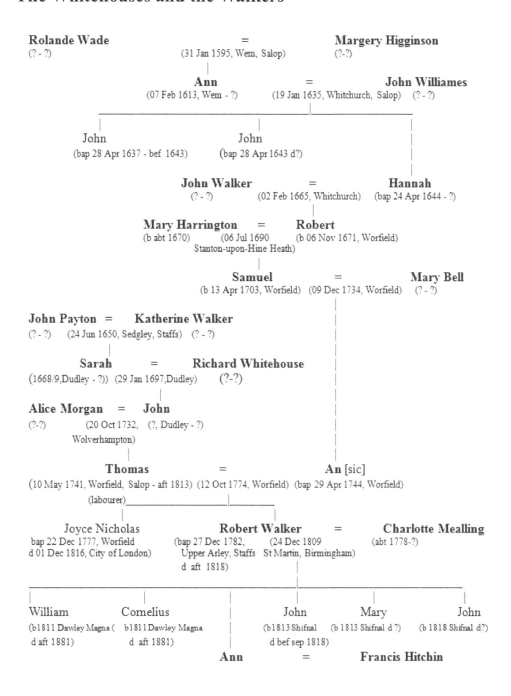

Rolande Wade   =   Margery Higginson
(? - ?)   (31 Jan 1595, Wem, Salop) (?-?)

Ann   =   John Williames
(07 Feb 1613, Wem - ?) (19 Jan 1635, Whitchurch, Salop) (? - ?)

John   John
(bap 28 Apr 1637 - bef 1643) (bap 28 Apr 1643 d?)

John Walker   =   Hannah
(? - ?) (02 Feb 1665, Whitchurch) (bap 24 Apr 1644 - ?)

Mary Harrington = Robert
(b abt 1670) (06 Jul 1690 (b 06 Nov 1671, Worfield)
Stanton-upon-Hine Heath)

Samuel   =   Mary Bell
(b 13 Apr 1703, Worfield) (09 Dec 1734, Worfield) (? - ?)

John Payton = Katherine Walker
(? - ?) (24 Jun 1650, Sedgley, Staffs) (? - ?)

Sarah   =   Richard Whitehouse
(1668/9,Dudley - ?)) (29 Jan 1697,Dudley) (?-?)

Alice Morgan = John
(?-?) (20 Oct 1732, (?, Dudley - ?)
Wolverhampton)

Thomas   =   An [sic]
(10 May 1741, Worfield, Salop - aft 1813) (12 Oct 1774, Worfield) (bap 29 Apr 1744, Worfield)
(labourer)

Joyce Nicholas   Robert Walker = Charlotte Mealling
bap 22 Dec 1777, Worfield (bap 27 Dec 1782, (24 Dec 1809 (abt 1778-?)
d 01 Dec 1816, City of London) Upper Arley, Staffs St Martin, Birmingham)
     d aft 1818)

William Cornelius   John   Mary   John
(b1811 Dawley Magna (b1811 Dawley Magna (b1813 Shifnal (b 1813 Shifnal d ?) (b 1818 Shifnal d?)
d aft 1881) d aft 1881) d bef sep 1818)

Ann   =   Francis Hitchin

Although I think of this branch of the family predominantly in terms of the Whitehouses, the earliest entry is that of Rolande Wade of Wem, in north Shropshire, whose daughter's husband, John Williames, may have been born in Whitchurch, an adjoining parish. This town was known to the Romans as *Mediolanum,* a name given to no fewer than 47 towns in the Roman world, the most famous being Milan. The name probably refers to the fact it is built on level ground and for this we can make a comparison with Wem, which indicates perhaps that it is a marshy site. The Saxon name of Whitchurch - a common one - is thought to indicate that it had a stone church (rather than a white one.) In mediaeval times it was an important ecclesiastical centre.

We do not know where John Walker came from, but his son, Robert, was born in Worfield, in the south-eastern corner of Shropshire. Robert moved up to Stanton-upon-Hine to fetch his bride, Mary Harrington, and returned to Worfield, where his son, Samuel, was born, lived and married Mary Bell, whose provenance is unknown.

Meanwhile, another Walker family had settled in Sedgley, in the next county, Staffordshire, where a member of that family, Katherine, married John Payton in 1650. They must have moved south to Dudley in Worcestershire because their daughter, Sarah, married the first Whitehouse to come upon the scene - Richard. John, son of Richard and Sarah, met and married Alice Morgan in Wolverhampton but by 1741 they had moved to Worfield and it was here that their son, Thomas, married An Walker, daughter of our previously mentioned Samuel and Mary.

A daughter of Thomas and An, Joyce Nicholas, was born in Worfield, but they moved a few miles south, and just into Staffordshire, for the birth of their son, Robert Walker, in Upper Arley, in 1782. Robert married Charlotte Mealling in Birmingham and it was their third child, Ann, who married Francis Hitchin.

Dawley Magna and Shifnal, where Robert's and Charlotte's children were born, are close to one another and are both in the south-eastern corner or Shropshire.

We must now pause for breath and consider a few details arising from the above account.

First, it will be noticed that I have been unable to find ancestors for several of the wives. This is largely because when baptisms are recorded, the father's first name and surname are invariably given, whereas usually the mother's first name only is written down. Unless you can find a firm marriage date for the couple, the mother's surname is likely to remain unknown. In Scotland the task is much easier: by law a Scotswoman retained her maiden name throughout her life, sometimes even at burial. Certainly when her children are born the maiden name is given, sometimes confusing the researcher, who imagines she is unmarried.

Even if a marriage can be found it is sometimes very difficult to trace the ancestry of either party. In the case of Charlotte Mealling this is particularly frustrating. The only woman of that name alive at the right time is traceable to Dorset. To frustrate matters even further, two of the three possible fathers for Charlotte came from the Midlands. It is very tempting to guess that Charlotte's father moved from Gloucestershire or Worcestershire down to Dorset and that she later moved north. This solution, although possible, is unsound.

Next, towards the end of the 18th century the occupations of ordinary people begin to be recorded in parish registers. (We have already seen this among my Hammond ancestors.) For example, Robert Walker Whitehouse is described at his children's baptisms as either a gardener or a servant. This must mean that he worked in the grounds of a big house, especially as his daughter Ann was born at Old House, Dawley Magna. His father, Thomas, is described as a labourer. (This last piece of information was obtained from Mr Keith Percy, who has made an extensive study of the Whitehouse name.)
From 1841, the date of the first detailed Census, one can of course expect to find details of professions and occupations.

Then there is the question of middle names. Before the 19th century it is rare for ordinary people to have a middle name. From the 1800s the practice becomes more common. Sometimes it may be done to honour an important godfather and this may be the case in the instance of Robert Walker Whitehouse. It is more likely, however, that his middle name is an acknowledgment of his Walker ancestry. We shall meet this practice again when we come to deal with Deftys.

Fourthly, a word of warning. The Whitehouse lineage I have proposed above has to be regarded with some care. The truth is that the name Whitehouse is very common in the Midlands and is not always capable of 100% checking. Nevertheless, I have done my best and reckon that the results are as accurate as I can make them. We have already met a Whitehouse as the first wife of my grandfather, Harry Charles Hammond. We shall meet the name again later in this chapter.

Finally, a word on the origins of the name, Whitehouse. I read somewhere that it derives from a word like *Whitehalse,* meaning 'white neck'. This seems pretty fanciful to me and the most obvious solution is almost certainly the correct one.

The Powells

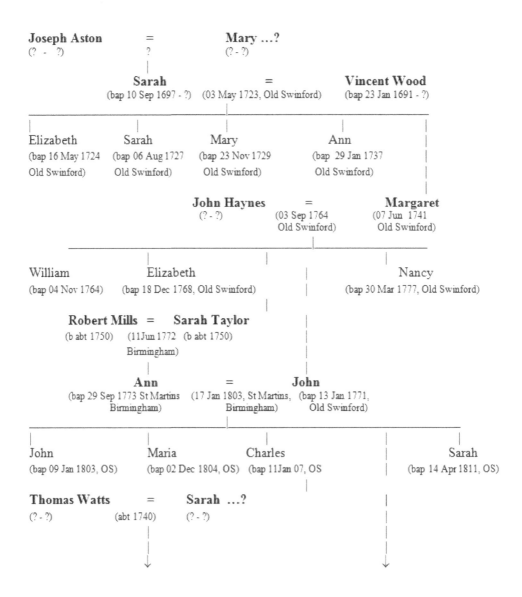

Joseph Aston   =   **Mary ...?**
(? - ?)   ?   (? - ?)

                          |

                  Sarah   =   **Vincent Wood**
            (bap 10 Sep 1697 - ?) (03 May 1723, Old Swinford) (bap 23 Jan 1691 - ?)

Elizabeth   Sarah   Mary   Ann
(bap 16 May 1724   (bap 06 Aug 1727   (bap 23 Nov 1729   (bap 29 Jan 1737
Old Swinford)   Old Swinford)   Old Swinford)   Old Swinford)

            John Haynes   =   **Margaret**
            (? - ?)   (03 Sep 1764   (07 Jun 1741
                               Old Swinford)   Old Swinford)

William   Elizabeth   Nancy
(bap 04 Nov 1764)   (bap 18 Dec 1768, Old Swinford)   (bap 30 Mar 1777, Old Swinford)

        Robert Mills = **Sarah Taylor**
        (b abt 1750)   (11 Jun 1772 (b abt 1750)
                        Birmingham)

                  Ann   =   **John**
        (bap 29 Sep 1773 St Martins   (17 Jan 1803, St Martins,   (bap 13 Jan 1771,
                Birmingham)   Birmingham)   Old Swinford)

John   Maria   Charles   Sarah
(bap 09 Jan 1803, OS)   (bap 02 Dec 1804, OS) (bap 11 Jan 07, OS)   (bap 14 Apr 1811, OS)

Thomas Watts   =   **Sarah ...?**
(? - ?)   (abt 1740)   (? - ?)

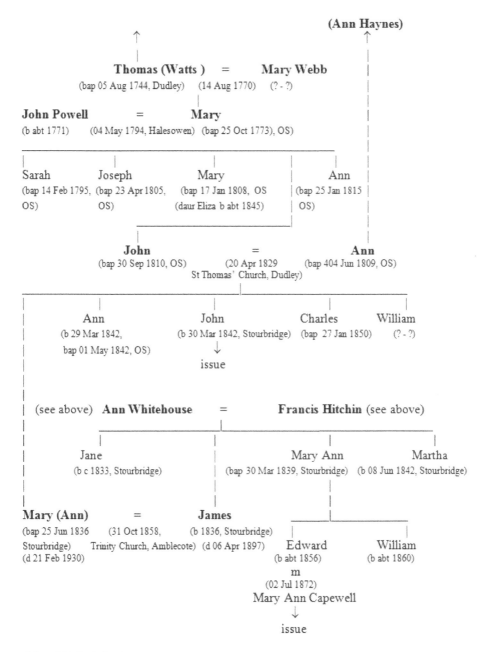

(Ann Haynes)

Thomas (Watts)   =   **Mary Webb**
(bap 05 Aug 1744, Dudley)   (14 Aug 1770)   (? - ?)

John Powell   =   **Mary**
(b abt 1771)   (04 May 1794, Halesowen)   (bap 25 Oct 1773), OS)

Sarah	Joseph	Mary	Ann
(bap 14 Feb 1795,	(bap 23 Apr 1805,	(bap 17 Jan 1808, OS	(bap 25 Jan 1815
OS)	OS)	(daur Eliza b abt 1845)	OS)

John   =   **Ann**
(bap 30 Sep 1810, OS)   (20 Apr 1829   (bap 404 Jun 1809, OS)
St Thomas' Church, Dudley)

Ann	John	Charles	William
(b 29 Mar 1842,	(b 30 Mar 1842, Stourbridge)	(bap 27 Jan 1850)	(? - ?)
bap 01 May 1842, OS)	↓ issue		

(see above)   **Ann Whitehouse**   =   **Francis Hitchin** (see above)

Jane		Mary Ann	Martha
(b c 1833, Stourbridge)		(bap 30 Mar 1839, Stourbridge)	(b 08 Jun 1842, Stourbridge)

Mary (Ann)   =   **James**
(bap 25 Jun 1836   (31 Oct 1858,   (b 1836, Stourbridge)
Stourbridge)   Trinity Church, Amblecote)   (d 06 Apr 1897)
(d 21 Feb 1930)

Edward	William
(b abt 1856)	(b abt 1860)

m
(02 Jul 1872)
Mary Ann Capewell
↓
issue

OS = Old Swinford

57

The Powells enter the genealogical table fairly late and the fact that although the 1841 Census shows John to have been born in Worcestershire, and no ancestor to him has yet been found leads to the conclusion that the origins of the family are perhaps to be found outside the Midlands. This in turn raises the question of whether or not there is a Welsh connection here. For of the two origins given for the name, one is 'son of Paul', while the other is '(m)apHowell', which means 'the son of Hoel.' This formation is in line with other names of Welsh origin, such as 'Prichard,' 'Probert' and Preece; 'map' is cognate with Scots/Irish 'mac/mc'. The question is open.

The other names and places seem quite firmly linked to the Birmingham area and the name Aston reveals eventual origin in a well-known area. Dudley, Halesowen and Stourbridge are close to each other. Amblecote was a small village just outside Stourbridge.

The earliest family where occupations are given is that of the first John Powell. Details of the 1841 Census are given below:

1841 Census LYE HO 107/1198

ASHCROFT (LOWER LYE)

				[Real ages - following baptismal records]	
John Powell	70	Nailer	Y	[70	]
Mary Powell	69		Y	[69	]
Sarah Powell	40	Nailer	Y	[46	]
Joseph Powell	30	Nailer	Y	[36	]
Mary Powell	24	Paper Maker	Y	[33	]
Nancy Powell	20	Paper Maker	Y	[20	]
Eliza Powell	5		Y		

[Eliza was the daughter of Mary, father unknown.
John Powell junior, b 1810, had married Ann Haynes in 1829 and was living elsewhere.
'Nancy' is a diminutive of 'Ann.']

Lower Lye is just outside Stourbridge.
Making nails was a cottage industry in which the whole family could be involved. I am not clear what was the task of a paper maker.

For Francis Hitchin and his family, here is the 1851 Census:

1851 Census HO107/2035 53:

'Stourbridge   Old Swinford

[4] Bury's Yard	Francis Hitchin	Head	Mar	38	Engineer, Engine Fitter	Shrop	Long
(High St)	Ann Hitchin	Wife	Mar	39			Wales UK
	Jane Hitchin	Daur	U	18	Dressmaker	Worcester	Stourbridge
	James Hitchin	Son	U	14	Engine Fitter's Apprentice	do	do
	Mary Ann Hitchin	Daur	U	13	Scholar	do	do
	Martha Hitchin	Daur	U	9	do	do	do'

James junior, as will be confirmed later, followed in his father's trade

But this Census entry contains a shock. Ann Whitehouse is shown as being born in Wales, UK.
How can this be? Fortunately the 1861 Census remedies the situation:

1861 Census: RG9 2065 folio 36:

'171 1 Berry's [sic] Yard 1 [inhabited] house

Francis Hitchin	Head	Mar	50	Engine Fitter	Salop	Longwaist [sic]
Ann Hitchin	Wife	Mar	48	Wife	do	Bridgnorth
Maryan [sic] Hitchin	Daur	Un	22		Worcs	Stourbridge
Edward Hitchin	Grdsn	Un	5	Scholar	do	do
William Hitchin	Grandsn	Un	1		do	do'

Here Ann is clearly shown as being born at Bridgnorth. This lies some ten miles south of Dawley Magna, where she was in fact born, but at least it is in the right county. It is possible (as I have learned from other instances) that the family moved from Shifnal, where later children were born, to Bridgnorth, and that this was the home she remembered. Long Waist, where Francis was born, is incorrectly spelled but is easily recognisable. On reflection, I think that the entry 'Wales' is a corruption of an entry 'Waste' and refers with 'Long' to the entry for Francis.

Edward and William are the illegitimate children of Mary Ann. Father unknown.

The Later Hitchin Family

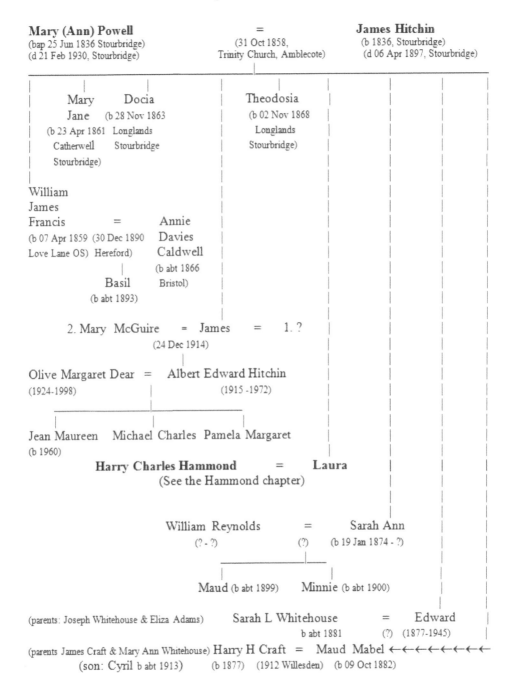

Mary (Ann) Powell (bap 25 Jun 1836 Stourbridge) (d 21 Feb 1930, Stourbridge)   = (31 Oct 1858, Trinity Church, Amblecote)   **James Hitchin** (b 1836, Stourbridge) (d 06 Apr 1897, Stourbridge)

Mary Jane (b 23 Apr 1861 Catherwell Stourbridge)   Docia (b 28 Nov 1863 Longlands Stourbridge)   Theodosia (b 02 Nov 1868 Longlands Stourbridge)

William James Francis (b 07 Apr 1859 Love Lane OS)   = (30 Dec 1890 Hereford)   Annie Davies Caldwell (b abt 1866 Bristol)

Basil (b abt 1893)

2. Mary McGuire = James = 1. ? (24 Dec 1914)

Olive Margaret Dear (1924-1998)   =   Albert Edward Hitchin (1915 -1972)

Jean Maureen (b 1960)   Michael Charles   Pamela Margaret

Harry Charles Hammond   =   Laura
(See the Hammond chapter)

William Reynolds (? - ?)   = (?)   Sarah Ann (b 19 Jan 1874 - ?)

Maud (b abt 1899)   Minnie (b abt 1900)

(parents: Joseph Whitehouse & Eliza Adams)   Sarah L Whitehouse b abt 1881   = (?)   Edward (1877-1945)

(parents James Craft & Mary Ann Whitehouse) Harry H Craft = Maud Mabel ←←←←←←←←
(son: Cyril b abt 1913)   (b 1877)   (1912 Willesden)   (b 09 Oct 1882)

60

When James Hitchin married Mary Ann Powell in 1858 she had been a servant for at least seven years, because in 1851, when she was 15, she features as a nurse-maid in a household with three other servants in High Street, Stourbridge. The couple were married in Trinity Church, Amblecote. She is described on the certificate as a servant and was given away by William Powell, who was probably her brother, although her father was still alive. The bride's address is shown as Love Lane and the Powell family were still there in 1861, at the time of the Census. James is described as an engineer and Francis, his father, as a fitter. I am not sure what precisely was meant by those terms in 1858.

In 1859 William James Francis, their first child, was born in Love Lane. This may mean that James and Mary Ann were living with the Powells. We know a little about William: he married, went to live in Hereford and had at least one child. By 1901 he had moved with his family back to Stourbridge, where he is described as a grocer's manager. He was present at his sister Laura's wedding to Harry Charles Hammond, where he probably gave her away, as their father, James, had died in 1897.

In 1861 Mary Jane Hitchin was born. The family had moved to Catherwell Street, Stourbridge.   We know nothing of her except that she survived until at least 1881.

We now come to the mystery surrounding Docia, the next daughter, who was born in 1863, by which time the family had moved to Longlands, still in Stourbridge.

I well remember my grandmother, Laura, telling me that she had had two sisters named Theodosia. The first had died after her dress burst into flames when she was standing in front of an open fire. This story made a great impression on me as a young child and when I came to write the family history I decided to investigate.
There had indeed been two daughters similarly named: one is called Docia on her 1863 birth certificate and the second Theodosia, born in 1868. It seemed that I was on the right track, especially as Docia is not mentioned on the 1871 Census return, nor on any other subsequent returns; Theodosia appears on both the 1871 and 1881 Censuses.
The problem arises because although I have checked the death records from 1863 to 1871 no evidence can be found of Docia's death. Surely the death of a child could not have been concealed from officialdom. Yet the evidence of my grandmother and the naming of Theodosia indicate that Docia must have died. Perhaps I shall never solve this mystery.

James Hitchin was the next child, also born at Longlands in 1866. A few years ago I learned more about him because one of my correspondents, Jean Morgan (née Hitchin), turned out to be a granddaughter of James. She lives in Kinver, near to Stourbridge, and has been very helpful, especially in the finding the graves of James, our great-grandfather, and Edward, his son, of whom more later. On the 1881 Census James is described as a porter and in 1891 he was an asylum attendant at St Helen, Sutton, Lancashire. In 1891 he was still unmarried.

After Theodosia comes my grandmother, Laura. In 1881 both sisters were at home in Cecil St, Stourbridge with the rest of the family, but in 1891 they were working as servants in

Worcester, as, respectively, nursemaid and housemaid. It was of course quite common for Victorian girls to leave home to go into service but less usual for two sisters to be employed by the same employer, in this case a widow living on her own means with two daughters (one aged 18 and described as a scholar) and two sons.

Laura never revealed (to me) that she had been a housemaid. In fact, she was inclined to give herself airs, implying that her family was middle-class. Her father, she said, always wore gloves and gave to the poor at Christmas. This may be true but I suspect that is more likely to reflect her experiences as an employee.

The 1901 Census, which took place a few months before Laura's marriage to Harry Charles Hammond, shows that she had travelled up to London and was staying in the house of her future brother-in-law's mother, Mary Ann Craft.

The complicated story of the Whitehouses and the Crafts should now be told.

First, the 1901 Census:

1901 Census 1379/40

24 Alfred St (3 doors away from William George Hammond and family):

Mary Anne Craft	Head	Widw	54			Worcestershire, Stourbridge
Walter Arthur* do	Son	S	23	Plumber	Worker	Middlesex, Northwood
Harry Charles Hammond	Boarder	Widr	43	Dock Foreman do		Hants, Andover
Charles Harry Hammond	Boarder	Widr	47 [? sc 40] Widd[?] Attending			
				Ships' Hatchway	Worker [faintly] Harb	
						Hants, Andover
Harry George Hammond	Boarder	S	16	Lighterman	Worker	
				(apprentice)		
				[faintly] Barge		Essex, West Ham
Laura Hitchin	Visitor	S	30			Worcestershire, Stourbridge

*Presumably this is the Arthur W Craft of the 1881 and 1891 Censuses

Missing is Louisa Ellen Hammond, 15, sister to Harry George. She may have been in service somewhere. Both were children of Charles Harry, whose wife had died of pneumonia in 1890.

Note that Harry Charles Hammond is here shown as a widower, but on his marriage certificate to Laura Hitchin he appears as a 'bachelor,' The marriage took place in Stourbridge and my grandmother would not have wanted it to appear that this was grandfather's second marriage!

Now for the **Crafts** and **Whitehouses**

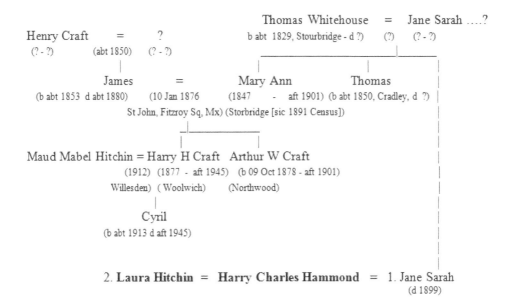

2. **Laura Hitchin** = **Harry Charles Hammond** = 1. Jane Sarah
(d 1899)

The above chart shows how the families were inter-related. It also explains why Laura Hitchin was in London in 1901: Mary Ann Craft (née Whitehouse) would have told the Hitchins back in Stourbridge (her birthplace) that her sister (Jane Sarah) had died and that Harry Charles Hammond was now 'available.' Ten years later the family relationship was cemented by her son Harry H Craft's marriage to Maud.

Furthermore, reference back to one of the grandmothers of Laura and Maud Mabel will remind us that she too was a Whitehouse. It is not known whether she was related to Thomas Whitehouse, father of Mary Ann and Jane Sarah.

But there is more still. Laura's younger brother, Edward, also married a Whitehouse, Sarah L, whose parents were Joseph Whitehouse and Eliza Adams. (See p 60) I do not know how or whether Joseph was related to the other Whitehouses.

I knew, or at least met, all three of Laura's younger siblings.

First of all, Sarah. I must have been quite young when I saw her at my grandmother's house because I asked her if her husband was still living; to which she replied: 'I hope so!'

Here is the family on the1901 Census:

RG 13/2669 Folio 59 page 1

'Stafford[shire], Kinver, St Peter

2 Enville Road

William Reynolds	Head	M	32	Game Keeper	Worker	Claverly, Shrops
Sarah Ann "	Wife	M	27			Stourbridge, Worcs
Maude "	Daur	S	2			Kinver, Staffs
Minnie "	Daur	S	1			Kinver, Staffs'

Later, my mother, Madeline Defty, went with Laura Hitchin to visit Sarah at Kinver. Madeline later told of a row that developed between the sisters over whether one of them was at a family event. Thereafter during the whole visit they would not speak to each other except through Madeline!

Next, Edward Hitchin.

Edward Hitchin was Edward Hammond's god-father and was a great favourite with the latter. His wife, Sarah, was an invalid, suffering from what I suppose would be called bowel cancer. They had no children.
My mother, Madeline Defty, told me that he had attempted suicide at one time and this was confirmed by information I received in July 2000 from Jean Morgan, who sent me a report on his death and the subsequent Inquest:

'Letters show a clear intent to take his life. He had attended doctor's surgery. Tuberculosis and arthritis were diagnosed. He thought he had a stomach growth. In fact he had had an ulcer. He had worked for 30 years for Lunt Bros as manager of a coal business.
'He had been a member of Stourbridge Institute and Social Club and a Bowling Club Council Member. He had been a churchwarden at St John's Church. He is buried in Stourbridge Borough Cemetery.

'Mourners included:
Mrs S L Hitchin - wife
Mrs L Hammond - sister
Mrs S Reynolds - sister
Mrs M Craft - sister
Mr H Craft   )
Mr W Whitehouse   ) brothers-in-law
Mr C H Whitehouse   )

4 nephews:
Mr EH Hammond
Mr T Hammond   [I am inclined to think that T Hammond represents 'Ted' and that therefore my father appears twice on the list.]

64

| L Surrell | [?] |
| Mr M H Surrell | [?] |

Niece
| Mrs E Chambers | [?]' |

The identities of L Surrell, Mr M H Surrell and Mrs E Chambers not yet known.

On 2 October 2000 I visited the cemetery with Jean Morgan and discovered Edward's grave. There was an engraved flower vase (see photo), with a dedication 'from his sisters' (viz Laura, Sarah, Maud.)   There was no mention of his wife and I wonder where is she buried.

While we were there Jean and I looked for a headstone for Edward's father, James Hitchin. We found nothing on the plot. This seems strange because when he died in 1897, his wife and presumably all his children (except Docia) were alive.

As for James's wife, Mary Ann, she survived him by 37 years, dying in 1930. Here she is with the younger members of her family in 1901:

1901 Census:

Stourbridge, Part of Stourbridge St Thomas

Albert St   [Part of inhabited house]

Mary Hitchin	Head	Wid	65	Monthly Nurse [overwritten 'sick']		Worc	Stourbridge
Edward do	Son	S	23	Leather Dresser	Worker	do	do
Maud M do	Daur	S	18			do	do'

And here are the details of her death certificate:

'Widow of James Hitchin General Fitter. Cause of death: '[d 21 Feb 1930] 1-(w) myocardial degeneration (not M) Certified by A R Sharrod [?] M.B.' 'Laura Hammond Daughter Present at the death 18 Brampton Road East Ham E6'

Laura Hitchin used to say that Mary Powell had very long tresses of hair and that I was taken as a baby to her; she was blind at the time but could feel me.
It was alleged by my mother, Madeline Defty, that Laura and Mary, her mother, did not get on. Madeline related to me the following story.
When my father, Edward Hammond, was a little boy he was one day in the garden, dressed in a new sailor suit. His grandmother, Mary, was with him. My father managed to get some mud on his clothes. Mary encouraged to smear more mud on his suit, whispering: 'Go on boy. Put some more on.'

Finally, the last member of the family, Maud Mabel. I knew this sister, her husband (uncle Harry) and their son, Cyril, quite well because they used to visit my grandparents' house. They lived at Pinner or Wembley. Harry Craft was a great comic and was very popular with my father. I suppose I must have seen them several time during the 1940s but I know nothing of their subsequent history. I think it likely that Laura, my grandmother, hoped that my father's sister, Grace, and her cousin, Cyril, might marry, but nothing came of any such plans.

In fact Grace, who was my godmother and took her duties as such quite seriously, had a number of suitors. One, whom I was encouraged to call Uncle Fred and who, I believe, was a ship's officer, gave my parents two pictures made of butterflies' wings, representing views of Rio de Janeiro. These pictures hang today in one of our bedrooms - a monument to political incorrectness. None of my aunt's romances prospered.

It was rumoured that any prospective husband would be expected to live in my grandparents' house and look after them

Because of the quarrels which I mentioned right at the beginning of this history, I lost track of Aunt Grace after 1951. In the 1980s, after my mother died, I found that she had late in life married a widower named John Wells. He was a freemason and took her to many functions. I hope she had happiness during these years because she was very kind to me.

I may seem to have been unsympathetic towards my grandmother, Laura Hitchin; certainly many of the criticisms of her seem to have stemmed from my mother.
On reflection, despite the quarrels that occurred in the family and the resentment shown by my mother, she emerges as a somewhat self-centred woman who tried to keep up appearances but was basically well-meaning. There was clearly a quarrelsome side to her nature but quite a generous side too. She was also capable of laughing at herself, especially when she came out with such classic Stourbridge quotes as 'Have yer washed yer?'

The Deftys of County Durham

The Early Deftys

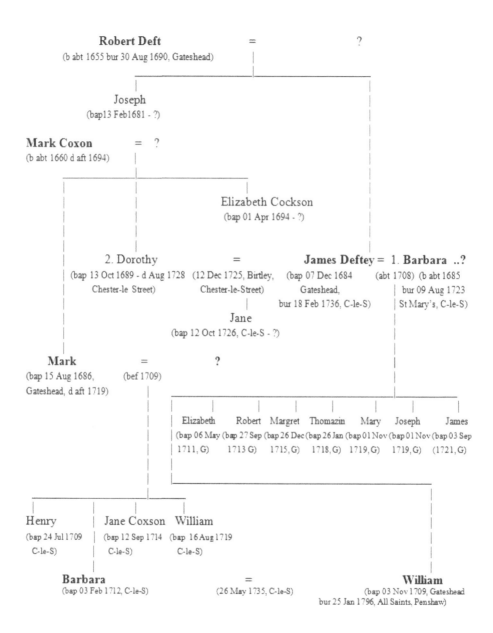

Robert Deft   =   ?
(b abt 1655 bur 30 Aug 1690, Gateshead)

Joseph
(bap13 Feb1681 - ?)

Mark Coxon   =   ?
(b abt 1660 d aft 1694)

Elizabeth Cockson
(bap 01 Apr 1694 - ?)

2. Dorothy   =   **James Deftey** = 1. **Barbara ..?**
(bap 13 Oct 1689 - d Aug 1728   (12 Dec 1725, Birtley,   (bap 07 Dec 1684   (abt 1708) (b abt 1685
Chester-le Street)   Chester-le-Street)   Gateshead,   bur 09 Aug 1723
                                  bur 18 Feb 1736, C-le-S)   St Mary's, C-le-S)

Jane
(bap 12 Oct 1726, C-le-S - ?)

Mark   =   ?
(bap 15 Aug 1686,   (bef 1709)
Gateshead, d aft 1719)

Elizabeth	Robert	Margret	Thomazin	Mary	Joseph	James
(bap 06 May	(bap 27 Sep	(bap 26 Dec	(bap 26 Jan	(bap 01 Nov	(bap 01 Nov	(bap 03 Sep
1711, G)	1713 G)	1715, G)	1718, G)	1719, G)	1719, G)	(1721, G)

Henry   Jane Coxson   William
(bap 24 Jul 1709   (bap 12 Sep 1714   (bap 16 Aug 1719
C-le-S)   C-le-S)   C-le-S)

Barbara   =   **William**
(bap 03 Feb 1712, C-le-S)   (26 May 1735, C-le-S)   (bap 03 Nov 1709, Gateshead
                                       bur 25 Jan 1796, All Saints, Penshaw)

Robert Deft is our earliest proven Defty ancestor and the earliest certain Defty/Deft inhabitant of Gateshead.

In the 17th cent Gateshead parish records it is possible, with the eye of faith, to see some earlier Deft/Deft entries but they are very difficult to read and the evidence is not secure.

The following references to Deftys are found in documents of the Prerogative Court of Yorkshire Exch Deps:

> John Defte   17-18 Eliz Mich 5
> Prerog YK/PER/3373 York Arch Soc Rec Series 1585-94
> 1554-1568 YK/PER/3531

These may refer to Property Wills of John Defte of Skerne, Harthill in the Deanery Act Book

The Borthwick Institute of Historical Research, Grants of Probate and Administration, shows the following:

ORDER NO 5001

> 'On 1 December 1558 administration of the goods of John Defte late of Skerne, was granted to   Alice Defte, his relict [ie widow].'

There is also reference in the same order to:

> Thomas Defte of Skerne, Holderness Deanery:

'On 30 May 1580 administration of the goods of John Defte late of Skerne, deceased, was granted to Martin, John and Joan Defte, children of William Defte, late of Skerne'

Here are the references in the International Genealogical Index to 16th and 17th cent Deft/ys in the East Riding of Yorkshire:

Leconfield:

Jane Deft	bap 30 Jan 1599	Rychard Deft
Jane Deft	m 29 Nov 1601	Lancelot Sharpe
Richard Defte	m 22 Oct 1598	Elizabeth Ferrington
Robert Defte	m 4 Jun 1607	Johan Bursay

Hayton:

Abigaill Defte	bap 15 Sep 1615	[father] Petter [Defte]
Ann Deft	bap 15 Jan 1619	Petter
Katharine Deft	bap 2 Apr 1622	Peter
John Deft	bap 21 Apr 1625	Peter
John Deft	bap`16 Aug 1627	Peter
Margaret Deft	bap 11 Aug 1644	Peter
Margret Deft	m 16 Apr 1677	John Hayton
Peter Deft	bap 23 Apr 1648	Peter
Peter Deft	m 19 Apr 1640	Maragret Stevenson
Petter Defte	m 6 Nov 1614	Margaret Willows
Robert Deft	m 10 Aug 1619	Elsabeth Burmbye

(NB a curiosity: Robert Defts bap Dec 1701 at St Botolphs Without Aldgate [London] Lebert[?] Defts/Sarah)

Finally, an unattributed reference as follows:

Cicilia Deft = Thomas Wallis
     1585, Bransburton
              |
Joannas   1585

It seems probable that Skerne, Leconfield, Bransburton and Hayton were part of the Deanery of the former parish of Holderness, which lay on the coast, near the present-day Hornsea.

It is possible that a member of one of these families went north to Gateshead and was the father or grandfather of Robert Deft. This cannot at present be proved; on the other hand, there do not seem to be other Deft/ys, not related to Robert, who were in the Gateshead area about 1700.

The derivation of the surname Defte is certainly a puzzle. The name is generally ignored by reference books although its cognate, Dafte, occurs several times in mediaeval manuscripts. Both seem originally to have meant 'gentle' or 'meek' but the meaning is often changed to 'apt,' skilful' or 'neat.' Both too sometimes carry the sense of 'stupid' or 'foolish,' although the meanings of the words have now settled down so that 'daft,' especially in Scotland, retains the pejorative significance, while 'deft,' although rather rare these days, means clever, usually manually. Another suggested derivation is 'deaf,' which my Grandfather Defty certainly was!

A theory propounded by a correspondent in the 1980s (Hibbert) suggested a Dutch derivation (< Delft). I do not think this is tenable.
The name Deft/Defty is quite rare and the IGI lists baptisms and marriages of only 51 in the

whole of England (16th to 19th centuries). Burials would of course account for a few more entries.

I have found other variations of the name: Duffty, Diffty, Doffty.

The name is (still) almost entirely restricted to the North-East of England.

The name Coxon seems to me more likely to be derived from 'coxswain' than from any other source that I have seen mentioned.

Returning to the family tree shown above, we see that the names of several women are missing: the two wives of the Mark Coxons, father and son; the name of James Deftey's first wife, from whom I am descended; and the name of Robert Deft's wife. None of the relevant marriages has been found and only in the case of James's first wife is the first name given - Barbara; this was at the baptisms of her children. She died less than two years after the birth of her youngest child and therefore it is not surprising that with a large and still young family, James married again, to Dorothy Coxon. This second marriage produced only one child, Jane, whose fate is unknown.

But the Coxons appear again: James's eldest son, William married the niece of his father's second wife. They were not related by blood and so there would have been no impropriety.

Two of James's and Barbara's children, Joseph and Mary, were probably twins: they were baptized on the same day.

We have no information on the occupations of these early Deftys. It seems possible that Robert and his contemporaries, living in Gateshead, on the southern shore of the Tyne, might have been involved in shipping or shipbuilding, perhaps turning to the growing industry of coal-mining before they had moved south to Chester-le-Street. Mining is certainly a strong possibility because we know that two pits were open in the Gateshead area as early as 1645 and 1697. Chester-le-Street had a colliery until 1967 but I have no information as to when it was opened. Later generations of Deftys, living in the same area, are, as we shall see, described as pitmen.

Gateshead ('head of the road') refers to the end of the Roman Road, moving north from Yorkshire and through Chester-le-Street, known to the Romans as *Congangis,* and recorded in 1050 as *Conceceastre.* Across the river, Newcastle upon Tyne was first known as *Pons Aelii* - Hadrian's Bridge. (*Aelius* was his tribal name.)

The Ancestors of Isabella Rain

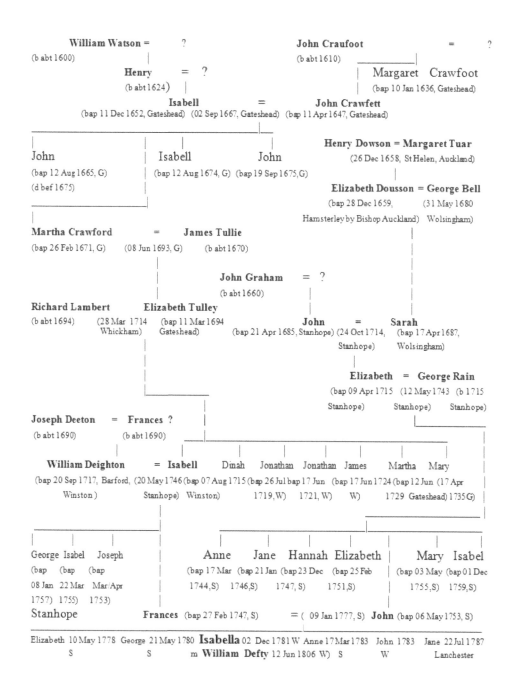

Elizabeth 10 May 1778 George 21 May 1780 **Isabella** 02 Dec 1781 W Anne 17 Mar 1783 John 1783 Jane 22 Jul 1787
     S   S   m **William Defty** 12 Jun 1806 W) S   W   Lanchester

This is a complex and perhaps contentious chart.

The first problem is that the families appear to be on the move quite often. Also, the suspicion remains that I may not have always read the descents correctly and may even have confused several families.

For example, it is possible that the various spellings of Crawford - Crawfett and Crawfoot - do not, as I believe they do, represent varying spellings or mishearing of the same name. Without access to each individual 17th century parish register it is difficult to be certain.

The problem of movement is perhaps not so serious: the parishes of Stanhope, Wolsingham and Hamsterley all lie on the river Wear and are within a few miles of each other, with St Helen Auckland a little further to the south-east. Even Winston, on the road between Darlington and Barnard Castle, is quite near to the others. Whickham, the parish of Richard Lambert lies immediately west of Gateshead, where his wife, Elizabeth Tulley, was baptized. The route connecting all these families would ultimately have been the remains of the old Roman road, Dere Street, running south-north through Lanchester and Ebchester.

The problem of identifying our ancestors' occupations still remains until we come to John Rain, who is described as a farmer at the time of his daughter's, Isabella's, baptism. This corresponds well with his location, Stanhope, which lies well up the valley of the Wear. The ancient parish was the largest in Co Durham but has since been split up into smaller constituents. The village itself lies on the river Wear and extends northwards and westwards into the heights of the Pennine chain.
John Rain's first two children were baptized in Stanhope; Isabella, the next child, was baptized in Wolsingham; then comes Anne, baptized in Stanhope and John in Wolsingham. It is possible that the Rains lived on the edge of Stanhope parish and there-fore chose twice to go to Wolsingham church. There is, however, another likely explanation: in the parish of Wolsingham, towards the border with Hammersley parish, a small enclave from Stanhope parish is shown. It may be that Rains lived inside this enclave and were thus technically part of Stanhope parish, although surrounded by Wolsingham parish. We met a similar situation when dealing with the Hitchins of Shropshire. In fact, though, Isabella's baptismal record shows that in 1781 the family lived at 'North Moor' and today at least that area is shown well to the north-east of the parish, very close to the boundary with Lanchester parish
An added complication is that the Rain family seem to have moved a few miles north-east to Lanchester by 1787, where their last child, Jane, was baptized. Perhaps they did not move at all but had their children baptized at three different churches.

The town of Lanchester is very close to Chester-le-Street where Isabella Rain married William Defty on 12 Jun 1806. It is to the Deftys that we must now return.

The *Pitmen*

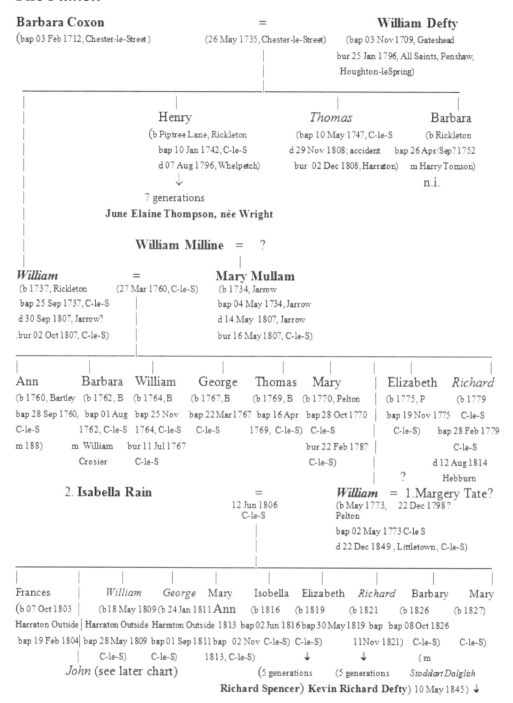

Barbara Coxon   =   **William Defty**

(bap 03 Feb 1712, Chester-le-Street)   (26 May 1735, Chester-le-Street)   (bap 03 Nov 1709, Gateshead

bur 25 Jan 1796, All Saints, Penshaw,

Houghton-leSpring)

Henry   *Thomas*   Barbara

(b Piptree Lane, Rickleton   (bap 10 May 1747, C-le-S   (b Rickleton

bap 10 Jan 1742, C-le-S   d 29 Nov 1808; accident   bap 26 Apr/Sep? 1752

d 07 Aug 1796, Whelpetch)   bur 02 Dec 1808, Harraton)   m Harry Tomson)

↓   n.i.

7 generations

June Elaine Thompson, née Wright

William Milline = ?

William   =   **Mary Mullam**

(b 1737, Rickleton   (27 Mar 1760, C-le-S)   (b 1734, Jarrow

bap 25 Sep 1737, C-le-S   bap 04 May 1734, Jarrow

d 30 Sep 1807, Jarrow?   d 14 May 1807, Jarrow

.bur 02 Oct 1807, C-le-S)   bur 16 May 1807, C-le-S)

Ann	Barbara	William	George	Thomas	Mary	Elizabeth	*Richard*
(b 1760, Bartley	(b 1762, B	(b 1764, B	(b 1767, B	(b 1769, B	(b 1770, Pelton	(b 1775, P	(b 1779
bap 28 Sep 1760,	bap 01 Aug	bap 25 Nov	bap 22 Mar 1767	bap 16 Apr	bap 28 Oct 1770	bap 19 Nov 1775	C-le-S
C-le-S	1762, C-le-S	1764, C-le-S	C-le-S	1769, C-le-S)	C-le-S	C-le-S)	bap 28 Feb 1779
m 188)	m William	bur 11 Jul 1767			bur 22 Feb 1787		C-le-S
	Crosier	C-le-S			C-le-S)		d 12 Aug 1814
						?	Hebburn

2. **Isabella Rain**   =   *William*   =   1.Margery Tate?

12 Jun 1806   (b May 1773,   22 Dec 1798?

C-le-S   Pelton

bap 02 May 1773 C-le S

d 22 Dec 1849 , Littletown, C-le-S)

Frances	*William*	*George*	Mary	Isobella	Elizabeth	*Richard*	Barbary	Mary
(b 07 Oct 1803	(b 18 May 1809	(b 24 Jan 1811	Ann	(b 1816	(b 1819	(b 1821	(b 1826	(b 1827
Harraton Outside	Harraton Outside	Harraton Outside	1813	bap 02 Jun 1816	bap 30 May 1819	bap	bap 08 Oct 1826	
bap 19 Feb 1804	bap 28 May 1809	bap 01 Sep 1811	bap 02 Nov	C-le-S)	C-le-S)	11 Nov 1821)	C-le-S)	C-le-S)
	C-le-S)	C-le-S)	1813, C-le-S)	↓	↓	(m		
John (see later chart)				(5 generations	(5 generations	*Stoddart Dalglish*		
				Richard Spencer)	Kevin Richard Defty)	10 May 1845) ↓		

74

In the eighteenth century the coal-mining industry expanded rapidly and continued to do so during the nineteenth century and the first half of the twentieth, by which time mining was taking place not only in the north-east of England but in many other counties, notably Lancashire, the Midlands, south Wales and even in southern counties, such as Kent and Somerset. Scotland also had many mines, for example in Fife, where the Afflecks lived. The first pits would have been open-cast, but gradually they were worked deeper, and in the case of those near the coast, gradually extended out under the sea-bed.

I have marked in *italics* the names of the men of my family for whose working in the pits I have documentary evidence. It seems certain, however, that Henry, George and Thomas Defty and others of their generation were also coal-miners.

As can be seen, Richard Defty, born in 1779, died in a pit accident in 1814 at Hebburn colliery, near Newcastle. One of the men in the pit changed the course of the air for ventilation; the pit fired, probably because of a spark, and Richard and ten others were burnt to death.

I shall say more about the conditions in the pits when we come to the story of the later. Deftys: in particular the two Johns shown at the bottom of the above chart.

June Thompson, my sixth cousin once removed, and her husband Warwick visited us from Australia a number of years ago. I have also been in touch with Richard Spencer, my fourth cousin once removed, for several years.

Tracing the parents of Mary Mullam proved quite difficult but since that surname is found with various spellings I have concluded, after much searching, that her father was a William Milline. At her baptism her mother is not mentioned but Mary is stated to be illegitimate. The marriage to William Defty on 27 Mar 1760 was by 'license' (note the spelling) and she was pregnant at the time, because Anne, her first daughter, was baptized six months later on 28 Sep. One of the witnesses at the marriage ceremony was a Henry Coxon, probably an uncle or cousin of William.

Although the life of a miner was undeniably hard it is surprising how well they survived - that is, if they managed to avoid a pit disaster. The two of my ancestors who worked as pitmen in the 18th and early 19th centuries lived on into their seventies; their wives, Mary and Isabella, likewise. The first William Defty, born in 1709, did even better: he died in 1796. It is true that we cannot be sure that he was a pitman, but it seems very likely.

There is a slight problem with Isabella's and William's first-born: Frances. She was born On 7 Oct 1803 and baptized at Tanfield on 19 Feb 1804. At that time Isabella and William were not married and as the father's name is not shown we cannot be absolutely sure that the child was William's. Certainly we seem to have the right mother because Frances was Isabella's mother's name.

Part of the problem (and also, incidentally, the solution) is that William's and Isabella's marriage occurred when he was 33, rather late for a marriage at that time. The inference could be that William had already been married - and I found a likely candidate: a Marjery Tate married a William Defty in 1798, just about the right date for a first marriage for William. The name Defty was and is rare enough to support this theory. What happened to Marjery? We do not at present know. She may have died in child-birth. If so, William met and had an affair with Isobella before marrying her in 1806.

The Ancestors of Margaret Gray

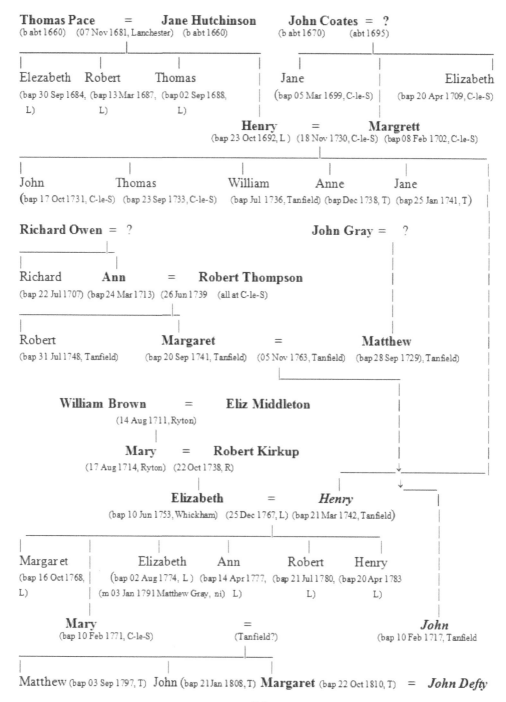

Thomas Pace   =   Jane Hutchinson   John Coates = ?
(b abt 1660) (07 Nov 1681, Lanchester) (b abt 1660)   (b abt 1670)   (abt 1695)

Elezabeth   Robert   Thomas   Jane   Elizabeth
(bap 30 Sep 1684, (bap 13 Mar 1687, (bap 02 Sep 1688,   (bap 05 Mar 1699, C-le-S) (bap 20 Apr 1709, C-le-S)
  L)   L)   L)

Henry   =   Margrett
(bap 23 Oct 1692, L) (18 Nov 1730, C-le-S) (bap 08 Feb 1702, C-le-S)

John   Thomas   William   Anne   Jane
(bap 17 Oct 1731, C-le-S) (bap 23 Sep 1733, C-le-S) (bap Jul 1736, Tanfield) (bap Dec 1738, T) (bap 25 Jan 1741, T)

Richard Owen = ?   John Gray =   ?

Richard   Ann   =   Robert Thompson
(bap 22 Jul 1707) (bap 24 Mar 1713) (26 Jun 1739   (all at C-le-S)

Robert   Margaret   =   Matthew
(bap 31 Jul 1748, Tanfield) (bap 20 Sep 1741, Tanfield) (05 Nov 1763, Tanfield) (bap 28 Sep 1729), Tanfield)

William Brown   =   Eliz Middleton
(14 Aug 1711, Ryton)

Mary   =   Robert Kirkup
(17 Aug 1714, Ryton) (22 Oct 1738, R)

Elizabeth   =   *Henry*
(bap 10 Jun 1753, Whickham) (25 Dec 1767, L) (bap 21 Mar 1742, Tanfield)

Margaret   Elizabeth   Ann   Robert   Henry
(bap 16 Oct 1768,   (bap 02 Aug 1774, L) (bap 14 Apr 1777, (bap 21 Jul 1780, (bap 20 Apr 1783
L)   (m 03 Jan 1791 Matthew Gray, ni) L)   L)   L)

Mary   =   *John*
(bap 10 Feb 1771, C-le-S) (Tanfield?)   (bap 10 Feb 1717, Tanfield

Matthew (bap 03 Sep 1797, T) John (bap 21 Jan 1808, T) **Margaret** (bap 22 Oct 1810, T) = *John Defty*

The information on the earliest ancestors shown here is sparse and consists largely of baptismal and marriage dates.

Because the areas where these people lived is well away from the coast the inference must be that they were involved in agriculture, although mining must have played an increasing part in their lives.

As before, known pitmen are shown in *italics* and many others should doubtless be so indicated. For example, it seems very likely that the three brothers of Henry Pace were also pitmen. The men of the Gray family also may have worked in the mines.

Most of the place-names mentioned have already appeared, but a new one is Urpeth:

> CHESTER-LE-STREET Baptisms: 'Feb 10 1771 Mary
> D[aughter]of Henry Pace of Urpeth pitman and Elizabeth.'

There are now two places that fit the bill: Low Urpeth and High Urpeth. Both lie about 2-3 miles to the north-west of Chester-le-Street.

There is one early marriage: Elizabeth Kirkup, born in 1753, seems to have been only 14 when she married Henry Pace in 1767, and 15 when her first child was born. This was neither reprehensible nor unusual at the time. It must be remembered that in certain southern states of the USA, 13 is still not an unusual age for girls to be married.

A few notes on the place-names occurring in this section.

Lanchester was the site of a Roman fort and the first syllable means 'long'.

Tanfield means 'field on the R Team,' and the river name itself is apparently from the same root as 'Tame,' 'Thames' and even 'Tamar,' signifying a dark river.

Ryton means 'rye farm'.

Finally, Urpeth means (incredibly) 'bison path' and was in use in 1297, by which time, presumably, the original meaning had been long forgotten.

The Family of John Defty and Margaret Gray

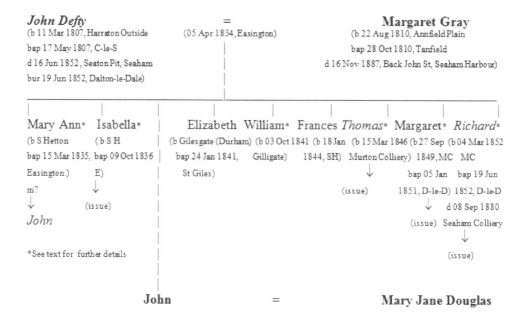

John Defty
(b 11 Mar 1807, Harraton Outside
bap 17 May 1807, C-le-S
d 16 Jun 1852, Seaton Pit, Seaham
bur 19 Jun 1852, Dalton-le-Dale)

= (05 Apr 1834, Easington)

Margaret Gray
(b 22 Aug 1810, Annfield Plain
bap 28 Oct 1810, Tanfield
d 16 Nov 1887, Back John St, Seaham Harbour)

Mary Ann* (b S Hetton bap 15 Mar 1835, Easington.) m? ↓ *John*

Isabella* (b S H bap 09 Oct 1836, E) ↓ (issue)

*See text for further details

Elizabeth (b Gilesgate (Durham) bap 24 Jan 1841, St Giles)

William* (b 03 Oct 1841 Gilligate)

Frances (b 18 Jan 1844, SH) ↓ (issue)

Thomas* (b 15 Mar 1846, Murton Colliery)

Margaret* (b 27 Sep 1849, MC bap 05 Jan 1851, D-le-D) ↓ (issue)

Richard* (b 04 Mar 1852 MC bap 19 Jun 1852, D-le-D d 08 Sep 1880 Seaham Colliery) ↓ (issue)

John = **Mary Jane Douglas**

So far we have been relying on parish records to provide us with information concerning baptisms, marriages and burials; occasionally, wills can provide important information, especially if they are accompanied by inventories of property left by the deceased.
With the advent of the nineteenth century, however, two more important sources of information become available.
First, in 1837 came the nationwide (in England and Wales) state registration of births, marriages and deaths. Scotland followed in 1855. Secondly, from 1841 onwards a detailed census is taken every ten years.
Thus I have copies of the birth certificates of most of the children of John and Margaret, starting with John, who was born in 1838.

As far as the census returns are concerned, 1841 reveals some very interesting information.

Census Return 1841, Durham City (CRO M27/12)

'1st from Claypath beginning at the Bakehouse Lane up the North Side of the Street through the Gilligate Toll Bar ending at **Defty's Public House,**
including Sands House and Williamson's House.'

Folio 18
1 [inhabited house]   [Born in County?]
    John   Defty   34   Coal Miner   Y
    Margaret do   34   Y
    Mary   do   7   Y
    Isabella   do   5   Y
    John   do   3   Y
    Elizabeth do   1   Y

[Neighbours are labourers, a blacksmith, calico weaver. Only one other miner close by.]

The information contained in the 1841 Census is limited but here we have a real gem. Not only do we have a detailed description of the area where the Deftys lived but we find that it is a public house. (This is confirmed by William's birth certificate where his father's occupation is described as 'publican.')

The location of this is now known. (Information from David Butler of the Durham CRO.) It was immediately to the east of what is now known as 'The Durham Light Infantryman', formerly 'The Bay Horse', later 'The Sun', and close to what is now an Esso Garage. Defty's Public House, which lay by the Toll Gate Bar, was known later as 'The Dun Cow.' It was closed in 1891. No doubt the pub was run by John's wife, Margaret. It appears that at this time there would have been little restriction on opening hours, except that the pub would be closed during the hours of divine service, ie perhaps between 11 and 12 am and 5 and 6 pm. The address was 112 Gilesgate.

An interesting and po-faced allusion to the practice of allowing ordinary persons to open a public house is found in *The Age of Reform* by Woodward, chapter 1, p 457, note 1

> 'The removal of some of the powers of the justices was not always
> a social advantage. Thus the freedom allowed to any rate-payer after
> 1830, to open a beer-house, on payment of two guineas,
> led to a great increase in the number of small and undesirable
> public houses.' [!]

The 1851 Census gives more detail: in particular, parishes are shown where each individual was born. This information can be cross-checked with birth certificates.

Census Return 1851 HO 107 2392 1-E Folio 166
Murton Colliery

John Defty	Head	Mar	45		Coal Miner	Durham Chester-le-Street
Margaret Defty	Wife	Mar	41			Durham Tanfield
Mary Ann Defty	Daur	U	17			Durham South Hetton
John Defty	Son		13			Durham Sherburn Hill
Elizabeth Defty	Daur		11			Durham Gilesgate
William Defty	Son		9			Durham Gilesgate
Frances Defty	Daur		7			Durham South Hetton
Thomas Defty	Son		5			Durham Murton Colliery
Margaret Defty	Daur		1			Durham Murton Colliery
Mary Gray	Visitor	Md		85	Mother-in-law	Durham Tanfield

John Defty would have moved to wherever his work took him. By 1851 the family is at Murton Colliery very close to South Hetton, near Easington where John and Margaret had been married.

We do not know why Margaret's mother was staying with them at the time. Perhaps it was to help look after the large family; perhaps John Gray had died of natural causes. I can find no evidence that he died in a pit disaster. If he was not living at the time of the census, Mary should have been shown as a widow.
The second daughter of the family, Isabella, is missing. She may have been in service somewhere. Isabella was to marry a miner, Charles Mullen, in 1860.

Mary Ann had an illegitimate child, called John Defty, in 1853. He too became a miner, as did eventually his son, William. John died aged 32 on 16th May 1885. A Master Shifter at Kimblesworth, he was killed by the breaking of a crab rope which engaged a repairing shaft. He and several others were thrown to the bottom of the pit, about 250 feet.

Two more men of the family became miners: Thomas, who was still alive in 1901; and Richard, not yet born at the time of the census, whom we shall discuss later.

Just over a year after the 1851 census, on 16 June 1852, disaster struck the family.

An explosion took place in Seaton Colliery, near Seaham, Durham. Six men and a boy were working at the place where the accident happened, and all of them perished. The names of the victims were:

Defty, John, aged 46
Halliday, Charles, aged 10
Pratt, John, aged 20, single
Simpson, Andrew, aged 18, brother of John
Simpson, John, aged 36, brother of Andrew, the brothers being the only support for their mother aged 86
Simpson, William, aged 27, left a wife and 2 children

The number of those who perished was, compared to other, later, disasters, quite small, but there are a number of features which shock the modern reader.
In the first place, the revelation that a boy as young as 10 was working in the pit.

The following extract is from *Troubled Seams* by John E McCutcheon, published in 1955.

> John Defty left a widow and nine [actually, eight - Richard was born later] children. Little Charlie Halliday a mere child of ten years, was a trapper boy [ie he opened and closed the trap] and the force of the explosion blew him against a wall thirty yards away and buried him in stone. It was of course a common thing in those days for children of tender years to be employed in the mines. Only ten years before this (1842) the Children's Employment Commission had made the most dreadful revelations......Children from five to eight years of age worked thirteen to sixteen hours a day for a wage of fivepence per day......
> formerly children used to be carried to the mines on their fathers' backs.
>
> The Inquest was. .....adjourned to "give the [newly-appointed] Governnent Inspector [of Mines, as a result of an Act of Parliament passed in 1850] an opportunity of being present."
>
> [We are informed] that the coalowners were bitterly opposed to this new measure and "a special clause was inserted in the Act expressly requiring the coal owners to allow the Inspectors entrance to and egress from the mine, because **Lord Londonderry [owner of Seaton Pit] had publicly declared that he would not allow an inspector to go down his pits, and that if an inspector did go down he might stay there.**" [My emphasis]

The second revelation concerns the lighting of the pits. It will be recalled that Sir Humphrey Davy had invented a safety lamp in 1815.
Troubled Seams again:

One revelation at [the] inquest will come as a shock…..and that is to learn
that at this deep Seaham pit naked lights were being used! Men at the
coal-face worked by candle-light!

Some of the reported alternative forms of producing light seem scarcely credible: for
example, the phosphorescence of decayed fish-skins was tried. Not unnaturally, this was
judged to be safe but inefficient.

The most common method was what was called a steel-mill,
the notched wheel of which, being made to revolve against
a flint, struck a succession of sparks which scarcely served to do
more than make the darkness visible. A boy carried the apparatus
after the miner……
Discussion at the inquest was also concerned with a similar problem,
namely the amount of air going into the pit. [A witness]….testifying on
behalf of the owners, considered the quantity of air circulating in the
mine….to be quite safe for men to work with candles.
[The] Inspector was more critical: "Unless more air is sent into the pit…
I would recommend its being worked with Davy lamps."   He stressed
the importance of more air being got into the pit…..
Nevertheless the warnings of the Inspector seemed to fall on deaf ears for
the jury, apparently unmoved, merely recorded a verdict of "Accidental Death."

I still find it difficult to come to terms with the circumstances of the death of my great-
great-grandfather and the callous attitude of the owners, exemplified by the remarks of
Lord Londonderry. It is also possible to feel shocked by the outlook of the parents who
allowed their young children to work in the pits.
It may be that we live in a 'nanny state' but surely this is infinitely preferable to a society
where lives are squandered so easily.
The toll of deaths from coal-mining accelerated in the second half of the nineteenth century
and continued to do so in the twentieth. Even in the 1950s there were disasters, such as that
at Easington in 1951 and Creswell in 1950 when the deaths were in the 80s.
Fifteen years later came the last calamity, that of Aberfan, where 144 persons, many of
them children died as a result of the collapse of a tip.
Even today we read of pit disasters in Eastern Europe and China.
I have been unable to find out details of the effect of the death of John Defty on the rest of
the family. But by a supreme piece of irony, his last son, Richard, who had been born three
months before John's death, was baptized on the day he was buried.
Even this is not the end of the story. For Richard was to die in an even greater disaster in the
same pit on 8th September 1880, when 164 men were killed.

Before coming to the end of this section it is important to show how involved in the
business of mining were my relatives in the Defty family. I know of 18 men who were
pitmen. At least 6 of them perished in the mines. We shall meet more in the next section.

The Ancestors of Mary Jane Douglas (1)

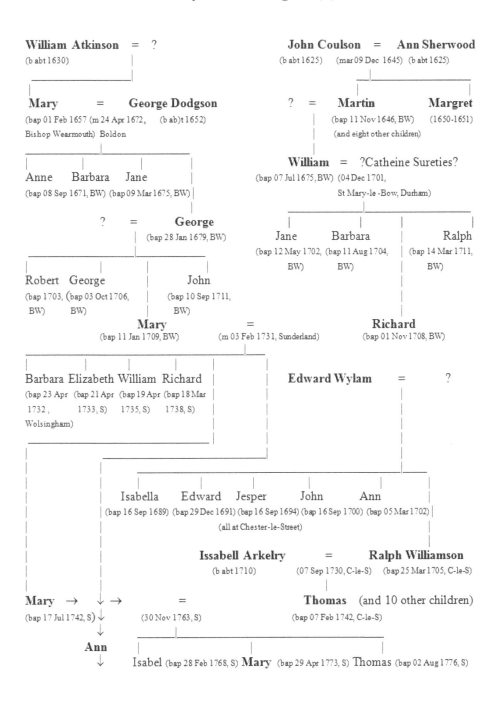

William Atkinson = ?
(b abt 1630)

Mary = George Dodgson
(bap 01 Feb 1657 (m 24 Apr 1672, (b ab)t 1652)
Bishop Wearmouth) Boldon

Anne   Barbara   Jane
(bap 08 Sep 1671, BW) (bap 09 Mar 1675, BW)

? = George
(bap 28 Jan 1679, BW)

Robert George   John
(bap 1703, (bap 03 Oct 1706,   (bap 10 Sep 1711,
BW)   BW)   BW)

John Coulson = Ann Sherwood
(b abt 1625)   (mar 09 Dec 1645) (b abt 1625)

? = Martin   Margret
(bap 11 Nov 1646, BW)   (1650-1651)
(and eight other children)

William = ?Catheine Sureties?
(bap 07 Jul 1675, BW) (04 Dec 1701,
St Mary-le -Bow, Durham)

Jane   Barbara   Ralph
(bap 12 May 1702, (bap 11 Aug 1704,   (bap 14 Mar 1711,
BW)   BW)   BW)

Mary = Richard
(bap 11 Jan 1709, BW) (m 03 Feb 1731, Sunderland) (bap 01 Nov 1708, BW)

Barbara Elizabeth William Richard
(bap 23 Apr (bap 21 Apr (bap 19 Apr (bap 18 Mar
1732,   1733, S)   1735, S)   1738, S)
Wolsingham)

Edward Wylam = ?

Isabella   Edward   Jesper   John   Ann
(bap 16 Sep 1689) (bap 29 Dec 1691) (bap 16 Sep 1694) (bap 16 Sep 1700) (bap 05 Mar 1702)
(all at Chester-le-Street)

Issabell Arkelry = Ralph Williamson
(b abt 1710)   (07 Sep 1730, C-le-S) (bap 25 Mar 1705, C-le-S)

Mary → ↓ →   =   Thomas (and 10 other children)
(bap 17 Jul 1742, S) ↓   (30 Nov 1763, S)   (bap 07 Feb 1742, C-le-S)

Ann
↓   Isabel (bap 28 Feb 1768, S) Mary (bap 29 Apr 1773, S) Thomas (bap 02 Aug 1776, S)

83

From this point the ancestor charts become more complicated, largely because, thanks to the survival of the parish records of County Durham, there is almost an *embarras de richesse* of information, all of which is interesting for one reason or another.

Very early on we have the emergence of the Coulson family, whose name figures so prominently in the designation of my immediate ancestors. They and most of the other families on the tree came from the Sunderland area and a word of explanation is necessary concerning the two parishes whose names appear.
The ancient parish was called Bishop Wearmouth - the name being self-explanatory. The mediaeval church, which is situated in the centre of Sunderland, became too small to accommodate the growing population which was employed in the industries of Wearside: ship-building and related manufacturing enterprises which grew up around the mouth of the river.

In 1719 a new parish, named Sunderland was established near the coast. An attractive Renaissance style church was built. So, whilst all the early baptisms and marriages were celebrated at Bishop Wearmouth church, by 1731, Richard Coulson and Mary Dodgson were married at the new church. In the adjoining church-yard many of my ancestors were buried. (A plan exists, giving details of the place of burial of a number of them.) The church was nearly derelict the first time I visited Sunderland in the 1980s but since then has been restored and is now a listed building. ('Before' and 'After' photos show the improvement.)

(Taken in 1987 and 1996)

During the eighteenth and nineteenth centuries a large number of houses were built for men working in the shipyards. I have a copy of a painting dating from about 1850, executed as if from a hill-top to the south of the dockland area. It shows a wonderful panorama of houses,

84

ships, railways and factories. The individual streets where my family lived are clearly shown: Woodbine St, Henry St East, East St, and many others. By the 1980s all this area had been demolished and although the street names are still there the neighbourhood is now occupied by modern factories and warehouses.

The parish of Boldon is situated slightly to the south west of South Shields.

There are one or two doubtful entries. For example, 'Catheine Sureties,' who married William Coulson in Durham in 1701, is almost certainly a corrupt entry; I have not been able to check the original parish entry (as opposed to consulting the IGI). On the other hand, no alternative has appeared.

The entry 'William Wylam' is a conjecture, but it seems reasonable to accept the next generation (who appear with the surname of Williamson) as descended from him. The name 'Arkelry' is puzzling and I have found no other examples of it. Wolsingham appears as the baptismal parish for Barbara, eldest child of Richard Coulson and Mary Dodson. I cannot account for this apparent anomaly, but the name Barbara appears in the previous Coulson generation; I think it confirms the descent.

At the base of above chart we see the sisters Mary and Ann Coulson who figure significantly in the next diagram but one.

The Ancestors of Mary Jane Douglas (2)

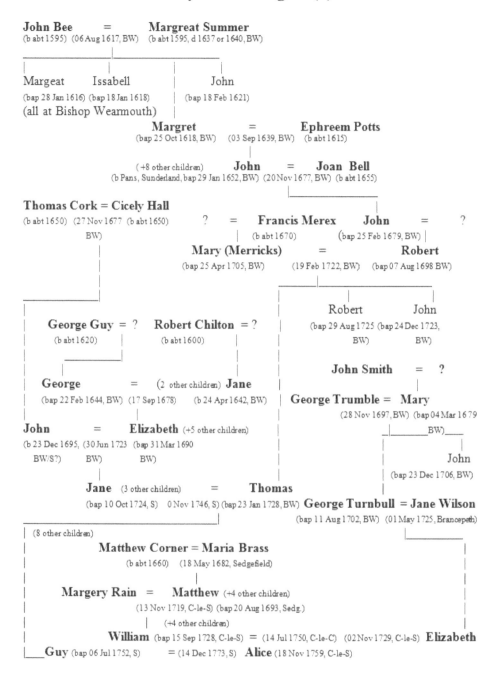

John Bee = Margreat Summer
(b abt 1595) (06 Aug 1617, BW) (b abt 1595, d 1637 or 1640, BW)

Margeat   Issabell   John
(bap 28 Jan 1616) (bap 18 Jan 1618)   (bap 18 Feb 1621)
(all at Bishop Wearmouth)

Margret = Ephreem Potts
(bap 25 Oct 1618, BW) (03 Sep 1639, BW) (b abt 1615)

(+8 other children) John = Joan Bell
(b Pans, Sunderland, bap 29 Jan 1652, BW) (20 Nov 1677, BW) (b abt 1655)

Thomas Cork = Cicely Hall
(b abt 1650) (27 Nov 1677 (b abt 1650)   ? = Francis Merex   John   =   ?
            BW)   (b abt 1670)   (bap 25 Feb 1679, BW)

Mary (Merricks) = Robert
(bap 25 Apr 1705, BW) (19 Feb 1722, BW) (bap 07 Aug 1698 BW)

Robert   John
(bap 29 Aug 1725 (bap 24 Dec 1723,
     BW)   BW)

George Guy = ?   Robert Chilton = ?
(b abt 1620)   (b abt 1600)

John Smith = ?

George = (2 other children) Jane   George Trumble = Mary
(bap 22 Feb 1644, BW) (17 Sep 1678) (b 24 Apr 1642, BW)   (28 Nov 1697, BW) (bap 04 Mar 1679

John = Elizabeth (+5 other children)   BW)
(b 23 Dec 1695, (30 Jun 1723 (bap 31 Mar 1690
  BW/S?)   BW)   BW)   John
                                                              (bap 23 Dec 1706, BW)

Jane (3 other children) = Thomas
(bap 10 Oct 1724, S) 0 Nov 1746, S) (bap 23 Jan 1728, BW) George Turnbull = Jane Wilson
                                              (bap 11 Aug 1702, BW) (01 May 1725, Brancepeth)

(8 other children)

Matthew Corner = Maria Brass
(b abt 1660) (18 May 1682, Sedgefield)

Margery Rain = Matthew (+4 other children)
(13 Nov 1719, C-le-S) (bap 20 Aug 1693, Sedg.)

(+4 other children)

William (bap 15 Sep 1728, C-le-S) = (14 Jul 1750, C-le-C) (02 Nov 1729, C-le-S) Elizabeth
Guy (bap 06 Jul 1752, S)   = (14 Dec 1773, S) Alice (18 Nov 1759, C-le-S)

A new parish now briefly appears: Brancepeth, apparently the birthplace of Jane Wilson. We have no other details of her. The parish lies between Durham city and Wolsingham

The name Cork is sometimes incorrectly shown on the IGI as Cort or even Conk. Examination of the parish records, however, reveals that there is no doubt that Cork is the correct name. The marriage of John is recorded on the IGI as also taking place in Sunderland but this must have been where one of the parties lived.

George Guy was born about 1620. Note how the surname reappears as a first name in the next century, and even later, as we shall see in the following chart.

Some unusual spellings of names are revealed in this section. Ephreem Potts and Margret had eight children and three of them are shown as Jann (Jean), Eliner and Isable.
The surname Merex appears under two other guises: Merricks and (not shown) Meocks. George Trumble's elder son is shown as George Turnbull, and this was probably the correct form. His brother, however, is shown as John Trumble.

The name Potts also survives as a christian name - in this case until 1904.

I have shown John Potts' birthplace as Pans, Sunderland. This is not strictly true; it is Jann, his sister, whose birth entry shows Panns; but it seems logical to assume the same location for all the children.
Panns is now known as Panns Bank and it lies on the southern shore of the River Wear, to the east of Wearmouth Bridge. The area used to be noted for the panning of salt which was used in both the glass-making industry and for general purposes. Descriptions of a similar area at South Shields, on the Tyne, for example by Daniel Defoe in the 18th century, show that choking fumes were produced when the brine was heated by inferior coal and that the fumes could be seen from many miles away.
Some years ago I came across a reference to the Panns in a transcribed Burial Register at the Durham Record Office. It was so poignant that I made a note of it:

> '1621 30 Dec
> John, a child from the Panns, foresworn of his father, forsaken of his mother.'

I hope he did not come from the Potts family

The Ancestors of Mary Jane Douglas - the Mariners (3)

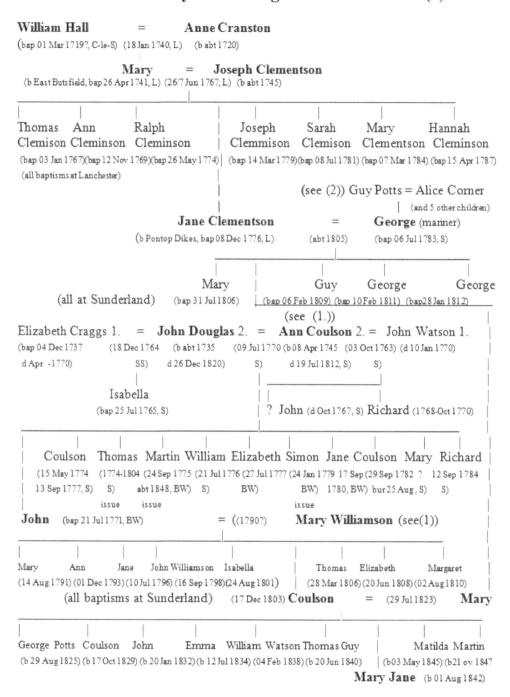

William Hall　　　　=　　　**Anne Cranston**
(bap 01 Mar 1719?, C-le-S)　(18 Jan 1740, L)　(b abt 1720)

　　　　　　　　　Mary　　=　**Joseph Clementson**
　(b East Butsfield, bap 26 Apr 1741, L)　(26/7 Jun 1767, L)　(b abt 1745)

Thomas	Ann	Ralph		Joseph	Sarah	Mary	Hannah
Clemison	Cleminson	Cleminson		Clemmison	Clemison	Clementson	Cleminson

(bap 03 Jan 1767)(bap 12 Nov 1769)(bap 26 May 1774)│　(bap 14 Mar 1779)(bap 08 Jul 1781) (bap 07 Mar 1784) (bap 15 Apr 1787)
(all baptisms at Lanchester)

　　　　　　　　　　　　　　　　　　　(see (2)) Guy Potts = Alice Corner
　　　　　　　　　　　　　　　　　　　　　　　　│ (and 5 other children)

　　　　Jane Clementson　　　　=　　　**George** (mariner)
　(b Pontop Dikes, bap 08 Dec 1776, L)　(abt 1805)　(bap 06 Jul 1783, S)

	Mary		Guy	George		George
(all at Sunderland)　(bap 31 Jul 1806)　(bap 06 Feb 1809) (bap 10 Feb 1811) (bap 28 Jan 1812)

　　　　　　　　　　　(see (1.))
Elizabeth Craggs 1. = **John Douglas** 2. = **Ann Coulson** 2. = John Watson 1.
(bap 04 Dec 1737　(18 Dec 1764　(b abt 1735　(09 Jul 1770 (b 08 Apr 1745　(03 Oct 1763) (d 10 Jan 1770)
d Apr -1770)　SS)　d 26 Dec 1820)　S)　d 19 Jul 1812, S)　S)

　　　　　Isabella
　　　(bap 25 Jul 1765, S)　　　│ │　? John (d Oct 1767, S) Richard (1768-Oct 1770)

	Coulson	Thomas	Martin	William	Elizabeth	Simon	Jane	Coulson	Mary	Richard
	(15 May 1774	(1774-1804	(24 Sep 1775	(21 Jul 1776	(27 Jul 1777	(24 Jan 1779	17 Sep	(29 Sep 1782	?	12 Sep 1784
	13 Sep 1777, S)	S)	abt 1848, BW)	S)	BW)	BW)	1780, BW)	bur 25 Aug, S)	S)
		issue	issue				issue			

John　(bap 21 Jul 1771, BW)　　　　= ((1790?)　**Mary Williamson** (see(1))

Mary	Ann	Jane	John Williamson	Isabella		Thomas	Elizabeth	Margaret
(14 Aug 1791)	(01 Dec 1793)	(10 Jul 1796)	(16 Sep 1798)	(24 Aug 1801)		(28 Mar 1806)	(20 Jun 1808)	(02 Aug 1810)

(all baptisms at Sunderland)　(17 Dec 1803) **Coulson**　=　(29 Jul 1823)　**Mary**

George Potts	Coulson	John	Emma	William	Watson	Thomas	Guy		Matilda	Martin
(b 29 Aug 1825)	(b 17 Oct 1829)	(b 20 Jan 1832)	(b 12 Jul 1834)	(04 Feb 1838)	(b 20 Jun 1840)				(b 03 May 1845)	(b 21 ov 1847

　　　　　　　　　　　　　　　　　　Mary Jane　(b 01 Aug 1842)

This last chart before we come to the 19th century Deftys and Douglases begins with two families: the Halls and the Cranstons. I have a note that William Hall was baptized on 1 Mar 1719 at Chester-le-Street, but I cannot now find any authority for that. Anne Cranston presumably came from Lanchester, as that is where they were married. Their daughter, Mary - the only child I have found, although there must have been others - appears in the Lanchester baptismal register. Her father is shown as living at East Butsfield, a few miles to the south-west of Lanchester. There is an abbey nearby.
Mary was married to Joseph Clementson in 1768:

> Lanchester Marriages (1767-8): 'June 27th Joseph Clemison
> & Mary Hall both of this Parish.'

The marriage date was probably 1768; it will be remembered that the change in calendar had occurred only a few years earlier and people had probably not yet become accustomed to the new year beginning in January and not March.

Mary died in 1819:
> LANCHESTER burials (indexed): '1819.10.25 Clemitson Mary Pontop High
> Stables   75.'

The age at death is not quite accurate, but that is not uncommon at this time

A curiosity is the eccentric spelling of the name Clementson: no fewer than four variations being found in one family. Even if orthography had been thoroughly settled by this time, the parish priest or his clerk would still only have written down what they thought they heard and experiments can show that a strong regional accent will distort the sound intended.

Joseph Clementson was a miner and it is probable that his three sons followed that occupation. His third daughter, Jane, married a keelman. Or perhaps they weren't married. I have found no evidence of a marriage and the following record of the baptism of their second daughter - the first Mary seems to have died as a baby - would seem to indicate this:

Birth and Baptism Sunderland OPR:
> 'Mary Pots b 31 July 1806 bapt 26 July 1807 dr of George Potts Keelman
> n[ative] of this parish by Jane Clementson of Swalwell.'

Swalwell is on the Tyne so that at some time the Clementson family must have moved.

We come now to the important account of the Douglas family. Most of the following information comes from Vera Stammers and her book *Echoes of the Past*.

Briefly, the story goes as follows.

John Douglas as a ten-year-old boy was present at Culloden in 1746. This was the site of the last battle to be fought on British soil. A combined army of Hanoverian forces and Lowland Scots met the Highland supporters of Bonnie Prince Charlie and decisively beat them. Charles, also known as the Young Pretender, fled 'over the seas to Skye' and thence to France. The remnants of his army also fled westwards and scattered to various points of the kingdom and also to the Continent. The Highlanders who remained were harshly pursued and hunted down.

It is alleged that John Douglas, a member of the Black Douglas clan and son of an aristocrat who was killed in the battle, joined the Duke of Perth's party that also travelled westwards, sailed round the north coast of Scotland and eventually arrived in France where they remained in exile. On their way, they discharged some of their number at Newcastle-upon-Tyne and Sunderland. It seems that the young John Douglas was one who was deposited on Wearside, where he settled and became a keelman.

John married twice, first to Elizabeth Craggs and then to Ann Coulson, who had previously been married to a John Watson.

A word is necessary on the keelmen of the Tyne and the Wear. The following is taken from an account which has reached me from Geoff Nicholson.

> Keelmen worked on the 'keels', or specialised wherries which carried coal on the rivers Tyne and Wear from up-river staithes at the end of the wagonways from the collieries down to the sea-going colliers lying near the river mouth. In the case of the Tyne, colliers could not go above the low mediaeval bridge at Newcastle but even if they had managed to do so (after it was swept away by floods in 1771, for instance), shoals and sandbanks would have rendered the river unnavigable in practice. Keelmen were therefore an essential part of the coal trade and without them the coal field would have come to a halt. This gave them what would now be called 'industrial muscle,' which they were by no means reluctant to use.......

> ....Strikes, or 'stands' as they were then known, were of frequent occurrence in all branches of the coal industry in the mid-eighteenth century. The 'Flying pickets' of the 1750s were every bit as well organised as their modern counterparts have been and, when faced by determined employers, a 'stand' could be a very lengthy and violent affair. [A strike......] started in mid March and lasted until May 7th, a period of seven weeks, marked out by disorder and riots in Newcastle, as had been a similar strike the year before. What had the authorities really worried, however, was the proclamation of the Pretender [Bonnie Prince Charlie] on April 27th by striking keelmen in the fields near Elswick [now part of west Newcastle]. **Many keelmen were of Scottish extraction and sympathies and the Jacobite rebellion of 1745/6 was still fresh in everyone's memory.*** Clearly something had to be done quickly to prevent events getting out of hand. The next day, April 28th, two things were done: (1) Newcastle Corporation placed an advertisement in the

local papers offering a reward of £100 for the discovery of the ringleaders and (2) the employers….drew up their 'Black-list' of strikers…..

….Each keel had a crew of three 'bound' men - that is, those who had signed a bond, rather like a miner's bond, committing them to work for one employer for a year and laying down their pay and condition for that time. On each keel there would also be a boy, called the 'Pee-Dee', who would not be bound….

….Many of the [keelmen's] names are interesting because they sound Scottish. Even when the surname does not give it away, a name such as Alexander or David (names of the old kings of Scotland) or Andrew (Patron Saint of Scotland) is a strong pointer…The keel men were known by their Scots 'Blue Bonnets' or 'Tam O'Shanter-style' hats, which are alluded to in the well-known song 'The Keel-Row' which, for its Tyneside imagery, is sung to an old Edinburgh tune.

* My emphasis

So it can be seen that if and when John Douglas arrived on the Wear in the late 1740s a Scottish environment was already present.

It is nevertheless necessary to investigate the supposed Scottish ancestry of John Douglas and discuss its validity.
There are certain indicators. First of all, it is clear that the tale was current early in the 19th century. It came down to me via my maternal grandmother, Catherine Hood, whose mother-in-law was Mary Jane Douglas, a formidable character, by all accounts. Catherine told me that I was descended from the Black Douglases through Mary Jane, known throughout her life, apparently, as 'Miss Douglas', in the Scottish fashion. Mary Jane herself was the great-granddaughter of John. Additionally, as we shall see, she named her children according to the Scottish manner.

Secondly, the story has been thoroughly researched by Vera Stammers (née Kinmond). She herself is descended from John Douglas, brother of Mary Jane. She has yet to establish firmly the parentage of the first John Douglas, but it is surely significant that similar stories have come down through the generations and two hundred years.

Thirdly, Martin Douglas, the fourth son of John Douglas, alludes to the story in his autobiography, a copy of which is in my possession. It is full of bravado and derring-do. But it also has useful information concerning the life and times of the Douglases and of Sunderland.

The following chart will illustrate how the three sources are related to the first John Douglas.

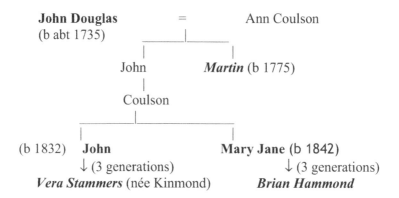

John Douglas   =   Ann Coulson
(b abt 1735) |
                    |
            John   *Martin* (b 1775)
                |
            Coulson
        _____|_____
        | |
(b 1832) **John**   **Mary Jane** (b 1842)
    ↓ (3 generations)   ↓ (3 generations)
Vera Stammers (née Kinmond)   ***Brian Hammond***

There are, however, problems with the story.

According to some accounts, which I have been unable to substantiate, Ann Coulson was the heiress to a fortune. It is rather difficult to reconcile that fact with the following:

Sunderland Burial Register:
> '[1812] Ann Douglas P[oor] H[ouse]   Wife of John Keelman. [Died] July 19 [Buried] July 21. [Aged] 67 years.'

I suppose it is possible that 'PH' has been wrongly interpreted.

John's death is well documented in that his funeral on 26 Dec 1820 was from Low St, Sunderland, the address of son Martin.

It may be felt that more facts have to be proved to make the account more than just an interesting story. On the whole, the positive elements incline me to accept it as believable.

Turning now to the detail of the children of John Douglas and Ann Coulson we find that their eldest son, John was a pitman. This is revealed in the Sunderland baptismal register for 1803, when his son, Coulson, was born:

> 'Coulson Douglas [b 21 Nov 1803] bap 17 Dec 1803 2 son of John Douglas Pitman, native of Sunderland by his wife Mary Williamson N[ative] of Sunderland.'

John married his first cousin, Mary Williamson, as will be seen from the following simplified chart.

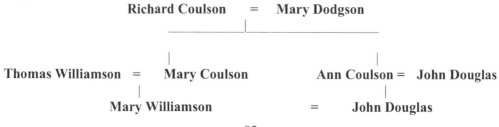

Richard Coulson   =   **Mary Dodgson**
        _____|_____
        | |
        | |
Thomas Williamson = **Mary Coulson**   **Ann Coulson** = **John Douglas**
        | |
    Mary Williamson   =   **John Douglas**

A word now about the use of Coulson as a first name. We can see that the process started with the sons of John Douglas and Ann Coulson. Their second son, Coulson, lived for three years only. Eight years later, in 1782, another son was born, whom they named Coulson but he died less than a year later.

Thereafter, and well into the late 19th century, I have discovered 16 boys whose first name was Coulson. This figure includes my own grandfather, Coulson Douglas Defty. In addition, 5 other boys were given Coulson as a middle name. I believe this practice has been carried on into modern times.

Thomas, Martin and Simon, children of John and Ann, are all known to have married and had children. Of the others, apart from those already mentioned, I have no information.

John, the eldest son, the pitman, was buried in October 1812 in the churchyard of Holy Trinity Church, Sunderland and the position of the grave is shown on the *Survey of Sunderland Churchards*, published by the Durham County Record Office. Also shown on the survey are John's daughter Jane and his son Coulson, whom we shall deal with soon.

The Deftys and Douglases of the Nineteenth Century, and Later

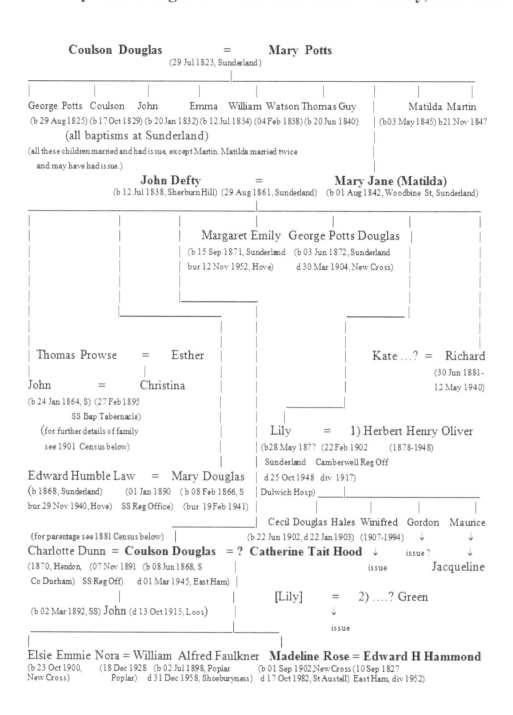

Coulson Douglas = **Mary Potts**
(29 Jul 1823, Sunderland)

| George Potts | Coulson | John | Emma | William | Watson | Thomas | Guy | | Matilda | Martin |

(b 29 Aug 1825) (b 17 Oct 1829) (b 20 Jan 1832) (b 12 Jul 1834) (04 Feb 1838) (b 20 Jun 1840)   (b 03 May 1845) b 21 Nov 1847

(all baptisms at Sunderland)

(all these children married and had issue, except Martin. Matilda married twice
and may have had issue.)

John Defty = **Mary Jane (Matilda)**
(b 12 Jul 1838, Sherburn Hill) (29 Aug 1861, Sunderland) (b 01 Aug 1842, Woodbine St, Sunderland)

Margaret Emily   George Potts Douglas
(b 15 Sep 1871, Sunderland   (b 03 Jun 1872, Sunderland
bur 12 Nov 1952, Hove)   d 30 Mar 1904, New Cross)

Thomas Prowse = Esther   Kate ...? = Richard
                                            (30 Jun 1881-
John = Christina   12 May 1940)
(b 24 Jan 1864, S) (27 Feb 1895
SS Bap Tabernacle)
(for further details of family   Lily = 1) Herbert Henry Oliver
see 1901 Census below)   (b 28 May 1877 (22 Feb 1902   (1878-1948)
                                 Sunderland   Camberwell Reg Off
Edward Humble Law = Mary Douglas   d 25 Oct 1948 div 1917)
(b 1868, Sunderland) (01 Jan 1890 (b 08 Feb 1866, S   Dulwich Hosp)
bur 29 Nov 1940, Hove) SS Reg Office) (bur 19 Feb 1941)
                                 Cecil Douglas Hales Winifred Gordon Maurice
(for parentage see 1881 Census below)   (b 22 Jun 1902, d 22 Jan 1903) (1907-1994) ↓   ↓
Charlotte Dunn = **Coulson Douglas** = ? **Catherine Tait Hood** ↓   issue ?   ↓
(1870, Hendon, (07 Nov 1891 (b 08 Jun 1868, S   issue   Jacqueline
Co Durham) SS Reg Off) d 01 Mar 1945, East Ham)
                                 [Lily] = 2) ....? Green
(b 02 Mar 1892, SS) John (d 13 Oct 1915, Loos)   ↓
                                            issue

Elsie Emmie Nora = William Alfred Faulkner   Madeline Rose = Edward H Hammond
(b 23 Oct 1900, (18 Dec 1928 (b 02 Jul 1898, Poplar   (b 01 Sep 1902, New Cross (10 Sep 1827
New Cross)   Poplar) d 31 Dec 1958, Shoeburyness)   d 17 Oct 1982, St Austell) East Ham, div 1952)

As the nineteenth century progresses more and more information becomes available to the family historian and therefore the selection process becomes more complex. But a number of important events demand mention. We have already seen that in 1852 one of my great-great-grandfathers, John Defty, became the victim of a pit disaster.

By a curious coincidence, two years before this, in 1850, another of my great-great-grandfathers, living a few miles away from John, in Sunderland, was drowned in a tragic accident. This is a contemporary press account.

Durham Chronicle, 2nd February, 1850

SHOCKING CATASTROPHE AT SUNDERLAND - THREE MEN DROWNED
A most melancholy spectacle was witnessed at Sunderland on the afternoon of Tuesday last, by a large number of persons; when 3 men found a watery grave, in attempting to pass a rope aboard a keel, which had come ashore on the south side of the south pier. It appears that a schooner - "the Pearl" - and three keels were being towed out to sea, at half past three o'clock in the afternoon; and that when going out of the river, the sea suddenly rose to a considerable height, and at the same time the towing-rope broke off the steamer. The keels and schooner were presently driven ashore on the south side of the pier. Two of the keels were taken in tow by steamers - one was put off to sea, and the other safely brought back into the river. The third keel - laden with iron, and belonging to Hartlepool - was driven ashore. A rope was instantly procured by several persons on the beach, with the intention of passing it aboard to rescue the owner of the keel; when 4 persons - who it appears had got entangled in the rope - were thrown down by the retiring surge, and with one exception - one who drifted out to sea and was picked up by a steam-tug - were all drowned! The names of the sufferers were Coulson Douglas (a master mariner), **a man of noted daring,*** [Robert]Reah (a fireman in a steam boat), [Robert] Chisholm (a sailor). Only one body, that of Douglas, has been picked up at the time we write. The cause of the rapid rise of the sea was variously accounted for: the most probable assumption is, that a strong easterly wind had sprung up, or that the westerly gale of the previous day had produced the swell.

* emphasis by BDH

At an inquest held a few days later the jury returned a verdict of accidentally drowned.

We also have some details of a petition which Coulson's wife, Mary, sent to Trinity House.

To the Honorable the Master, Wardens & Assistants of the Corporation
of Trinity-House of Deptford-Strand

Mary Douglas 43 living at East Woodbine St at Sunderland
Widow of Coulson Douglas
That your petitioners Husband went to Sea at the age of 12 years in the year
1815 and was employed in the Merchant Sea Service for 35 years in the
following ships and others and in the annexed stns

ship/vessels name				
1815	SARAH apprentice		Coasting & foreign	
1833	LIBERTY	179 tonnage)		”
”	HINDE	176 ”) 16 years	”	
”	DOUGLAS	272 ”) Master of	”	
”	BRUCE	306 ”) those Ships		”
1849	THOMAS BAKER 231 ”)			”

That your petitioners Husband left off the sea in 1849 in consequence of
ill health and lost his life ['died' was crossed out] January 29th 1850 and
she has children viz 2 boys under 12 and two girls under 14.

Thomas Guy Douglas	20 June 1840
Martin Douglas	21 Nov 1847
Mary Jane Douglas	1 Aug 1842
Matilda Douglas	3 May 1845

That your petitioner has no annual income

[her signature]

[written in margin]   she has 9 children altogether - five above age.

[written in top of form to the side and partly hidden by binding]

The Deceased lost his life on 29th January 1850 in attempting to[_____]
The [_____] of a small [_____] which came on them
behind Sunderland Pier witness[.......]

We do not know the result of this petition but in 1871 Mary was living with her son
William Watson Douglas and her granddaughter Elizabeth Thurlbeck at 35 Henry St East
Sunderland.

Of the six sons of Coulson Douglas and Mary Potts all had careers connected with the sea, many of them as master mariners. Even the youngest, Martin, who perhaps did not become a mariner, is shown by the 1901 Census to have repaired ships' engines.

Furthermore, of their daughters, Emma married a pilot and Mary Jane a ship's stoker. Only Matilda married landsmen.

The naming of the children of Coulson and Mary reveals a strong sense of family connections. This, as we shall see when we come to examine the Hood family and more especially the Afflecks, is a characteristic of Scottish naming patterns and is a strong indication that the Douglas family were convinced of their Scottish ancestry.

George Potts Douglas is named after his maternal grandfather. We might have expected him to have been called John, after Coulson's father, and the two-year gap between his parents' marriage and his birth leads me to suspect that an elder child, named John, may have been born some time in 1824; and that this boy died before January 1832, when another boy was named John. Coulson was clearly named after his father, reflecting the descent from Ann Coulson.

Emma's name is a mystery; I have found no ancestor of that name. It was of course, quite a popular name in Victorian times.

William Watson's name is intriguing. There is no ancestor that I can find bearing that name. But Ann Coulson's first husband's surname was Watson and this could reflect a mistaken interpretation of Coulson's ancestry.

Thomas Guy is a conflation of Thomas (Potts), born in 1728, and (George) Guy, born about 1620.

Mary Jane was named after her mother and her mother's mother (Jane Clementson.) Interestingly, her birth certificate shows a third christian name - Matilda. This unexpected name was dropped by the time of her father's death - see above - perhaps because by then another daughter had been born and named Matilda.

Martin was named after his colourful great-uncle - he who by his own account spent much of his time chasing and defeating the French!

Excluding the descendents of Mary Jane Douglas, Coulson Douglas and Mary Potts had at least 20 grandchildren. Most of their descendents have not been documented by me but many of their stories have been chronicled by Vera Kinmond in her book, *Echoes of the Past*. It seems likely that a good number of relatives out there remain to be discovered.

I turn now to my great-grandparents, John Defty and Mary Jane Douglas.

How did they meet?

It is clear that after their father's death in 1852, John and William Defty both abandoned the idea of coal-mining as a career, although their younger brothers, Thomas and Richard both became pitmen, the latter dying in 1881.

By the time of his marriage in 1861, John had moved from the village of Murton Colliery into Sunderland, where he was living in the dockland area, in East Street. He was employed as a stoker, presumably on a vessel. Mary Jane was living nearby, in East Woodbine Street, perhaps in the house where she was born. A witness at her wedding was her elder brother Thomas, who may have 'given her away.' Both fathers (Coulson Douglas and John Defty) are correctly shown as deceased.

What else do we know about Mary Jane and John?

Here is a photo of Mary Jane. She appears just as formidable as her daughter-in-law, my grandmother, described her. A no-nonsense person if ever there was one.

I imagine that it was her influence or at her insistence that her children were named following the usual Scottish pattern, which goes as follows. (I have inserted the name of each child as it would normally be expected.)

First son named after his paternal grandfather	John
Second son named after his maternal grandfather	Coulson
Third son named after his father	John
First daughter named after her maternal grandmother	Mary
Second daughter named after her paternal grandmother	Margaret
Third daughter named after her mother	Mary Jane

The next children are likely to be named after great-grandparents.
This is how the seven Defty children were named, in order of birth:

John   **Mary** Douglas   **Coulson** Douglas   **Margaret** Emily   **George Potts Douglas**   Lily   Richard

The first four children were named conventionally, with the addition of Douglas as appropriate. Margaret's second name (the one by which she was generally known) is a puzzle. Although there were a number of Emmas in the family (descendents of other Douglases), no Emily among the ancestors has been found. Perhaps it was the name of a friend of the family, possibly a god-mother, although no evidence of a baptism has been found.

The third son could not be called after his father as the name John had already been used, so he was named after his maternal great-grandfather, George Potts, again with the addition of Douglas. William (Defty) might have been expected, but I think we can see the hand of Mary Jane here!

The third girl could not be named after her mother (though we might have expected Jane.) The name of Lily is also a puzzle: again, the source of the name may have been a friend of the family.

Richard is almost certainly named after his father's youngest brother, Richard Defty, who the previous year (1880) had perished in a pit disaster.

It is noteworthy that the names of three of the children incorporated Mary Jane's maiden name: Douglas.

This second photograph, a wedding group shows a contrast between Mary Jane and John: she appears to be scowling; he is smiling. I am not thoroughly sure whose wedding this is but by the clothes and the ages of Mary Jane and John I surmise that it is Richard Defty's, which occurred on 23 April 1910. The bridesmaid would be Margaret Emily (who never married) because Mary Douglas was married in 1890 and Lily in 1902. Mary Jane appears to be in part mourning and this could be for her son, George Potts Douglas Defty, who died of tuberculosis in 1904. The man to the left of the bride's father, in a top hat and smoking a cigar, is probably my grandfather, Coulson Douglas Defty.

The photograph may have been taken behind the Deftys' family home, 152 Jerningham Road, New Cross, a photograph of which, taken in the 1980s, is shown below:

Another photo that was taken at the same time few clearly shows the name 'Duglas' above the door. This misspelling seems curious until we remember that Mary Jane could not write - evidenced by the X mark shown on the birth certificate of her second child, Mary Douglas - and that she was prime mover in the naming of the house. That the house has the Douglas name would also indicate that John and Mary Jane owned the house - they did not rent it.

How the family managed to acquire such an attractive house is something of a mystery. The addresses established from birth certificates and Census returns marks quite a swift ascent after a few years away from the dockland area, moving gradually towards the centre of Sunderland. By 1891 the family had removed to New Cross, south London; first to Somerville Rd and then to 152 Jerningham Rd.
Is this rapid rise in social status marked by a similar change in John's occupation?

In 1861 he was a stoker; by 1881 he was a chief engineer:

   1881 Census Milton in Gravesend Fiche no 0875 162 13411207

   V[essel] Dorcas
   Douglas George Ridley   M 26 Master   Durham Sunderland
   Deffty [sic] John   M 46 Chief Engineer Durham Durham

By 1891 Mary Jane says she is the wife of an engine fitter (probably confusing him with her son, Coulson, who is also so shown) and in 1901 he describes himself as a 'shipping director.'

101

The clue to this change in the family circumstances may be found in the detail of the 1881 Census. George Ridley Douglas, master of the 'Dorcas' was a nephew of Mary Jane. It was probably his family connection with the Douglases which ensured his movement into the world of ownership. Martin Douglas, son of Mary Jane's great-uncle, is shown in the 1856 Sunderland Directory as a 'Ship Owner.'
Family tradition has it that John either owned or was director of a company which owned a vessel called the 'Val de Travers.' Such a vessel certainly existed in his time but I have been unable to establish a firm connection with it.

It would be satisfying to record that John and Mary Jane enjoyed a happy life together in middle and old age. Unhappily, such is not the case. Around 1900 things seemed to be going badly wrong.

The 1901 Census is the first indication of this that I found, nearly twenty years ago. The 1901 Census had not then been released but on payment of a fee, and giving an assurance that I was a descendent of the family, I was able to obtain the following:

1901 Census:

152 Jerningham Rd, New Cross:

Mary J Defty	Head	Wid[?!]		59		Sunderland
Margaret E	do	Daur	S	29		do
William Howard		Visitor	M	38	Marine Engineer	Newcastle-on-Tyne
Elizabeth	do	do	M	29		do
Mary D Lane[*]		do	M	33		Sunderland
Lily Defty		Daur	S	23		do

*sc Law, ie the married daughter of John and Mary Jane,

It was some time before I worked out that Lane was a mistake for Law and that this was the married Mary Douglas Defty. The three Defty girls are thus all present; whilst of the sons, John, George and Richard, I found out late,   are accounted for at other addresses, though not at present Coulson.
The surprise, however, is in the first line. Mary Jane describes herself as Head of Household; and Widowed. This cannot be true because John did not die until 1913.
Did she believe he was dead? Or is this a cover-up to save her having to admit she did not know where he was. It was not of course unusual for a seaman, or one connected with the sea, to be absent from home.

In 2002 I was able to search for John and eventually found him:

1901 Census:

RG 13/338 Folio 58, Page 1

Birkenhead, St Mary

18 Chester St

[Head of household   William Brewitt   Head M 67   Restaurant Keeper [overwritten 'Coffee Ho']]

                         [age]   [place of birth]
John Defty Lodger M NK [crossed out, replaced by '39'] Shipping Director [overwritten 'Nav Shore[?]] NK

What on earth does all this mean?
'NK' means 'not known' and it is quite possible that if John was not present when the form was first filled in that an amendment was subsequently made. But 39! John was in his 63rd year when the Census was taken. Above all, what was John doing in Birkenhead? Unless he was on shipping business.

In my view his absence from home signals some domestic problem.

Worse was to follow in the family. On 22 February 1902, Lily married Herbert Henry Oliver and by then she must have been pregnant because Cecil Douglas Hales Oliver was born on 22 June 1902. The child died in January 1903 but the couple had three more children before they were divorced in 1917. The youngest of these, Maurice, became the father of Jacqueline Oliver.

Let us now deal with the rest of the family at this critical time.

George Potts Douglas Defty, a marine engineer, who had been ill with tuberculosis since 1899, died in 1904 at 152 Jerningham Road.

John Defty, the eldest son, a mariner in the merchant service, may have been thought to have married beneath him, to judge by his treatment in his father's will. (See below.) Here is his family, according to the 1901 Census:

1901 Census
'RG13/4735 Folio 142 page 25

103

23 Westpole [?] 3 rooms - 12 occupants!

Name		Relation	Status	Age	Occupation	Worker	Birthplace		
Thomas Prowse		Head	M	53	**Iron Foundry Labourer**	Worker	Devon, Kingsmore		
Esther	do	Wife	M	46			Durham, S Shields		
George	do	Son	S	16	General Labourer	do	do	do	
Anthony	do	Son	S	15	Apprentice Iron Moulder	do	do	do	
William	do	Son		6			do	do	
Christina Defty		Daur	M	27			do	do	
John W do		Grandson		5			do	do	
Gladys W[?] do		Granddaur		3			Yorks	Middlesbro'	
Thomas do		Grandson		1			do	do	
Harry Crawford		Son-in-Law	M	25	Iron Foundry Labourer	do	do	do	
Ann	do	Daur	M	21			do	do	
Robert	do	Grandson		3 mths			do	do	

High-lighted above are shown the wife and children of John Defty, Coulson's elder brother. We have to remember that the relationship is to the head of household.

The same Census reveals that John himself was at that time 2nd mate aboard the 'Plato' in a London Dock.

Mary Douglas had married Edward Humble Law in 1890. By 1901 he was a chief engineer. In 1904 he reported the death of his brother-in-law, George, so he and Mary must have been living at 152 Jerningham Road.

Margaret Emily, as we have seen, was living at home in 1901, unmarried. We shall meet her again in 1941 and later.

What of Coulson Douglas Defty, my grandfather?
In 1983, when researching my mother's family, I found to my great surprise that my mother, Madeline Rose Defty, and her elder sister, Elsie Emmie Nora Defty, had both been born illegitimate, in 1902 and 1900, respectively. There was no evidence that Coulson and my grandmother, Catherine Tait Hood, had ever married.
Bearing in mind the mores of the time, and the severe penalties for bigamy, this had to mean that he was already married to someone else.
After considerable searching I found the answer:

'1891 Marriage solemnized at the Register Office in the District of South Shields in the County of South Shields [sic] and Durham

Seventh	Coulson Defty	23 years	Bachelor	Engineer	16 Chichester Road South Shields	John Defty	Engineer
November 1891	Charlotte Dunn	21 years	Spinster	---------	85 Ellesmere St South Shields	Andrew Dunn (deceased)	Master Mariner

Married in the Register Office etc
In the Presence of us   **M E Defty,** William E Sharman

I have high-lighted one of the witnesses because this must be Margaret Emily, Coulson's sister. Why was she and no other of the family at this register office wedding?

The following 1881 Census shows Charlotte's family ten years earlier:

1881 Census
RG11/5005/119 p 111:

37 Ellerslie Ter
Monkwearmouth, Co Durham

Andrew Dunn	Head	M	Male	43	Glasgow, Lanark, Scotland	Master Mariner (Seaman)
Charlotte Dunn	Wife	M	Female	31	Sunderland, Durham,England	
William Dunn	Son	U	Male	18	Fraserburgh, Aberdeen, Scotland	Joiner
Elizabeth Dunn	Daur		Female	16	Sunderland, Durham, England	Domestic Servant
Charlotte Dunn	Daur		Female	12	do	Scholar
George Dunn	Son		Male	12	do	do
Margaret J Dunn	Daur		Female	7	do	do
Thomas H Dunn	Son		Male	1	do	

For a discussion of her whereabouts in 1901, see the chapter on the Hood family.

This was obviously a hurried wedding because Charlotte was eight months pregnant at the time, as is shown by the following birth certificate:

1892 Birth   in the Sub-district of   Westoe in the Counties of South   Shields and Durham

When and where Born	Name	Sex	Name, and surname of father	Name, surname and maiden surname of mother	Occupation of Father	Signature, description and residence of informant	When reg
Second March 1892 98 South Westoe Woodbine Street Westoe W.S.D.	John	Boy	Coulson DEFTY	Charlotte DEFTY formely DUNN	Marine Engineer (Merchant Service)	C. Defty mother 98 South Woodbine St	7thApril 1892

This marriage and the subsequent birth have great implications.
First of all, if Margaret Emily knew about these matters, surely the rest of the family must eventually have found out.
What must have been the attitude of Mary Jane in particular when in 1900 Coulson was known to have abandoned his wife for my grandmother and in 1902 fathered a second child by her?
My Aunt Nora once said she was born in Jerningham Road. This was not true, but both she and my mother were born in New Cross, at different addresses, but at quite short distances from the Defty home.
Did the Deftys know that my grandmother already had an illegitimate child, Richard, by another, unknown man? They surely must have.

To my mind all these events occurring at the end of the nineteenth century and the beginning of the twentieth all indicate what we would now call a dysfunctional family.

On 18th December 1902, at the age of 64 and three months after the birth of my mother, John Defty signed his will, a copy of which was given to my grandfather:

THIS IS THE LAST WILL AND TESTAMENT of me JOHN DEFTY
of Douglas House 152 Jerningham Road New Cross in Surrey Engineer

1. I revoke all testamentary dispositions made by me and I APPOINT my sons COULSON DOUGLAS DEFTY and RICHARD DEFTY my Executors and Trustees.

2. I give to my wife a legacy of FIFTY POUNDS to be paid to her as soon as possible after my death to provide for immediate necessities.

3. I give to my son Richard my silver watch and I give to my three daughters Mary Douglas and Margaret Emily and Lily or such of them as shall survive me all my linen and all my plate plated goods and jewellery. I give to my sister in law Matilda Conder[1.] my painting of my father in law[2.] and the frame belonging to it I Give to my son Coulson Douglas my painting of my brother William[3.] and also my gold Albert chain I give my photo of myself and the frame belonging to it to my daughter Mary Douglas I give my photo of my mother in law[4.] and the frame belonging to it to my daughter Margaret Emily and I give my photo of my own Mother[5.] and the frame belonging to it to my daughter Lily.

4. I give to my wife (but without prejudice to the last preceding clause) all my household furniture books pictures and prints and all articles in and about my house at the time of my death intended for domestic use or ornament for her own use and benefit.

5. I GIVE AND BEQUEATH to my wife for her own use and benefit the house in which I now reside namely Douglas House 152 Jerningham Road New Cross for the whole of my estate and interest therein.

6. I GIVE DEVISE and BEQUEATH to my Trustees all the residue of my real and personal property upon trust to sell and realize the same and out of the proceeds and any ready money of which I may die possessed pay my funeral and testamentary expenses and my debts and to stand possessed of the remainder of such money upon trust to invest the same with power to vary any investment from time to time.

7. My trustees shall hold my residuary trust estate on trust to pay the income to my wife during her life or until she shall assign mortgage charge or encumber or attempt to assign mortgage charge or encumber the same or part of it or until she shall become bankrupt or receiving order be made against her or until she shall do or suffer something whereby such income or some part of it would through her act or default or by operation or process of law or otherwise if belonging absolutely to her become vested in or payable to some other person or persons.

8. I direct that subject to the foregoing directions my Trustees shall stand possessed of the   capital of my residuary Estate and the income of it in trust for my children in equal shares but nevertheless subject to the following special directions that is to say:-

(a) In case any one or more of my children shall die during my lifetime leaving children surviving who shall attain the age of twenty-one years such children shall on attaining that age take equally between them if more than one the share which their his or her parent would have taken if living at my death.

(b) The share of my son George Potts Defty shall be reinvested and my Trustees shall pay to him out of capital or income Two pounds per month until he shall mortgage charge [etc………..
…..] such capital or income or part of it would through his act or default or by operation or process of law or otherwise if belonging absolutely to him become vested in or payable to some other person or persons and any unapplied part of his share and any unapplied shall fall back in to residue and so   augment the remaining shares I my residuary estate.

(c) **The share of my son John Defty shall not in any event be payable or paid to him personally but shall be reinvested and my Trustees shall apply both capital and income for the maintenance education and advancement or in any manner they think fit for the personal benefit of any or all of the lawful children of my son John Defty who may survive me whether for the time being and from time to time over or under the age of twenty one years and I expressly direct that my trustees shall have absolute discretion in regard to the application of the share in question both capital and income and shall be at liberty to so appropriate the same as to give to one or more of children of my son John a larger benefit than the other or others or if they think fit so as to at any time exclude one or more from all participation.**

9. The expression "my Trustees" shall be taken to mean my Trustees already named or the survivor of them and the executors administrators of such survivor or other the Trustee or Trustees of my Will for the time being however constituted.

Dated this Eighth day of December One thousand nine hundred and two Signed by the above named John Defty as his (signed) John Defty last Will in the presence of us both being present at the same time who in his presence at his request and in the presence of each have subscribed our names….[etc]

THIS IS A CODICIL to the above written Will of me John Defty.

10. I appoint my daughter Mary Douglas Law and her husband Edward Humble Law my Executrix and Executor and Trustees to act jointly with my two sons appointed by Clause 1 of my Will.

11. My sister in law Matilda Conder having died I revoke the gift made to her by Clause 3 of my Will

12. My son George Potts defty having died[6.] I revoke the provisions of Clause 8 (b) of my Will

13. Except as altered by this Codicil I hereby confirm my above written Will.

Signed by the Testator as a Codicil to his above written Will…[etc]

[1.]   née Douglas, sister of Mary Jane
[2.]   Coulson Douglas
[3.]   William Defty (1841-1892)
[4.]   Mary Potts
[5.]   Margaret Gray
[6.]   30 March 1904

I have high-lighted the section concerning the exclusion of John Defty (but not his children) because I find it puzzling. We do not know what John could have done to offend his father (or mother?) Instead of the eldest son being made an executor, he is excluded from all benefits and his younger brother is preferred; and the latter had seemingly abandoned his wife and child and now had two illegitimate children.

John Defty died on 13 December 1913 and the events surrounding his death are something of a mystery. He died at 1 Preston Street, Brighton, of cerebral haemorrhage - the third attack in twenty-four hours. One story (from his granddaughter - Elsie Emmie Nora) is that he died in his bath. His daughter, Margaret Emily, was present at his death.

108

What were they doing in Brighton?

His body was brought back to London and buried in Brockley cemetery in a grave already occupied by his brother, William, and his son, George Potts Douglas Defty.

Mary Jane lived until she was nearly 85, dying on 30 July 1927 at 39 Troutbeck St, New Cross. Presumably 'Duglas' had by then been sold. She too is buried in the family grave in Brockley cemetery.

It is time to move on to the next generation.

On a Sunday in 1941 the following notice appeared in the personal columns of the *News of the World:*

'DEFTY - Would John Defty, last heard of in the Durham, South Shields or Newcastle area, Coulson Defty, last heard of in the Forest Gate area of London, and Lilian Florence (née Defty), last heard of in the Camberwell area of London, being the two brothers and sister of Mollie [sc Mary Douglas] Law (née Defty,) of Hove, or their issue please communicate with Nye and Donne, 58, Ship Street, Brighton, solicitors.'

My aunt Nora (Elsie Emmie Nora) had spotted this advertisement and she quickly told her father, Coulson Defty.
The sequel is an intriguing commentary on the Defty family relationships. Aunt Nora told me some years later that she and her father, Coulson, travelled to Brighton (this being in the middle of the second World War, when travelling, especially to coastal areas, was controlled.)
In the solicitors' office they met Coulson's sister, Margaret Emily Defty, still unmarried, who at first refused to recognise Coulson as her brother and Nora as her niece. Eventually she did so and Coulson received part of the estate of his deceased sister - some £500, worth in modern terms, about £10,000.
John Defty, Coulson's elder brother, had died in 1925, and in 1941 three of his five children were alive. I cannot say whether they received any of his legacy.
Richard Defty had died in 1940. He left no children.
Lily's married name was Green, not Florence, and I cannot say whether she responded to the advertisement. She died in 1948.

In the years following 1945 my mother and I met aunt Emmie, as we knew her. She was living in a comfortable flat in Waterloo Street, Hove. My mother, Madeline - known in the family as Lena - and I were impressed by fine furniture she had presumably acquired from her mother and therefore we were not surprised when, at her death in 1952, she left what in those days was a considerable sum of money:

Her nieces Nora and Madeline each received £500.

Her niece, Winifred Rushton (née Oliver), who turned out to be a daughter of Lily Defty and her first husband, Herbert Henry Oliver, also received £500.

Two friends received, one £500 and the other £1000.

Emily's landlady received £1000.

£500 was bequeathed to the National Lifeboat Institution.

An undisclosed sum, the residue, was left to the King George's Fund for Sailors.

Not counting the last, unknown, amount, her bequests total £4,500 - perhaps £90,000 in present-day terms.

My grandparents did not benefit much from their bequest. They gave up the house in Chandos Road, Stratford, where they had lived for nearly 30 years, and lived first with Richard Hood, my grandmother's son, whom Coulson had unofficially adopted, and his wife in Dagenham. About 1943 they came to stay with my parents and me in East Ham. My grandfather, who took to dressing snappily in his old age, and who had in earlier years had frequented race-courses, died in 1945. I remember him as a taciturn, very deaf man who spoke with a Sunderland accent.

I have considerable detail of Coulson's merchant service. He used to tell me that he had been to Odessa, in the Crimea; there may be a connection here with another member of the Douglas family: according to Vera Stammers (née Kinmond) George Ridley Douglas, a first cousin of Coulson Douglas Defty died in 1891 at Turganrog, on the sea of Azov.

In April 1913, a few months before his father died, Coulson was discharged from a firm of steamship owners. The discharge says he has been with the firm for twenty-two years and has held the position of Chief Engineer for twenty of those years, having proved himself a 'steady, sober and attentive officer.'

I do not know what his immediate future was. On 7 May 1920 he was demobilized from the Royal Engineers, having enlisted on 3 May 1919, as Lance Corporal. His trade is shown as 'plumber.'

My grandmother, about whom I shall say more in the chapter on the Hood family, died in 1950.

Finally, my uncle, John Defty, my mother's half-brother, of whom I had never heard before I began preparations for this account. Did my mother and my aunt know about him? Did my grandfather know his son had been killed in action?

Here is the Army Record of John Defty (52400), copied from documents at the Public Record Office.

He enlisted on 11 Nov 1914 Sunderland into the Royal Garrison Artillery. Age given as 22 years 8 months. Address given as 28 Ripon Street, Rothes [?] Sunderland. Trade: boilermaker [shipyard?]

Medical examination shows height 5' 9" [he was therefore, six inches taller than his father], chest (expanded) 36 and half". Weight 144lb. Not married. Next of kin Charlotte [surname later shown to be Jefferson] ,[* See below]16 Valley Road, Harrogate. Relationship: mother
Statement of Service:

Joined at Newhaven 12.11.14.
Posted as a gunner to 3 Depot R[oyal]G[arrison]A[rtillery] 24.12.14.
Then to 36 Co[mpan]y RGA on 14.1.15.
Posted 2 Depot RGA on 1.6.15.
Posted overseas 6.6.15 Fort Rowner.
Posted to 13 Trench B[at]t[er]y on formation from Base. Posted TH School 1st Army 12.8.15. Posted 2nd Trench   Bty   13.8.15.
Killed in action 13.10.15.

There is correspondence during the war and afterwards concerning his medals. He was awarded the 1914-1915 Star. His mother applied for the Victory Medal. It is not known if this was awarded.

There are revealing omissions on the form which Charlotte had to fill in on 1 April 1919. Charlotte Jefferson says her son has no brothers or sisters, nor half-brothers or half- sisters; that his father is dead. The section asking for names of grandparents, nephews and nieces and uncles and aunts by blood is left blank. The form is signed by Charlotte and countersigned by a Church of England clerk in orders.

Now, at this time not only was his father, Coulson Douglas Defty alive, but also his grandmother, Mary Jane Douglas; as also were his half-sisters, Elsie Emily Nora Defty and Madeline Rose Defty.

Are we to assume that his father never knew of his death; nor his grandmother; nor his half-sisters?

We know the name of Charlotte's husband/partner, J P Jefferson, from a letter the latter wrote 3 Feb 1916, returning a map sheet to Officer i/c Records, Dover. Presumably this gave the location of John's death.

If Charlotte had married Mr Jefferson then she had committed bigamy, something that Coulson Douglas Defty had avoided because, so far as is known, he never married Catherine Tait Hood.

Familyhistoryonline shows a picture of the War Memorial at Harrogate on which a J Defty is shown. Given that on his enlistment he gave the name of his next of kin as Charlotte (Defty), living at Harrowgate, this must surely be our John Defty.

On this melancholy note we come to the end of the Defty saga.

The Hood Family

The Dallases and the Hoods

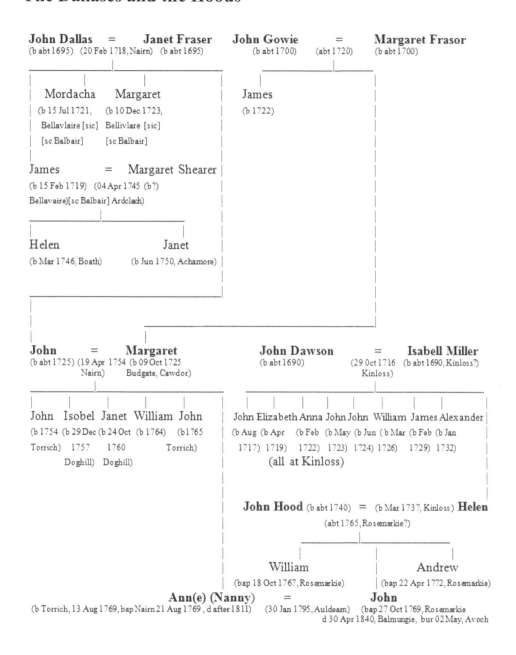

John Dallas = **Janet Fraser**
(b abt 1695) (20 Feb 1718, Nairn) (b abt 1695)

John Gowie = **Margaret Frasor**
(b abt 1700) (abt 1720) (b abt 1700)

Mordacha Margaret
(b 15 Jul 1721, (b 10 Dec 1723,
Bellavlaire [sic] Bellivlare [sic]
[sc Balbair] [sc Balbair]

James
(b 1722)

James = Margaret Shearer
(b 15 Feb 1719) (04 Apr 1745 (b?)
Bellavaire)[sc Balbair] Ardclach)

Helen Janet
(b Mar 1746, Boath) (b Jun 1750, Achamore)

John = **Margaret**
(b abt 1725) (19 Apr 1754 (b 09 Oct 1725
Nairn) Budgate, Cawdor)

John Dawson = **Isabell Miller**
(b abt 1690) (29 Oct 1716 (b abt 1690, Kinloss?)
Kinloss)

John Isobel Janet William John
(b 1754 (b 29 Dec (b 24 Oct (b 1764) (b 1765
Torrich) 1757 1760 Torrich)
Doghill) Doghill)

John Elizabeth Anna John John William James Alexander
(b Aug (b Apr (b Feb (b May (b Jun (b Mar (b Feb (b Jan
1717) 1719) 1722) 1723) 1724) 1726) 1729) 1732)
(all at Kinloss)

John Hood (b abt 1740) = (b Mar 1737, Kinloss) **Helen**
(abt 1765, Rosemarkie?)

William
(bap 18 Oct 1767, Rosemarkie)

Andrew
(bap 22 Apr 1772, Rosemarkie)

Ann(e) (Nanny) = **John**
(b Torrich, 13 Aug 1769, bap Nairn 21 Aug 1769 , d after 1811) (30 Jan 1795, Auldearn) (bap 27 Oct 1769, Rosemarkie
d 30 Apr 1840, Balmungie, bur 02 May, Avoch

In contrast to the suppositions of Scottish ancestry that were characteristic of the Douglas sections of the Defty family history, there is no doubt about the lineage of the Hoods and other forebears of my grandmother, Catherine.

She was born in Aberdeen but the earlier Hoods came from further north, in particular from the stretch of coast running west-east from Inverness and the immediate hinterland, before the ground rises to the Highlands proper.

To judge from the large number of small parishes which are found in this area, it must have been well-populated in historical times. Unfortunately, many parish registers begin later than those in England - some not before the first quarter of the eighteenth century - though the pattern is varied.

Because of this I do not know the year of birth of the first John Hood on record, nor where he was born, although since his children were born at Rosemarkie, on the so-called Black Isle - actually a peninsula running eastwards from near Inverness - it is possible that he came from that area. If, like his son John, he was a ferryman, his work could easily have taken him along the coast to Kinloss, where he married Helen Dawson about 1765.

One interesting point to mention here is that it is often easy to establish the parentage of a child, such as the sons of John and Helen, because, unlike in England, the baptismal register almost invariably names the mother as well as the father, giving her unmarried name.

For example:

> OPR Nairn/CAWDOR
>
> '1725
> GOWIE Lords Day Octor 10th
> Margaret Daur to John Gowie and Margaret Frasor in Budgate
> born the 9th inst was baptized in face of the congregation'

Before I was aware of this, I seemed to be faced with the likelihood of a large number of children born out of wedlock!

In fact, as I mentioned when writing about Mary Jane Douglas, it was customary in Scotland for a married woman to keep her maiden name throughout her life. Sometimes women were even given their unmarried names in the burial register.

I have never been given a satisfactory reason for this. My own view, for which I admit to having no evidence, is that it is a relic of the supposed matriarchal society of the Picts, who until they became defeated by, and fused with, the invading Scots from Ireland (and also the Vikings) ruled over much of present-day eastern Scotland.

The Dallases, who presumably came originally from the village of that name - which   is in the same general area - must have been much affected by the events which led up to Culloden. Balbair, where James's son, Mordacha (stated, incidentally, to be a girl in the baptismal register, although this is surely a boy's name) and Margaret seem to have been living, was the place where the Duke of Cumberland encamped. On 15th April 1746, the rebel Jacobites advanced from the north-west, hoping to make a pre-emptive strike on the government forces. They arrived just before dawn and, realising that they were too late to catch their enemies unawares, they retreated and were subsequently defeated on the 16th on Culloden Muir, a few miles to the south-west.

We have no detailed knowledge of the effect the terrible aftermath had on my family; they would presumably not have been classed as Highlanders, but the general upheaval in the area must have affected them. James Dallas and his wife, Margaret Shearer had moved a few miles eastwards to Boath and then Achamore; but John Dallas and Margaret Gowie were married in 1754 in the parish of Nairn. Margaret had been born at Budgate, just outside Cawdor, and the family went to live at the farmstead at Torrich, overlooking the coast-road along which Cumberland's forces had come before the encounter at Balbair.

The wedding of John and Margaret is recorded:

> OPR Nairn
> '19 Apr [1754]
> Matrimonially John Dallas and Marght Gowie both in this Parish who having been thrice proclaimed were married'

Of their six children three are known to have been born at Torrich and two at nearby Doghill. The birthplace of one other child is unknown.

The baptism of my ancestor Anne (family name 'Nanny') Dallas is recorded as follows:

OPR Nairn

'August 21st 1769. John Dallas in Torrich and Margaret Gowie his wife had a child baptized named Anne Witnesses Alexr Mclean in Torrich [margin Dallas] and Alexr McWatt in Ardclach and William McIntosh in Torrich Anne Cameron in the parish of Ardclach Anne Cumming in Torrich and Anne Grant in Urchney [= Urchany]. The child was born Aug 13th. Current.'

As one of the ladies in the Aberdeen Family History Shop once said: 'That must have been quite a party!'

The mention of Ardclach reminds me that John Dallas's sister was married there. Sheila and I visited the location in December 1995. There is a bell tower and an abandoned church lies in the valley below the tower. There is also a cemetery there. A more modern church lies a mile or so to the north-west.

Several years later, when our daughter, Katharine and her family were living at Kinloss, we were invited on to the farm at Torrich. The present buildings date from the 19th century but the farm may once have been an important place. It seemed to me that there was evidence of some fortification. Above the farmstead lies a significant eminence - the Hill of the Ord ('conical hill'). The first syllable of the name Torrich is thought to be cognate with 'tor' in the south-west of England. It may even imply 'castle'. '-rich' could reflect an importance the place once had.

Now for a list of the place-names mentioned with their possible meanings. (Ref: *The Dictionary of Place Names in Scotland* - Mike Darton)

Nairn	(river) of the alder trees
Balbair	settlement of the level clearing
Ardclach	high stone(s)
Budgate	? (English?)
Cawdor	-?water
Rosemarkie	headland of the horse (cf Cornish 'ross' and 'margh')
Kinloss	headland of ?
Doghill	? (English?)
Auldearn	? + river Earn
Balmungie	settlement + proper name?
Boath	herdsman's hut
Achamore	big flat space (rather than 'flat space near the sea')

The Bairds and the Taits

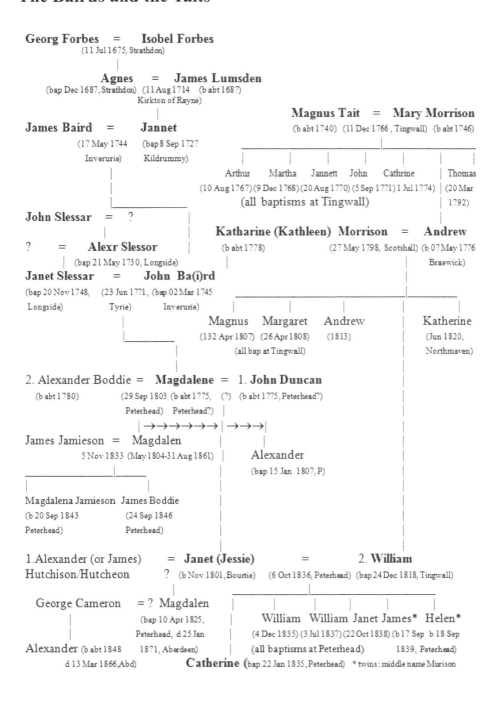

Georg Forbes   =   Isobel Forbes
          (11 Jul 1675, Strathdon)

                    Agnes   =   James Lumsden
          (bap Dec 1687, Strathdon)   (11 Aug 1714   (b abt 1687)
                                Kirkton of Rayne)

                                                    Magnus Tait   =   Mary Morrison
James Baird   =   Jannet   (b abt 1740) (11 Dec 1766, Tingwall) (b abt 1746)
     (17 May 1744   (bap 8 Sep 1727
      Inverurie)   Kildrummy)

                                    Arthur   Martha   Jannett   John   Cathrine | Thomas
                          (10 Aug 1767)(9 Dec 1768)(20 Aug 1770)(5 Sep 1771)1 Jul 1774) | (20 Mar
                                  (all baptisms at Tingwall) | 1792)

John Slessar   =   ?

?   =   Alexr Slessor   Katharine (Kathleen) Morrison   =   Andrew
        (bap 21 May 1730, Longside)   (b abt 1778)   (27 May 1798, Scotshall)(b 07 May 1776
                                                                              Braewick)
Janet Slessar   =   John Ba(i)rd
(bap 20 Nov 1748,   (23 Jun 1771, (bap 02 Mar 1745
 Longside)   Tyrie)   Inverurie)

                            Magnus   Margaret   Andrew | Katherine
                          (132 Apr 1807)(26 Apr 1808)   (1813) | (Jun 1820,
                                  (all bap at Tingwall) | Northmaven)

2. Alexander Boddie =   Magdalene = 1. John Duncan
   (b abt 1780)   (29 Sep 1803 (b abt 1775,   (?)   (b abt 1775, Peterhead?)
              Peterhead) Peterhead?) |
                              | →→→→→→ | →→→ |
James Jamieson = Magdalen | |
     5 Nov 1833 (May 1804-31 Aug 1861) | Alexander
                                    | (bap 15 Jan 1807, P)

Magdalena Jamieson James Boddie
(b 20 Sep 1843   (24 Sep 1846
Peterhead)   Peterhead)

1.Alexander (or James)   =   Janet (Jessie)   =   2. William
Hutchison/Hutcheon   ?   (b Nov 1801, Bourtie) (6 Oct 1836, Peterhead) (bap 24 Dec 1818, Tingwall)

   George Cameron   = ? Magdalen
          | (bap 10 Apr 1825, | William   William Janet James* Helen*
          | Peterhead, d 25 Jan | (4 Dec 1835) (3 Jul 1837)(22 Oct 1838)(b 17 Sep b 18 Sep
Alexander (b abt 1848   1871, Aberdeen) | (all baptisms at Peterhead)   1839, Peterhead)
   d 13 Mar 1866, Abd)   Catherine (bap 22 Jan 1835, Peterhead)   * twins: middle name Murison

117

This section of the story is about two branches of the family, the Bairds and the Taits, who were united in 1836.

The Baird, Forbes and Slessor families came chiefly from Aberdeenshire, essentially a lowland area through which flow four great rivers and their tributaries: the Deveron to the north and the Ythan, Don and Dee to the east. To the west, Strathdon, where the Forbes family lived, lies on the edge of the highland region. Further east, the Lumsdens came from Kirkton of Rayne, a few miles to the north of the mountain Bennachie, the probable site of the famous battle of *Mons Graupius,* in which the Romans defeated the Caledonians in AD83. In fact, in order to control the Caledonian tribes, the Romans built a series of forts and camps to guard the mouths of the main valleys leading from the Highlands. For our purposes we can say that these started near the unfinished fortress at Inchtutil, just south of Blairgowrie, moving in a north-easterly direction towards Aberdeen; then curving in a north-westerly arc towards the north coast.

The Bairds first appear in 1744 at Inverurie. John Baird, or Bard, met and married Janet Slessar at Tyrie. This must have been a very small parish. At any rate, it now seems to be represented by one settlement, Tyrie Mains, a few miles to the south-west of Fraserburgh, although there is a small watercourse, the Tyrie, near by.
The Slessars came from Longside, a few miles west of Peterhead.

From now on the relationships between the various members of this branch of the family become rather complicated.
John's and Janet's only recorded child was Magdalene, who was born about 1775, probably at Peterhead. She is the first of seven of my family to have borne that name. The last two are my mother, Madel(e)ine and one of our grandchildren, Elizabeth Madeline Hammond.
Given the usual custom for naming girls in Scotland, I am convinced that further, earlier, Magdalenes could be found if the parish records existed. The most obvious candidate would be Janet Slessar's mother (Alexr's wife).
We know that Magdalene Baird married twice: her first husband, or partner - we have no evidence of a marriage ceremony - was John Duncan. This is confirmed by the baptism of their daughter, Janet/Jessie/Jean:

> Peterhead: 'Novr. 30th. 1801 John Duncan in Block-house had a Daughter Baptized called Jean.' [The last name is in a different hand.]

and by Jessie's death:

> Death cert:'1859 District of St.Nicholas, Burgh of Aberdeen (168.2/24) on January 8th (7h.56m.am) at 139 Gallowgate, Aberdeen Jessie Tait Aged 58. Wife of a Street Pavior Daughter of John Duncan, farmer(deceased) and of Magdalene Duncan M/S Baird (dec) Cause of death Consumption, some years. No medical attendant. Burial Place Spital Cemetery, Aberdeen. As certified by Andrew Blackie. Informant Catherine Tait. Daughter. Present' Aged 59.

Once more we can be grateful for the comprehensive nature of Scottish records which enabled me to extend my searches.

The person reporting the death is my great-grandmother, Catherine Tait, shown at the bottom of the previous chart.

A pavior is a setter of paving stones.

I have seen Jessie's grave in the Spital (= hospital) Cemetery. Dying of consumption (tuberculosis) was only too common in poor urban areas.

John Duncan must have died soon after Jessie was born because in 1803:

OPR ABERDEEN 1803 p 297
> 'Sept 29   Upon the Twenty Ninth day of September One Thousand and Eighteen hundred and Three By the Revd Mr Robert Day minister Alexander Boddie Maggn Baird of the Trinity Chapel of Ease in Aberdeen were lawfully Married in the East Church of Aberdeen after due proclamation of Banns Alexander Boddie Carrier in Peterhead and Magdalane Baird in Aberdeen Daughter of John Baird Farmer in Peterhead In Presence of these Witnesses Thomas Youngson Stabler in Aberdeen and George Reed Servant to Mr Kilgour in Peterhead'

and

OPR PETERHEAD, Co Aberdeen (232/2)
> Marriages: '1803 September 29th Alexander Boddie, Carrier in Peterhead and Magdalen Baird in Aberdeen.'

The marriage is recorded twice because the bride and groom were living in two different parishes, Peterhead and Aberdeen. This must mean that after Jessie's birth Magdalene had gone to live in Aberdeen. In fact, Jessie was probably born in Bourtie. (See below.)

The couple had two known children: Magdalen and Alexander. Magdalen also had two children, Magdalena and James. At this point these descendents become well removed from those of John Duncan. No doubt there are other Magdalenas who came from this second marriage, perhaps even into the twentieth century.

We return now to the direct line.

Reference to the baptism of Janet/Jessie/Jean Duncan has already been made above. Unfortunately there is still some confusion. The IGI differs from the reference quoted above. It reports that on 30 Nov 1801 a Jean Duncan was baptized in Bourtie, the father's name being John Duncan. This date accords with that mentioned above, where, however, there is no mention of Bourtie only of 'Blockhouse.'

Now, I have found a settlement called Blockhouse lying about 2 miles due east of Bourtie. Is this the same place? Is this the same father? Duncan was and is a very common name and it is possible that an error has been made .For this same reason it has proved impossible to find John Duncan's parents.

Janet/Jessie/Jean also had two marriages or *liaisons*. (I shall call her Jessie from now on.)

The first was with James (or possibly, Alexander) Hutcheon or Hutchison whom she probably met in Peterhead, since that is where their daughter, Magdalen, was born in 1825. Ten years later in 1836, Jessie married William Tait, also in Peterhead:

> OPR PETERHEAD: '6 Oct 1836 William Tait Labourer and Janet Duncan both of this parish'

William Tait was probably born at Tingwall, Shetland. The exact location of his birth is not absolutely certain; on the 1851 Census a ditto mark makes it seem that he was born in Aberdeen. I am sure this was an error made by the enumerator. The same Census does however make it clear that this is 'our' William. The ancestry and relationship are confirmed by his death certificate:

> 'Died: William Tait Aged 64. Pauper formerly a Quarryman. Widower of Janet Duncan..Son of Andrew Tait, Seaman (deceased) and of Catherine Tait M/S Morrison (deceased). ..Cause of Death Cardiac Disease. Some years As certified by Alex: Robertson M.D...Informant. John McPherson, Governor's Clerk..'

In 1993 I wrote to the Shetland Islands Council and received the following letter dated 04 Mar 1993: '..there is..an entry of approximately two lines in the parish register which states that Mr Andrew Tait and Kathleen Morrison were married in Scotts Hall on 27 May 1798..I have also taken the liberty of highlighting Braewick on the map, and Scotts Hall which is in the area of Laxfirth..I believe that Scotts Hall is what you referred to as Scottshoul [which was how I thought it was spelled].'

On 24 May 1997, during the course of an archaeological visit to Shetland, Sheila and I visited the Library and Museum in Lerwick. Here I learned that Scotts Hall, where Andrew Tait and Katharine Morrison were married in 1798, had been on the site of Laxfirth House, which was built in the middle to late 19th cent. About 1600 the same site had been known as 'Tait's Boed.' This word meant 'bothy' but not in the sense usually found, ie where the labourers lived, but in the sense of a substantial 2-storey building, perhaps a fishing station. The Tait mentioned could have been a fish factor or merchant. My informant in the Museum suggested we go to see the present owner of Laxfirth House, Miss Ena Leslie. This we arranged by phone.
At 1.30, leaving the rest of the party, we took a taxi first to the village of Breiwick, where Andrew Tait is said to have lived. After some enquiries we learned that there had been until quite recently Taits still living in Breiwick.
We next paid a visit to Breiwick's oldest inhabitant, 93-year-old Mary Anderson. She was knitting and was wearing a leather pouch, known as the Shetland knitting belt, the pad stuffed full of horse-hair, with holes into which the long needles could be stuck. She invited us into the house, where she had been born. It was warm, tidy and clean. She had a dog. There were photographs of her family, including her grandfather. She had never been

outside the Mainland of Shetland and had only visited Lerwick and Scalloway and the immediate area. She seemed very content. We took pictures of her.

The taxi driver then took us to Laxfirth House. Miss Leslie invited us into a house filled with so many articles that Sheila later said that it was a complete Antiques Road-Show. Miss Leslie told us that her niece was preparing a history of the house and had considerable evidence. She said that in the early days the site had been a smugglers' den. A baillie had committed suicide on the site because of his involvement with the smugglers. We took photos of Miss Leslie and the house. During alterations to the house evidence had been found of an earlier construction. Was this Scottshall? Finally, we briefly visited the Shetland Family History Society, situated near the Museum, where I saw the film of the Tingwall Parish Register and was able to confirm the entry, especially that the place of marriage was Scottshall. (Is that where Katharine Morrison lived?)

On Monday 26 May the tour took in the Tingwall site and the church, which we photographed, the latter from a distance. Discovering that the present church dated from about 1790, we asked to stop again at Tingwall on 27 May, exactly 199 years to the day after Andrew and Katherine were married at Scottshall.

In the library I examined the Court Book of Shetland, 1615-1629, edited by Gordon Donaldson, Shetland Library, Lerwick 1991. ISBN 1873998007, p8:

8 August 1615
> Gilbert Tait in Laxfurde decerned to pay to Robert Sinclair, lawful son of the deceased William Sinclair of Ustanes £30 for the price of 3 barrels beer as half of 6 barrels 'equallie coft [(cost?)] be thame baith, run [(?)] be the said Gilbert and sauld at Brassound this last somer, quhairof he promeisit him compt, rekinning and payment; juramente octore asente reo [be on the oath of pursuer and with consent of defender] attour decernes 30s of expenssis and ordanes preceptis.'

The earliest Tait relation I could discover was Magnus, a name redolent of Viking connections and a reminder that until the fourteenth century Orkney and Shetland had belonged to Norway. It would be unlikely that any earlier ancestor could be discovered because parish records probably begin in the early eighteenth century. I say 'probably' because the usually reliable *Philimore Atlas and Index of Parish Registers* is defective in its coverage of Orkney and Shetland. We do know, however, from the quotation shown just above this paragraph, that Taits lived on Shetland in the seventeenth century.

Magnus Tait and Mary Morrison had seven children, born between 1767 and 1792. At Tingwall, just north-west of the capital, Lerwick. Andrew was the second youngest. That he was a seaman is known from his son William's death certificate. (See above).

Andrew and Katherine (or Kathleen) Morrison had five children, all of them born at Tingwall, except the last, Katharine, who was born at Northmaven, at the north of the main island.

Tingwall is historically important as it was the traditional meeting place of the island - compare this with Dingwall in Scotland and the Isle of Man parliament: Tynwald.

We do not know how or why William moved first to Peterhead and then to Aberdeen. Perhaps his father moved the family to the mainland in the early years of the nineteenth century. William is described first as a labourer, then as a quarryman and then a *pavior,* apparently meaning one who lays paving stones.

The 1851 Census shows the Tait family on 31st March:

Parish of West Aberdeen, 168A
Simpsons Court, Gallowgate
Schedule 119

					[Aberdeenshire Aberdeen]	
William Tait	Head	Mar	40	Quarrier	do	do
Janet do	Wife	Mar	50		do	Peterhead
Magdalene do	Daur	U	24	Flax Spinner	do	do
Catharine do	Daur	U	16	Lint Spinner	do	do
William do	Son	U	13	Tobacco Spinner Aberdeenshire Peterhead		
Janet do	Daur	U	11	Comb maker (Stainer)	do	do
James do	Son	U	9	Tobacco Spinner [...?}	do	do
Elizabeth Fraser	Lodger	U	18	Wool spinner	Aberdeenshire	do
Alexander Cameron Grandson U 2					do	do
Alexʳ McKay		Lodger	U15	Wool Spinner	Caithness	

As I said earlier, the ditto entry to William Tait must be an error.

Magdalene, Janet's (Jessie's) illegitimate daughter by James or Alexander
Hutcheon/Hutchison has been taken into William's family.
James (Murison) Tait's age should read 12. His twin sister, Helen (Murison) Tait is
missing from the Census.
Alexander Cameron, shown as William's grandson, is Magdalene's (illegitimate) son by
George Cameron. He died at the age of 17 and is buried in the Spital Cemetery, S3, with a
well-preserved granite stone:

Erected by
George Cameron
in memory of his son
ALEXANDER
who died March 13th 1866. Aged 17 years

The inscription continues

Also of
Jessie Duncan
Grandmother of Alexander Cameron
Who died Jan 8th 1859 aged 59 years

also of
Magdaliene Hutcheon
Mother of the said Alexander Cameron
who died Jan 25th 1871 aged 44 years [actually 46 years]
On the reverse side of the stone:

This is also the
burying ground of
James Wm Hood Master Mariner
sacred to the
memory of his infant daughter
Elizabeth Nix
Who died 2nd Feb 1867
aged 5 months

Information from The Record of Burials in the City of Aberdeen Environmental Health Dept confirmed the information on this headstone; it also revealed that three other persons unrelated to my family were also interred in the grave. Finally, because of the wording it seemed to show that James Wm Hood was not buried there.   But we shall be dealing with James William and his daughter in the next section.

Passing now to the 1861 Census we find:

Registration District: St Nicholas, Aberdeen
Registration Number: 168A
Address: 188 George Street
Household schedule number:2/35

Magdalina Hutchison	Head	Female	36		Peterhead, Aberdeenshire
Catherine Tait	Half Sister	Female	24	Flax Millworker	Peterhead, Aberdeenshire
Jessie Tait	Half Sister	Female	20	Comb Worker	Peterhead, Aberdeenshire
James Tait	Half Brother	Male	19	Brass Finisher	Peterhead, Aberdeenshire
Alexander Cameron	Son	Male	12	Booksellers Assistant	Aberdeen, Aberdeenshire
Jessie Fraser	Boarder	Female	13	Flax Millworker	Banff, Banffshire

(This information is taken from the transcription by *Ancestry*.)
Comparing this Census with the 1851 Census, we see that there are three notable absences: William and Janet Tait and their daughter, Helen. Janet had died in 1859 but we do not know what has become of William. Helen is again missing from the Census; she must be working away from home, perhaps in service. Janet Tait is now called Jessie.
James's age is again incorrectly shown; it should read 22.
The rest of the information is logical enough. A new lodger has replaced Elisabeth Fraser and one is tempted to speculate that the present boarder is her daughter.

The question of the twins, Helen and James, raises some doubts. Nevertheless, James reported the death of Alexander Cameron on 13th March 1866 at 5 Short Loanings and is described as the deceased's 'half-uncle.' Furthermore, 'Helen Tait Aunt' was present at the death of Lizzie Vix Hood (sc Elizabeth Nix Hood) on 2nd Feb 1867 at 6 Short Loanings.

Returning to William Tait, he was present at the marriage of his daughter, Catherine, in 1864. Here is the transcript of the ceremony:

> ...At Hanover Lane Aberdeen After Banns according to the Terms of the Free Church of Scotland...William Hood   Seaman (Mate)(Merchant Service) age 25..St Clements Street..[father].John Hood porter at a Foundry [mother] Elizabeth Hood M.S. Nix (deceased)...Catherine Tait Flax Mill Worker (Spinster)..age 27..6 Short Loanings..[father] William Tait Stone dresser [mother] Jessie Tait M.S.Duncan (deceased) Signed John Stephens Minister of Free John Knox's Aberdeen.
> Signed   WilliamTait

The mention of the Free John Knox Church reminds us of the Presbyterian schism which had occurred in 1843 with the emergence of the 'Wee Free.'

John Hood and the Colonial Connection

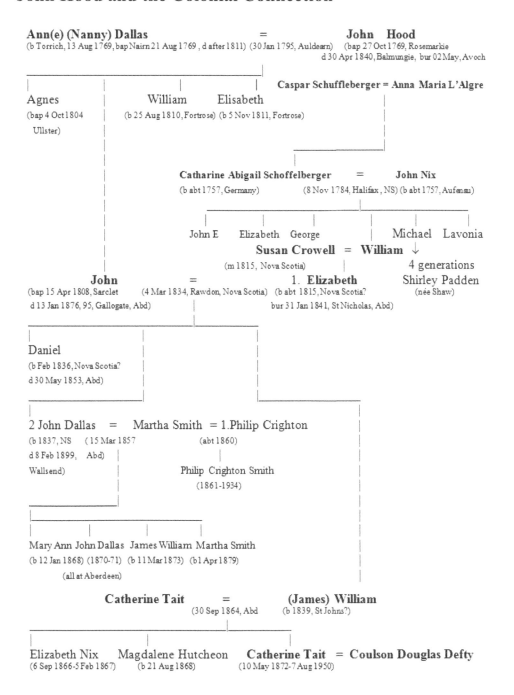

Ann(e) (Nanny) Dallas   =   **John   Hood**
(b Torrich, 13 Aug 1769, bap Nairn 21 Aug 1769 , d after 1811)   (30 Jan 1795, Auldearn)   (bap 27 Oct 1769, Rosemarkie
                                                                                           d 30 Apr 1840, Balmungie, bur 02 May, Avoch

Caspar Schuffleberger = Anna Maria L'Algre

Agnes   William   Elisabeth
(bap 4 Oct 1804   (b 25 Aug 1810, Fortrose) (b 5 Nov 1811, Fortrose)
  Ullster)

Catharine Abigail Schoffelberger   =   **John Nix**
(b abt 1757, Germany)   (8 Nov 1784, Halifax , NS) (b abt 1757, Aufensu)

John E   Elizabeth   George   Michael   Lavonia
                Susan Crowell = **William** ↓
                (m 1815, Nova Scotia)   4 generations
    John   =   **1. Elizabeth**   Shirley Padden
(bap 15 Apr 1808, Sarclet   (4 Mar 1834, Rawdon, Nova Scotia) (b abt 1815, Nova Scotia?   (née Shaw)
 d 13 Jan 1876, 95, Gallogate, Abd)   bur 31 Jan 1841, St Nicholas, Abd)

Daniel
(b Feb 1836, Nova Scotia?
 d 30 May 1853, Abd)

2 John Dallas   =   Martha Smith = 1. Philip Crighton
(b 1837, NS   (15 Mar 1857   (abt 1860)
 d 8 Feb 1899,   Abd)
 Wallsend)   Philip Crighton Smith
                                 (1861-1934)

Mary Ann John Dallas James William Martha Smith
(b 12 Jan 1868) (1870-71) (b 11 Mar 1873) (b 1 Apr 1879)
       (all at Aberdeen)

        Catherine Tait   =   **(James) William**
               (30 Sep 1864, Abd   (b 1839, St Johns?)

Elizabeth Nix   Magdalene Hutcheon   **Catherine Tait** = **Coulson Douglas Defty**
(6 Sep 1866-5 Feb 1867)   (b 21 Aug 1868)   (10 May 1872-7 Aug 1950)

125

John Hood and Anne Dallas were married in 1795 but even after extensive research I can find no births to the couple until 1804. There must be earlier children but they seem not to have been recorded. I can find no evidence that I have erroneously chosen another couple, especially as it seems unlikely that two John Hoods married two Anne Dallases; in any case, there is no record of the marriage of a second couple with the same names.

Of the four children we know about, Agnes was born at Ulbster, Caithness; John, my ancestor, at Sarclet, near Wick; and the last two, William and Elisabeth, at Fortrose, on Black Isle. These births are consistent with John's having been a ferryman, plying along the north-east coast of Scotland. In the case of William, his father is described as a 'ferrier' in the Rosemarkie (the parish church) register. I thought this was a mistake for 'farrier' until I came to Elisabeth's baptism, where John is described as a 'ferryman.'

In July 2000 Katharine and I travelled to Sarclet, just a few miles south of John o' Groats. The village still exists, but as a long row of cottages leading away from the cliffs. The little harbour as it was in the Hoods' time is now completely abandoned:

We have no information about the early years of John junior but in 1834 we find he has emigrated to Nova Scotia. This was first revealed when I examined Census returns which bore the name of his third son, my great-grandfather, James William Hood. James was at sea for the 1871 Census, but the 1881 Census reads:

Parish or District: Old Machar   City or County: Aberdeen   168-2/1881/11/110

33 Summer St   James Wm Hood   Head   Widr   41   Mariner   [Where born]
America St John's

           Magdelin H   "   Daur   Unm   13   Housekeeper   Aberdeen

           Catherine T   "   "   "   9   Scholar   "

James's wife, Catherine, had died earlier in the year and he was left with two daughters, the second of whom is my grandmother.

There are a great number of St John's in the New World and I did not know which to choose until I came across a Census showing James's brother John Dallas Hood:

1881 Census Wallsend   5071 112 97

'Wallsend 38 Clyde Street
Hood   John D   Head   M   34[sic]M   Seaman Laborer   **Novo[sic]Scotia**
[the rest of his family follows]   **NewPort U.S.[sc N.S?]**

I already knew from James's marriage to Catherine Tait (see above) that his mother's maiden name was Nix and I managed to find the following marriage:

Church Records: Rawdon Anglican: St Pauls:mfm 11814X:

    'John Hood of this parish and Elizabeth Nix of this parish, md by banns and consent of parents, 4 March 1834 wit: Wm Walker & John Hunter '

Working with these pieces of information, and getting in touch with the Nova Scotia authorities, I received the following information:

[Information received 12 Jan 1998 from Mrs Virginia Clarke, researcher in Nova Scotia:]

'...The name Nix is found in Hants County....Newport was a township in Hants County (Maybe the US is NS?) Nowadays, St Johns' is the capital city of Newfoundland, but across the Bay of Fundy from County Newport is Saint John, New Brunswick with ties and trade to that part of Nova Scotia....'

At this point it is appropriate to discuss the origins of my great-great-grandmother, Elizabeth Nix. In this I received valuable assistance from a distant relative, Shirley Padden, who now lives in Massachusetts, USA.

As can be seen from the table above, the Nixes were of German origin. John Nix was born in Aufenau in central Germany. He married Catharine Abigail Schoffelberger (or Schuffelberger). Here are the documentary evidence and his will:

05 APR 99
[From Shirley Padden]:

'John Nix B[orn] before 1764 in Aufenau, Germany. married Katherine Schoffelberger 8 Nov 1784, dau of Caspar Schuffelberger and Marie L'Algre. Marriage Index Book at PANS 1993 found NIX, John 6 [?] November 1784 and BERGER, Catherine Abigail (G) St George's Anglican.

'Records Dutch Church 1784 - St George's Anglican Church, Halifax - MG4, Volume 309 show marriage of John Nix and Katherine Schoffelberger 8 Nov 1784. Witnesses Adam Wolf, Adam Tsler [?], solemnized by Rev BM Houseal [?]

'A short reference on the Nix family is found in Hants County, NS by author John V Duncanson's book of Rawdon and Douglas - "Two Loyalist Townships in NS." John Nix was listed in the Rawdon Assessment of 1795. John Nix's will was proved at Windsor, NS on 5 Sep 1814. His wife Catherine inherited the Rawdon property. Daughter Elizabeth, wife of Francis Mason Jn. was named in the will and also a son[s Michael and] William and a son George, who [this last] inherited 250 acres formerly in possession of Thomas Pearson, Esq. HCEP#129A.'

'Last Will and Testament of John Nix – Rawdon (transcribed Shirley Padden, amended by Brian Hammond)

'In the name of God Amen

  I John Nix of the township of Rawdon in the County
of Hants, Province of Nova Scotia, Farmer
                    Being very sick and weak in body, but of
                    perfect mind and memory, thanks be given
                    unto God, calling, unto mind the mortality of
                    my body, and knowing it is appointed for all
                    Men to die, do make and ordain this my last
                    will and testament: that is to say principally
                    and first of all, I give and recommend my
                    soul into the hand of Almighty God that
                    gave it, and my body I recommend to the
                    earth; to be buried in decent Christian
                    burial, at the discretion of my Executors;
                    nothing doubting but at the general resur-
                    rection, I shall receive the same again,
                    by the mighty power of God. And as touching

such worldly estate wherewith it has pleased
God to bless me in this life, I give, devise,
and dispose of the same in the following
manner and form

First, I give and bequeath unto Catharine, my dearly
beloved wife the whole estate and property
real and personal belonging to me in
the said Township of Rawdon, and in
the said County of Hants for her term
of Life and at the decease of the said
Catharine wife of the said John Nix is
to descend to

[Page two]

My well beloved Sons Michael and William
and.[George?] is to be equally divided between them
Consisting of Three Hundred Acres
Forty Pounds to be paid by them out of
the above mentioned estate to my beloved
Daughter Elizabeth wife of Francis
Mason as follows eighteen months after
the decease of the said John Nix the
sum of 14 Pounds and nine months
after the said paid the sum of thirteen
Pounds, likewise at the expiration
of nine Months following the date
of the second payment the sum of
thirteen pounds is by them to be paid
Secondly All that track of Land to me belonging at
the place called nine mile river in the
County Halifax - Letter A No1 No 4 consisting of two hundred Acres to be equally
divided between the two above mentioned
Sons Michael and William
Thirdly To my well beloved Son George All that
certain track of Land formerly in the
possession of Thomas Pearson Esqre
Consisting of two hundred and fifty Acres
bounded on the North by lands granted to
John Lewis on the East and South by lands
unoccupied and on the West by lands granted
to John Bond Junr.

All debts, demands, dues coming upon the
said estate is to be paid and received by
Catharine, wife of John Nix

Signed, sealed, published pronounced
and declared by the said John Nix
as his last Will and testament
in the presence, and in the pre-
ence of each other, have here
unto subscribed our
Names

John McLalan [?]

William Canavan [?]   [seal]   John Nix

Francis Parker'

John Nix's first son, John E Nix, had clearly died before his father and it is from the third
son, William that I am descended. He it was who married Susan Crowle and whose first
daughter, Elizabeth, married John Hood. We do not have Elizabeth's date of birth but it
must have been pretty soon after her parents' marriage in 1815 (which was by licence and
witnessed by William's two remaining brothers, George and Michael) because in 1834
Elizabeth, who would have been 19 or younger, married John Hood with the consent of
[her] parents. This means that she was a minor (under 21 years). John himself would have
been about 26.
John and Elizabeth had three known sons:
Daniel/David Hood, born in February 1836 (confirmed by his gravestone 'aged 17 years
and three months.')
John Dallas Hood, born in 1837
James William Hood, born in 1839

Mrs Clarke (whom I quoted above) adds: ' ….. I checked the recently indexed 1838 census
for Hants County, NS.... only 4 of 18 counties have been published by the Genealogical
Association of Nova Scotia   and I find one John Hood, Newport Twp [Township?]
labourer. [In the household are]:

* 2 males (-6yr)   0 females (-6y)
  1 male (6-14y)   0 female   (6-14y)
  0 males (14y+)   2 females (14y+)**
    6 [5?] plus male head of house..'

This could work out thus:

Daniel Hood   (b 1836, aged 2) *
John Dallas Hood   (b 1837, aged 1) *
unknown male child   (b 1832, aged 6)
John Hood
Elizabeth Nix and another unknown female. **

James William would not have shown on the 1838 Census because he was born a year later.

Daniel Hood has caused me considerable trouble. He is sometimes shown as Daniel and sometimes as David. The worst confusion comes when you compare the St Nicholas (Aberdeen) burial register with the gravestone in Nellfield Cemetery, Aberdeen. In the register he is shown as 'David,' on the gravestone as 'Daniel.' (See the relevant chart later on in this narrative.)
Now, if you write David or Daniel quickly they can look very similar. This is how the confusion must have arisen. Unfortunately to resort to the usual Scottish naming pattern does not solve the problem, as neither name appears in the immediate ancestry of either the Hood family or the Nix family.

John Dallas Hood is much more straightforward because John Hood's father's wife's maiden name was 'Dallas.'

James William Hood's first   names are also obscure but are secure because we have the evidence of his marriage certificate to Catherine Tait. (See above.)
All three boys appear on the 1851 Aberdeen Census with their father and stepmother and new stepbrother, Andrew and stepsister, Barbara. Daniel is correctly shown but unfortunately all three boys are incorrectly shown as born in Aberdeen!

As for their mother, Elizabeth Nix, we have the following entry:

OPR ABERDEEN Co ABERDEEN [Burial Register of St Nicholas, Aberdeen]:
  '1841 January 31 Elizabeth Nick [sc Nix?] from the Hospital'

It seems that John Hood must have brought Elizabeth and their three sons back from Nova Scotia to Aberdeen between 1839 and early 1841 (when Elizabeth Nix died.) John and his family have not yet been found on the 1841 Census for Scotland.

A few paragraphs above I referred to the 1851 Census in which the boys' stepmother makes an appearance. It is now time to detail John Hood's other two marriages:

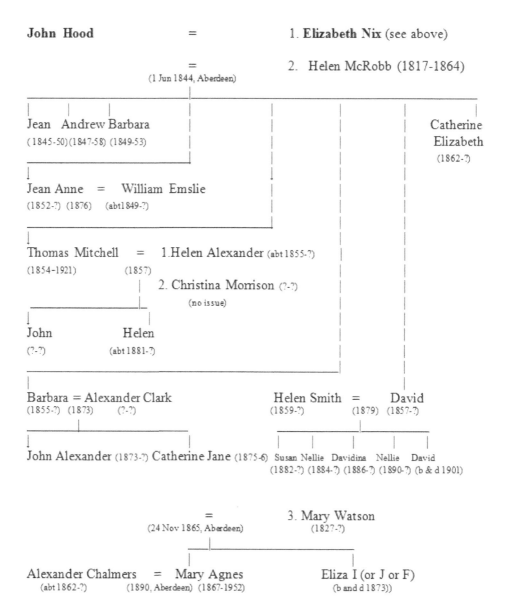

John Hood = 1. **Elizabeth Nix** (see above)

= 2. Helen McRobb (1817-1864)
(1 Jun 1844, Aberdeen)

Jean   Andrew Barbara
(1845-50) (1847-58) (1849-53)

Catherine
Elizabeth
(1862-?)

Jean Anne = William Emslie
(1852-?) (1876) (abt 1849-?)

Thomas Mitchell = 1. Helen Alexander (abt 1855-?)
(1854-1921) (1857)

2. Christina Morrison (?-?)
(no issue)

John Helen
(?-?) (abt 1881-?)

Barbara = Alexander Clark
(1855-?) (1873) (?-?)

Helen Smith = David
(1859-?) (1879) (1857-?)

John Alexander (1873-?) Catherine Jane (1875-6) Susan Nellie Davidina Nellie David
(1882-?) (1884-?) (1886-?) (1890-?) (b & d 1901)

= 3. Mary Watson
(24 Nov 1865, Aberdeen) (1827-?)

Alexander Chalmers = Mary Agnes
(abt 1862-?) (1890, Aberdeen) (1867-1952)

Eliza I (or J or F)
(b and d 1873))

132

Before we come to John Hood's three wives and his children we have to review the somewhat colourful life of John himself.

First of all, there can be no doubt that throughout we are dealing with the same person. John's parentage is clearly stated on all the relevant documents: John Hood and Ann Dallas. It is true that his father's occupation is   shown as 'farmer' on his death certificate and on his marriage to Mary Ann Watson, but I am convinced that these are mistakes for 'ferrier'; it may even be that John Hood senior did become a farmer after he retired from the sea. On his brother William's birth entry 'ferrier' appears and on his sister Elisabeth's entry 'ferryman'. Although John and his siblings were born at different places along the eastern coast, they all had the name Anne ('Nanny') Dallas as their mother and I consider it almost inconceivable that we dealing with two different families.
Furthermore, John was economical with truth over his age. From various documents which appeared throughout his life he seems to have grown younger rather than aged!
He could have been just as careless when giving other details.

John Hood's early life is not known. As a young man he must have emigrated to Canada, living perhaps in St John, New Brunswick, and then crossing to Newport, Nova Scotia and then on to Rawdon, Hants County, where he married Elizabeth Nix. If it is his family quoted above on the 1838 Nova Scotia Census, then he is shown as a labourer.

After his return to Scotland, we know that he became a fireman. Three years after the death of Elizabeth Nix:

OPR Aberdeen, Co Aberdeen (168/1/30) Marriages
>'1844 June 1st
>After due Proclamation of Banns, John Hood **fireman** in Aberdeen was on the
>First day of June One Thousand Eight Hundred and Forty Four. Married at
>Aberdeen to Helen McRobb Daughter of the late William McRobb, Shoemaker b
>1837 in Aberdeen by the Reverend Gavin Parker Minister in Aberdeen. In
>presence of these Witnesses James Milne and John Falconer both in Aberdeen.'

By the time of 1851 Census he had changed his job. Here now is the whole family:

1851 Census 1851/168A/(136)/2/6 at George Street, West Parish, Aberdeen, Co Aberdeen:

John Hood	Head	Marr	39	**Clerk Iron Works**	Born Invernessshire
Ellen Hood	Wife	Marr	30		B Moneymusk, Co Aberdeen
Daniel Hood	Son		15	Combmaker	B Aberdeen, Co Aberdeen
John Hood	Son		12	Combmaker	B Aberdeen, Co Aberdeen
William Hood	Son		11	Combmaker	B Aberdeen, Co Aberdeen
Andrew Hood	Son		3		B Aberdeen, Co Aberdeen
Barbara Hood	Daur		1½		B Aberdeen, Co Aberdeen

All three sons born to Elizabeth Nix are shown here, but with incorrect birth-places. Daniel is, however, correctly named.

A curious incident occurs in 1854. Thomas Mitchell Hood was born. He seems to have been named after the manager of the Footdee Iron Works who, as Thomas Mitchell, a widower, aged 68 in 1861, appears on the Census living in the Manager's House, next to John Hood and family.

By the end of 1858 both Barbara Helen and Andrew had died. Here is the entry for Andrew:

> '1858 District of St Nicholas, Burgh of Aberdeen (168/2/691) on September 9th at Porters Lodge, Foot-Dee Iron Works, Aberdeen (8.45pm) Andrew Hood Aged 11 years/Son of John Hood, **Gate Porter** Foot-Dee Iron Works and Helen Hood M/S MacRobb [sic]/ Cause of Death Erysipelas followed by inflammation of lungs for five days. Cert by George J Nicol MD who saw the dec 5 Sep.

Burial Place Nellfield Cemetery../Inf John Hood.Father.Presant [sic]'

Erysipelas, commonly known as 'St Antony's Fire' is a virulent streptococcal infection of the skin which, before the use of antibiotics, if not fatal, could be extremely disfiguring. I remember that in the 1930s there were frequent advertisements for creams to relieve the symptoms.

Some years ago, Sheila and I visited the site of the iron works in the parish of St Clements, Foot-Dee, known still as the Fittee (foot of the Dee). The area is well preserved and makes an interesting tourist venue.

On the 1861 Census the family are found still living in the porter's lodge of the Footdee Iron Foundry, with John as the Gate Keeper

On 6 July 1864 Helen, John's wife, died:

> Death of Helen Hood: '1864 District of St Nicholas, Burgh of Aberdeen (168/1/820) on July 6th at St Clement St Aberdeen Helen Hood aged 46. Married to John Hood, **Gate Keeper at an Iron Foundry**. Daughter of William McRobb, Farmer, (deceased) and of Jane McRobb M/S Davidson (deceased) Cause of death Cancer, 14 months and upwards As certified by

John Wood, Surgeon Informant John Hood, Husband. Present. Died at 0.30 am Aged 46 [56]'

Sixteen months later John married for a third time:

Marriage of John Hood and Mary Ann Watson:

> 1865 District of St Nicholas, Burgh of Aberdeen (168/1/311) on November 24th
> at Upper Kirkgate, Aberdeen. After Banns according to the Forms of the
> Established Church of Scotland.
> John Hood   Aged 50. **Gatekeeper at an Iron Foundry**
>   Widower
>   Usual residence St Clements Street, Aberdeen
>   Son of John Hood, Farmer (deceased) and of
>   Ann Hood M/S Dallas (deceased)
>   and of Mary Ann Watson Aged 40. Domestic Servant. Spinster
>   Usual residence 40 Upper Kirkgate, Aberdeen
>   Daughter of Alexander Watson, Linen Weaver (deceased) and
>   Isabella Watson M/S Gray
>
>   Signed   Ch: Skene, Minr of John Knox Church, Aberdeen
>   Witnesses   Alex: Watson   John McKay

John was by this time aged 57, not 50.

A child was born eighteen months after the marriage:

> '1867 District of St Nicholas, Burgh of Aberdeen (168/1/811) on May 29th at
> 13 Upper Kirkgate, Aberdeen [at 4.30 am]
> Mary Agnes Hood
> Daughter of   John Hood, Clerk at an Iron Work and of
>   Mary Ann Hood M/S Watson
> Marriage of Parents   1865, November 24th. Aberdeen
> Informant   John Hood. Father.'

The family is still at the ironworks.

Meanwhile, there had been another Census, in 1871:

1871 Scotland Census. Roll CSST1871_31
Registration number 168/1. Household Schedule number 54

47 Camerons [Court,]

John	Hood	Head	Mar	59	**Provision Dealer**	Caithnessshire	*Searth?*
Mary Ann	do	Wife	Mar	44		Kinkardinshire	Drumlithie
Jean Ann	do	Daur		18	Bookbinder	Aberdeen	
Thomas	do	Son		17	Engine Fitter's Apprentice		do
David	do	Son		13	Iron Moulder's	do	do
Mary Agnes	do	Daur		3			do

There are a number of important points to be extracted from this document, on which the hand-writing is unusually difficult to read.

We see that John has changed his occupation. Does this mean he has become a shop-keeper? Only a contemporary street directory will establish this.

More curious is his place of birth. Caithness is, for the first time, correctly given; but the town or village is nearly illegible on the sheet. To me it appears as *Searth* but the digitalised copy interprets the entry as *Sentle*. Neither of these is close to the real name: *Sarclet*.

Finally, the family have moved. Cameron's Court, now no longer existing, adjoining North Road.

Mary Agnes Hood, the last but one of John's children, survived until December 1952, that is, into my 24th year!

The last child of John and Mary Ann was born and died in 1873 but there is no reference to her except on the Nellfield cemetery gravestone. See below.

John Hood died in 1876:

Death Cert: 'John Hood **Insurance Agent**/Married to Mary Ann Watson, previously to Helen McRobb/1876/January/thirteenth/6h 0m. a.m. /60 years [sic]/John Hood/ Farmer (deceased)/ Ann Hood m.s. Dallas (deceased)/Bursting of a Blood Vessel/ Sudden death/Not Certified/[Signed] David Hood/Son and Inmate.'
[line 2] '95 Gallowgate Aberdeen'

Any doubt that this is the correct John Hood is dispelled by the confirmation that he was previously married to Helen McRobb. Again, we have an incorrect age given. John was by now in his 68th year. 'Insurance Agent'?

I discovered that his death was the subject of an inquiry. It turned out that there was nothing sinister about this: it was the natural legal result of the reporting of a sudden death:

REGISTER OF CORRECTED ENTRIES
FOR THE DISTRICT OF ST NICHOLAS
IN THE BOROUGH OF ABERDEEN

The following Report of result of a Precognition has been received touching the Death of John Hood, Registered under no.40 in the Register Book of Deaths,for the year 1876.

Name, Age & Sex	When and Where Died	Cause of Death	Burial Place
John HOOD Male	At 6 o'clock a.m.	Bursting of a	Nellfield Cemetery
	13th January	Blood vessel	
63 years [sic]	1876 In the Dwelling	(the main	Aberdeen
	No 95	artery of the	Robert Leslie
	Gallowgate Aberdeen	body)	74 Queen
	occupied by the	Francis Ogston	Cemetery Undertaker
	deceased	Junr M.D.	Aberdeen
		Aberdeen, made	
		a Post Mortem	
		examination	
		of the body	

City Procurator-Fiscal's Office   (Signed) Geo Cadenhead
                                                                    Procurator-Fiscal

                        January 25th 1876, at Aberdeen
                        Charles Stronach, Assistant Registrar
                                    (Initd) J.W.
John Watt Registrar

In other words, this is like an English Coroner's Report.

Here is an account of all of John's children from his three marriages:

To Elizabeth Nix:

Daniel	born 'America'	Feb 1836	died	Aberdeen 30 May 1853
John Dallas	'Novo [sic] Scotia/ New Port US [sc NS]' 1837			Tynemouth 8 Feb 1899
James William	America St Johns'	1839		? after 1881

To Helen McRobb:

Jean Ann	Aberdeen	Feb 1845	Aberdeen 2 Sep 1850
Andrew	Aberdeen	1847	Aberdeen 5 Sep 1848
Barbara Helen	Aberdeen	Aug 1849	Aberdeen 13 Nov 1853
Jean A	Aberdeen	1852	?
Thomas Mitchell	Aberdeen	1854	Airdrie 28 Aug 1921
Barbara Helen	Aberdeen	2 Nov 1855	?
David	Aberdeen	16 Nov 1857	? after 1901
Catherine Elizabeth	Aberdeen	6 Apr 1862	? after 1881

To Mary Ann Watson:

Mary Agnes	Aberdeen	29 May 1867	Leslie, Fife, 30 Dec 1952
Eliza I (or J or F)	Aberdeen	Apr 1873	Aberdeen Aug 1873

From the above list we see that John lost not only two wives during his lifetime but that 5 of his 13 children did not reach adulthood. This is probably no worse a proportion than any other family living in cramped urban conditions in the mid-nineteenth century. It also demonstrates how skewed statistics about longevity can be that do not take account of the heavy loss of young children.

Many of the above were buried in the same grave in the Nellfield Cemetery, Aberdeen. Here, in full, is what is inscribed on the grave-stone:

Erected by
John Hood
In Memory of his children
JEAN ANN   Died 22^d Septr 1850
Aged 5 years and 7 months
DANIEL Died 30th May 1853
Aged 17 years 3 months
BARBARA HELEN, Died 13th Nov 1853
Aged 4 years and 3 months
ANDREW Died 5 Sept 1858 aged 11 years
Also his wife HELEN M^{c}ROBB
Died 6th July 1864 Aged 46 years
The above JOHN HOOD died on the
13th Jany 1876 aged 64 years
Deeply regreted [sic] by his family

---------0----------

ALSO THE BURYING GOUND OF
JOHN HOOD JUN^R
WHOSE SON JOHN D HOOD DIED ON THE
16th SEPT^R 1871 AGED 19 MONTHS
ALSO HIS AUNT BARBARA MCROBB
WHO DIED 30th AUGUST 1887 AGED 64 YEARS

[on the reverse of the stone at the top]

IN MEMORY OF
ELIZABETH HOOD
Who died 5th DEC^R., 1856,
Aged 74 YEARS

Before we come to discuss the identity of this last person, Elizabeth Hood, we need to look at the corresponding entries in the St Nicholas Burial Register:

<u>Nellfield burials 1830-1900</u>

977 Hood. Miss[?]   **Elizabeth** 1849   Certificate 777

                   Janet, sister, 25 Sept 1849 ag. 68 years

                   Jane A., 25 Sept 1850   ag. 5 years 7 months

                      David, 31 May 1853 ag. 17 years

                   Barbara H, 14 Nov. 1853 ag. 4 yrs. 3 mnths.

                   Elizabeth, self, 8 Dec 1856 ag. 74 yrs

                   Andrew, 8 Sept. 1858 ag. 11 years

       McRobb,   Helen, 9 July 1864   ag. 46 yrs

       Hood,   John D., 20 Nov. 1871 ag. 1 yr. 7 mths.

                   Eliza, I or J or F, 29 Aug. 1873 ag. 4 mths

       Hood,   **John, brother,** 15 Jan 1876 ag. 64 yrs

       Clark,   Catherine I or J, 16 Nov. 1876 ag. 3 yrs

       McRobb   Barbara, 2 Sept. 1887 ag. 60 yrs.

I have put in bold script the main items discussed below. Now, comparing the Nellfield Cemetery stone, the St Nicholas Register and the Statutory Records (from 1855) we have:

St Nicholas Burial Register	Nellfield Gravestone	Stat Records (from 1855)
Janet Hood 25 Sep 1849	[no mention]	N/A
Jane A 25 Sep 1850	Jean Ann 22 Sep 1850	N/A
David, 31 May 1853	*Daniel* Died 30 May 1853	N/A
Barbara Hood, 14 Nov 1853	Barbara Helen Died 13 Nov 1853	N/A
Elizabeth Hood 8 Dec 1856	Elizabeth Hood died 5 Dec 1856	5 Dec 1856
Andrew 8 Sep 1858	Andrew Died 5 Sep 1858	9 Sep 1858
McRobb, Helen, 9 Jul 1864	Helen McRobb Died 6 Jul 1864	6 Jul 1864
Hood, John D, *20 Nov* 1871	John D Hood Died *16 Sep* 1871	*17 Nov* 1871
Eliza I [or J or F] 29 Aug 1873	[no mention] Neither birth nor death recorded	
Hood John, 15 Jan 1876	John Hood died 13 Jan 1876	13 Jan 1876
Clark, Catherine I [or J], 16 Nov 1876	[no mention]	16 Nov 1876
McRobb Barbara 2 Sep 1887	Barbara McRobb, 30 Aug 1887	30 Aug 1887

I used to prefer *David* Hood as being more likely than *Daniel*, especially as David recurs later in the Hood family. But discovery of the 1851 Census makes it clear that the name was Daniel, as shown on the stone. The entry in the Burial Register is an error.

I cannot explain the engraving on the stone of 16 *Sep* instead of *Nov* for the death of the younger John Dallas Hood. The Burial Records and the Statutory Registration agree on November, which must surely be the correct month.

The inclusion of two formerly unknown women, however, presents a real problem: I mean Elizabeth and Janet Hood.

It seems from the Burial Register that Elizabeth Hood was responsible for the acquisition, if not the purchase, of the plot. It is clear too that Janet Hood and our John Hood were respectively the sister and brother of Elizabeth. But this cannot really be the case, at least as far as Elizabeth is concerned. She died in 1856 and here is the entry in the Statutory Register of Deaths:

> District of St Nicholas, Burgh of Aberdeen 168 1/986
> on 5th Decem at 11 Exchequer Row, Aberdeen Elizabeth Hood   Aged 74 . Sick Nurse. Single
> Daughter of **Andrew Hood, Farmer Deceased and of Janet Hood M/S Ritchie (dec)**
> Cause of death Chronic Bronchitis for several years as cert by James H.Forsyth Physician who saw deceased 4 Decem
> Burial Place Nellfield Cem, Aberdeen, As cert by Ebenezer Bain, Undertaker
> Informant Jessie Youngson her x mark neice [sic] and occupier present.

(On the 1851 Census Elizabeth is shown living with her niece and her niece's husband.)

These parents are clearly different from the known parents of our John Hood: John Hood and Anne (Nanny) Dallas.

If Janet Hood was the sister of Elizabeth, her parents would also have been Andrew and Janet. Unfortunately she died six years before the start of Statutory Registration. She may have been found on the Roskeen 1841 Census: 1841 081/00 009/00 007:

Roskeen, Ross and Cromarty S Main St		[Whether born in County]	
Janet Hood	45	Ind[ependent means]	Y
John Goss	30	Merchant	N
Harriett do	25		Y
Mary Goss	3		Y
Harriett do	1		Y
Ann McKenzie	30	F[emale] S[ervant]	Y
Margaret Holm	15	"	Y

There is, however, no clear evidence that this is our Janet Hood.

Here is a possible solution: both of these women, if their ages at death are correctly shown, were born in the early 1780s - more than 25 years before our John Hood.
The chances are, therefore, that they were the *aunts*, not the *sisters*, of our John Hood.
In this case, Andrew Hood and Janet Ritchie could be the grandparents of our John.
Unfortunately, I can find no evidence of a marriage between an Andrew Hood and a Janet Ritchie. So the problem must for the present remain unresolved.

Finally, why was Janet's name not put on the stone? Did John, who had it erected, not know about her? Had there been a family quarrel? And why was Elizabeth's name alone put on the *reverse* of the stone?

James William Hood and his family

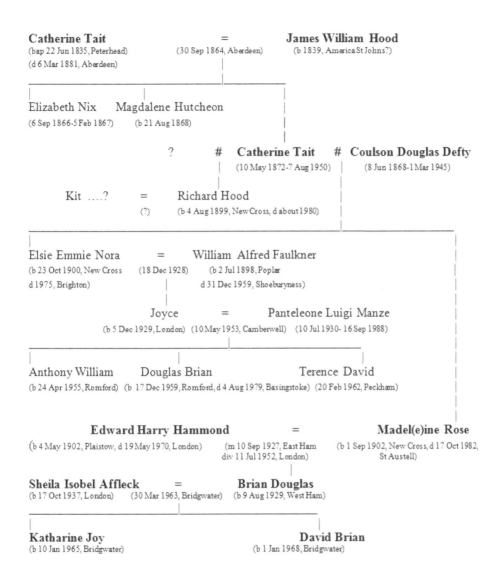

Catherine Tait   =   **James William Hood**
(bap 22 Jun 1835, Peterhead)   (30 Sep 1864, Aberdeen)   (b 1839, America St Johns?)
(d 6 Mar 1881, Aberdeen)

Elizabeth Nix   Magdalene Hutcheon
(6 Sep 1866-5 Feb 1867)   (b 21 Aug 1868)

?   #   **Catherine Tait**   #   **Coulson Douglas Defty**
(10 May 1872-7 Aug 1950)   (8 Jun 1868-1 Mar 1945)

Kit ....?   =   Richard Hood
(?)   (b 4 Aug 1899, New Cross, d about 1980)

Elsie Emmie Nora   =   William Alfred Faulkner
(b 23 Oct 1900, New Cross   (18 Dec 1928)   (b 2 Jul 1898, Poplar
d 1975, Brighton)   d 31 Dec 1959, Shoeburyness)

Joyce   =   Panteleone Luigi Manze
(b 5 Dec 1929, London)   (10 May 1953, Camberwell)   (10 Jul 1930- 16 Sep 1988)

Anthony William   Douglas Brian   Terence David
(b 24 Apr 1955, Romford)   (b 17 Dec 1959, Romford, d 4 Aug 1979, Basingstoke)   (20 Feb 1962, Peckham)

Edward Harry Hammond   =   **Madel(e)ine Rose**
(b 4 May 1902, Plaistow, d 19 May 1970, London)   (m 10 Sep 1927, East Ham   (b 1 Sep 1902, New Cross, d 17 Oct 1982,
div 11 Jul 1952, London)   St Austell)

Sheila Isobel Affleck   =   **Brian Douglas**
(b 17 Oct 1937, London)   (30 Mar 1963, Bridgwater)   (b 9 Aug 1929, West Ham)

Katharine Joy   **David Brian**
(b 10 Jan 1965, Bridgwater)   (b 1 Jan 1968, Bridgwater)

To begin with - the name by which James William is most frequently known.

On the 1851Census, aged eleven, he is called **William.**

He has not been found on the 1861 and 1871 Censuses. But on the 1881 Census he is shown as **James Wm.**

Meanwhile, at the births of his three children he appears respectively as **James William, William and William.**

On his marriage certificate, he is **William.**

On the death certificate of his wife, Catherine, in 1881 he is **James Wm**.

Finally, on the Spital Cemetery stone we have:

This is also the burying ground of **James Wm** Hood

The point is an important one because of knowing who to look for on the 1891 and 1901 Censuses. He has not yet been found. All I know is that he appears not to have been buried in the Spital Cemetery. As I said earlier, after his wife's death he may have given up the sea and moved south into England with his two daughters, Magdalena and Catherine.

The couple's first daughter was named Elizabeth Nix, a clear indication that James William's mother and John Hood's first wife was Elizabeth Nix.

Birth Cert:

'On 6th September 1866 at 6h 0m am at 77 Hutcheon Street [sic] Aberdeen **Elizabeth Vix Hood** was born; daughter of James William Hood (Seaman, Mate, Merchant Service) and Catherine Hood m/s Tait Married: 1864 September 30th Aberdeen. Informant James Wm Hood. Father' (166b/St Nicholas, Burgh of Aberdeen 1681/1311)

Unfortunately, the middle name was wrongly written as *Vix* and this error was repeated when the child died a few months later

Death Cert:

'..6h.30m.P.M..aged 5mos..Bronchitis 3 weeks as certified by Wm . Fraser Surgeon..Helen Tait Aunt Present..' Name shown as 'Lizzie **Vix** Hood'

Fortunately the Spital Cemetery stone corrects this:

'…sacred to the
memory of his infant daughter
Elizabeth Nix
Who died 2nd Feb 1867
aged 5 months'

Elizabeth died of bronchitis.

The second daughter, Magdalene Hutcheon, was born in 1868:

> Magdalene Hutcheon Hood/1868/August Twentyfirst/3 hrs. 4 m PM/30 Skene Square Aberdeen/F/William Hood Seaman - Chief Officer "Sir John Lawrence" Catherine Hood MS Tait/1864 September 30th Aberdeen [marriage]/Catherine Hood   Mother [informant]/ 1868 October 31st at Aberdeen/ John Leask Registrar

Two and a half years later she appears on the 1871 Census:

Census 1871 168 2 7/7   2/3 Apr 1871

> 5 Short Loanings, Aberdeen

Catherine Hood	wife	married	33	Seaman's wife	Aberdeenshire, Peterhead
Magdlina [sic] Hood	dtr	unm	2		Aberdeenshire, Aberdeen
William Leslie	boarder	unm	23	Shoemaker	?

It is difficult to account for her middle name. If we turn back to p122 we see that Magdalen Hutcheon (or Hutchison) were the first name and surname of Catherine's half-sister, as she was specifically described in 1871. She was still alive in 1868 and when she died in 1871 was described as a lodging-house keeper in Short Loanings, which was   where my grandmother, the third child of James William and Catherine, was born in 1872. It may be that Magdalen Hutcheon was the godmother of Magdalene Hutcheon Hood.
We have a photo of Magdalen:

probably taken in the early years of the 20th century.

Aunt Nora was a particular favourite of hers and we have this off-beat, enigmatic note which she sent to Nora in 1922:

October 22nd. 1922

> *This with many Happy Returns for*
> *23rd. dear Smiler*   [Nora's birthday]
> *It is a card box. Would never survive*
> *The Post Office coal slot, so I*
> *put it here.*
> *It used to hold my love letters.*
> *Now can hold yours.*
> *Which just symbols:- "Time was,*
> *Time is."*
> *May your Best One be as*
> *faithful as mine.*
>   *Auntie*

I wonder who was her 'best love' and what became of him. Perhaps they were married and he died during the First World War.

Unfortunately this is all I know about her because she seems to have disappeared at about the same time. My cousin Joyce Manze (née Faulkner and Aunt Nora's daughter) thinks she may have emigrated to New Zealand. I have been unable to confirm this. There is also a rumour that in her younger years she may have joined the suffragette movement. This too is unconfirmed. The last Census I have been able to find her on is the 1881 Census, where at 13 years old, and her mother having recently died, she is described as a housekeeper (ie for her father and nine-year old sister, my grandmother.) I have been unable to find her on either the 1891 or 1901 Censuses.

My grandmother, Catherine Tait Hood, was born 10 May 1872 at 6 Short Loanings, Gilcomston, Aberdeen. Here is the record of her birth, extracted in 1894 from the Register of Births:

Birth Cert: '...1872/May/Tenth/5h.40m.A.M./...William Hood/Seaman (First Mate) Catherine Hood/M.S.Tait/[Date and place of marriage]1864 September 30th/Aberd

My grandmother used to say that she was seven when her mother died; in fact she was not quite nine. Here is the statutory record of Catherine Tait's death:

> 'Catherine Hood/(married to James William Hood, Seaman)/ 1881/March /Sixth/8h.30m.p.m./33/Summer Street,/Aberdeen..44 years/William Tait/Stone-cutter(deceased)/ Jessie Tait/m.s.Duncan/(Deceased)/Abortio-13 days/Heamorrage [sic]./Exhaustion/ as cert. by J.Wight,/M.D./James Wm Hood/Widower/(present)'

It seems clear from the above that her death was the result of a miscarriage.

As we have seen, Catherine was still in Aberdeen with her father and sister when the Census was taken a few weeks later and we do not know what year the family left Aberdeen, nor the detail of what subsequently happened to her father and sister. But Catherine herself is found on the 1891 English Census:

1891 Census, England. RG12/079. Administrative County of Middlesex. Civil Parish: Tottenham. Urban Sanitary District: Wood Green. Folio ?

4 Brosley Villa

H Stubbings	Husband	M	54	Town Traveller	Essex etc
H E Stubbings	Wife	M	51		Middlesex etc
H E Stubbings	Son	S	27	Tobacconist	Essex etc
F E Stubbings	Son	S	21	Town Traveller	London etc
J A Stubbings	Son	S	18	Apprentice Electric Engineering	London etc
M Stubbings	Daur	S	12	Scholar	London etc
Cath Hood	**Servt**		**S**	**18**	
Scotland.					

It seems certain that the last entry is our Catherine Tait Hood. There were only two other Catherine Hoods born in Scotland 1870 - 1873 and they are both accounted for, living in Scotland in 1891.
Catherine used to describe herself to me as a fever nurse and I took this to refer to the time when she was living in London at the turn of the century. It seems confirmed on the Birth Certificate of Richard Hood (see below).   I have, however, searched the former LCC hospital records in South London around 1899 and have found no reference to her. It seems likely therefore that either she invented this to disguise her position as a house servant; or she may have been a nursemaid at some time in her early years.

Here is a picture of my grandmother, probably taken on the same occasion as her sister's (See above, p 145)

109.WESTERN R?
BRIGHTON.

I have no knowledge of where she was after this until the birth of her son, Richard Hood: 1899.

Birth in the Sub-district of Camberwell in the County of London:

When and where born informant	Name, if any When registered	Sex	Name and surname of father	Name, surname and maiden surname of mother	Occupation of father	Signature, description and residence of
Fourth August 1899 3 Emily Road	Richard	Boy	_____	Catherine Hood ___ Hospital Nurse	_____	C. Hood Mother 3 Emily Road (Old Kent Road)	Eighteenth August 1899

The all-important information about the father is omitted, in accordance with contemporary practice. The lack of entry about the mother's maiden name indicates that she was unmarried.

The question of Richard's father has not been resolved. He is alleged by my aunt Nora to have been one of the Lupinos, a famous stage family of the late 19th and early 20th centuries. He may not have been adopted legally by Coulson Douglas Defty: his mother once told me that Coulson once said he would not leave anything to Richard in his will, because 'he's not my son.' To which she alleges she replied: 'He's been a good son to you.' The choice of Richard as a first name does not help us at all.

Catherine once said to me that Richard Hood was her son by 'a form of (sc "former"?) marriage.' I wish now I had asked her to be more specific but I was in my late teens at the time and such things were not discussed in those days. Certainly, when I questioned my mother on the subject: ('Why is Uncle Dick's surname Hood not Defty?') I was brusquely answered that it would be explained later. It never was.

Catherine described the morning when, at the age of fourteen, he was to start an early shift on what became the LNER. she woke him up and he went downstairs. Later she had to wake him again because he had fallen asleep in a chair, holding his cap in his hands.

He was in the army on the Western Front during the First World War and was the victim of a gas attack.

Richard Hood was a life-long socialist and he told me that J H Thomas (one time Secretary of the National Union of Railwaymen) had betrayed the workers during the General Strike of 1926. He stayed an engine fireman all his working life; I do not think he even became a driver. When electric trains were introduced on his line, in the late 1940s, he said he did not want to become a 'sparks.'

A nice, gentle and quiet man, he was a favourite of his half-sisters, especially my mother, Madeline.

He was married twice and died about 1979.

In 1900 Catherine Hood gave birth to her second child:

1900. Birth in the Sub-district of St George Camberwell in the County of London

When and where born	Name, if any	Sex	Name and surname of father	Name, surname and maiden surname of mother	Occupation of father	Signature, description and residence of informant	When registered
Twenty Third October 1900 8 Odell Street	Elsie Emmie Nora	Girl	_____	Kate Defty ____ No occupation	_____	Kate Defty Mother 8 Odell Street Albany Street	Thirtieth November 1900

Once more there is no mention of a father but essentially this time Catherine gives her surname as Defty (and adds the interesting comment: 'no occupation'). She has moved a short distance from Emily Road. Presumably she has had to give up her nursing job in

149

order to look after Richard and now her daughter. I can only surmise that Coulson Defty is providing financial support.

The naming of the new baby is hard to explain. As far as I can judge there had been no child named Elsie or Nora in either the Hood or Defty families. It is tempting to deduce that *Emmie* is a chosen form of *Emily*, Coulson's sister, but there is no evidence for this. In any event, she was always known as Nora. I never heard either of her other names being used.

Aunt Nora was always more outspoken than her younger sister, but even she never revealed to me the truth about Richard's father. In 1928 she married William Faulkner, a policeman. My cousin Joyce was their only child, born in 1929, a few months after me. Aunt Nora died in Hove in 1975.

Six months after Aunt Nora's birth came the 1901 Census and one would expect to find Catherine Hood and her two young children somewhere in England, probably in London. In fact, extensive searches have failed to find them anywhere in the United Kingdom. Coulson Douglas has also not been found. One explanation is that they were all abroad at the time of the Census, which was taken on the night of 31st March. (For details of the 1901 Census see the **Defty** chapter, pp 102 and 103.)

Now, we have merchant navy discharge certificates for Coulson Defty and the relevant one shows that he was 1st Engineer aboard *SS Hardy,* registered at London for Home Trade from 23/10/1900 until 25/6/1901. He then seems to have been ashore until 11/7/02 when he became Chief Engineer on the *SS Val de Travers,* registered at Glasgow, also for Home Trade until his discharge on 31/12/02.

This latter ship was often talked about by my mother, aunt and grandmother, because it took them on several trips to the French channel port of Le Tréport, where the Deftys were remembered as late as 1948, when I visited the town. We even have a photograph, apparently taken on Le Tréport beach, some years later, showing unmistakably Catherine Hood, and her two daughters, Nora and Madeline. The photograph does not copy well but shows top left Catherine Tait Hood, my grandmother, wearing a broad-brimmed hat; next to her is my mother, always apparently known in the family as 'Titch'; then comes my aunt Nora. Richard Hood does not appear to be present but there a number of children in the photograph and he could be standing among the French boys.

This photograph was sent as a post-card from France to Mary Jane Douglas by her son-in-law, Edward Humble Law, the husband of Mary Douglas Defty. The reverse of the photo is shown below.

151

The French postage frank seems to show that it was sent on 13 August and the London mark, August 14. No year is discernible but the size of the children would indicate about 1912.

The meaning of the text of the message is obcure, except the reference to the *Val de Travers*.

Returning briefly to the 1901 Census, I must say that I cannot account for the omission of Catherine and her children in 1901: there may simply be errors in the Census Return. The matter is complicated by the fact that Coulson Douglas's real wife, Charlotte, and her son, John, are also absent from the 1901 Census and it is hardly likely that they too were in France!

And where, incidentally, was Catherine's sister, Magdalena, in 1901?

My mother was born in 1902. Here is the relevant entry:

When and where born registered	Name, if any	Sex	Name and surname of father	Name, surname and maiden surname of mother	Occupation of father	Signature, description and residence of informant	When
First September 1902 19A Clifton Hill	Madeline Rose	Girl	_____	Kate Defty of Independent Means	_____	K. Defty Mother 19A Clifton Hill	Eighteenth September 1902

Once more, no father is mentioned but Catherine has again adopted the Defty surname and now she is 'of Independent Means,' presumably supplied by my grandfather.

From various sources we have a number of addresses for Catherine, Coulson and their family:

                31 Aug 1908 - 94 Woodhouse Rd, LEYTONSTONE
                22 Apr 1913 - 20 Cheneys Rd, LEYTONSTONE
                05 Nov 1927 - 50 Chandos Rd, LEYTONSTONE

It is the last address that I knew quite well. It was a tram, later trolleybus, ride from East Ham. My grandparents lived in a rather dark basement flat, with the bedroom (which I never saw) on the ground floor. The basement was often in danger of flooding and a two-foot high concrete barrier was built to protect their home. That part of Chandos Rd has now been pulled down and rebuilt.

By a curious coincidence, when Catherine and her family were living in Leytonstone, a few minutes away, in Leytonstone Road, the future film director, Alfred Hitchcock, (born

1899) was growing up. His father kept a greengrocer's shop and the chances are that the family frequented that shop.

About 1941 the Deftys moved from Leytonstone to 278 Valence Avenue, Dagenham, the home of Richard Hood and his first wife. After a short while they moved to my parents' house in East Ham, where they lived upstairs in one room, which had its own gas stove and sink.   Here they both died, Coulson in 1945 and Catherine in 1950.

The fact that she and Coulson Defty were unmarried would have been easier to conceal in the early twentieth century, when few official documents were needed. They were very poor, living on two old-age pensions (in the 1930s: ten shillings = 50 pence a week each.) I remember that on Saturdays my mother and I used sometimes to go to Stratford and take my grandmother to the cinema - I   can still recall a fuzzy image of the singer, Grace Moore, in *One Night of Love* (!) ; this must have been in 1935 when I was about six years old. After the cinema we used to buy kippers from a market stall and take them home to share with my grandfather, Coulson, who was too deaf to go to the pictures.
My Defty grandparents used to go on holiday with Aunt Nora and her family. We, my parents and I, seem to have spent a number of holidays with my father's parents and his sister, my Aunt Grace.

Catherine always struck me as a mild-natured person. She was more communicative to me than my other grandparents and I regret now that I did not question her more about her past life. It must have been hard in the 1870s, living in a poor area of Aberdeen, where disease, particularly tuberculosis, was rife; and losing her mother when she was not quite nine years old.
She had a loud laugh and once told me that when a child she had to be removed from Chapel because of her amusement on seeing a well-dressed gentleman carrying a top hat trip and fall over.

My parents' troubled marriage did not long survive Catherine's death. They were divorced in early 1952, whilst I was teaching in France.

This concludes my account of the families of my four grandparents. It has taken me a quarter of a century to gather information and complete the narrative. There is still a great deal to examine and some mysteries remain: perhaps they will never be solved but I hope future generations will continue the story.

If I am asked what I have learned from the quest, the answer is: many lessons.
Most important are two things.
First, I have acquired a greater knowledge of history.
Secondly, and more importantly, I have learned that we need to understand people, if not according to their own terms, at least within the context of their own times, circumstances and needs.

153

Furthermore, I now understand more easily why many of our distant ancestors respected and worshipped their forebears.

In particular, I remember what Catherine Hood wrote in an early autograph book of mine:

> There is much that is good in the worst of us.
> There is much that is bad in the best of us.
> So it ill becomes any one of us
> To criticise the rest of us.

Book II

The Ancestors of Sheila Isobel Affleck

Introduction

The provenance of two of Sheila's four grandparents is somewhat simpler to relate than my own. The Affleck and the Butters families lived in the East Neuk part of Fifeshire for at least four centuries.

David Affleck was born in 1877 at The Elie (to give the town its proper name) in the ancient Kingdom of Fife. Four of his direct ancestors, also named David, had been born and raised in Pittenweem, just along the coast. Further back, two other ancestors, named James, came from the same area. Sheila's father, another David, came to London in the 1930s.

A few miles inland from Pittenweem and the adjacent village of St Monance is Carnbee, home of the ancestors of Isabella Butters, who became the wife of David Affleck, and thus Sheila's grandmother. The family must have moved to the coast in the early 19th century. We have a post-card reproduction of a painting entitled *Old Buttar*. (See *The Butters*). The subject is an old fisherman who is probably a member of Sheila's family.

By contrast, the story of the Parishes is much more complex and even now open to doubt. They appear to have lived in Devon from at least 16th to the 19th centuries. They then came to live in north-east London, where William Parish, Sheila's other grandfather, was born. There are some tragedies to relate but part of the story takes us back to the 16th century, and to the beginnings of parish registration.

William's wife, Hephzibah Clara Page had, through her father, James, links with Leicestershire. But the other side of the family came from Essex, arriving in London by the 1870s. A number of interesting stories arise from this side of the family, not least the colourful life of Lucy Mullins.

I knew all my grandparents very well. Sheila, however, remembers none of hers.
David Affleck died in 1944; she had seen him about the age of two but does not remember him.   Isabella Butters died a year before Sheila was born,
William Parish in 1934 and his wife, Hephzibah in 1940, when Sheila was only two and a half.

155

Acknowledgments

I have to thank a number of persons for help received in preparing this narrative. Whereas I had one cousin only to assist me in my researches, Sheila has many more and I have gratefully to acknowledge the assistance given me by David Keir Affleck, Jennifer McNaughton, Margaret Miles, Stanley Walker, Billy Parish and Geraldine Hooper. In addition, Anna Stevenson, the younger sister of Sheila's father, David, surviving until a few years ago, provided much information dating from the beginning of the 20th century. I have also to thank the researcher, Mrs Corkerton, who over a number of years searched the records in Edinburgh and provided me with much detail about Sheila's ancestors and my own.
Most important of all, however, is the information provided by Sheila's mother, Louie, whose remarkable memory has led to so much detailed discovery. Much of her evidence (on audiotape and videotape) could in the first instance be strictly described as anecdotal. So much, however, has later been confirmed by written sources that the information has proved to be very reliable.

_____

A Note on Scottish Naming Patterns

Reference will be made in the course of the narrative to the Scottish custom of naming children according to a set pattern. This pattern is not immutable but is so frequent that it needs some explaining. Briefly, the system goes like this:

> The first son is named after his *paternal* grandfather.
> The second son is named after his *maternal* grandfather.
> The third son is named after his father.
> The first daughter is named after her *maternal* grandmother.
> The second daughter is named after her *paternal* grandmother.
> The third daughter is named after her mother.

For the seventh and subsequent children the tendency is to go back a further generation or to choose a name of a great-aunt or great-uncle.
Here is an actual example, taken from the Afflecks and Butters:

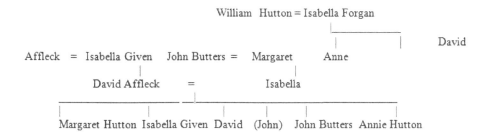

```
                    William  Hutton = Isabella Forgan
                                    |_____
                                    |             |
                                    |             |        David
Affleck  =  Isabella Given   John Butters =   Margaret      Anne
              |                             |
         David Affleck       =           Isabella
    _____
    |          |            |          |         |            |
 Margaret Hutton Isabella Given David  (John)  John Butters  Annie Hutton
```

(John) died early. Because there were already four Isabellas in the family, for the third girl a different name had to be chosen - that of a great-aunt. By now there was a tendency to have a middle name, often the surname that went with the first name.

The Afflecks of East Neuk (= 'nook' or 'corner')

First, a note on the surname.

> *This surname is of twofold origin: (1) from the barony of Auchinleck in Ayrshire and (2) from Affleck in Angus…The..Angus Afflecks were hereditary armour bearers to the Earls of Crawford.* ('The Surnames of Scotland', George C Black.)

Over thirty variants of the two alternatives are given by Black and they are found over much of Scotland. In Sheila's family for the past two centuries *Affleck* has been the norm but *Authenleck* is found as an alternative in the early 18th century.

There is a town Auchinleck in Ayrshire which we have not visited; presumably this is the seat of the barony referred to above.
We did, however, in 1992 find an Affleck Dairy; it is on the A97 near Huntly in Aberdeenshire. Here is a photo of Sheila standing by the entrance:

Far more interesting is Affleck Castle in Angus, at Monikie, between Broughty Ferry and Arbroath. It consists of a mediaeval tower with an 18th century manor house close by. Visitors are not welcome, for despite being a scheduled monument, it is privately owned. We managed to take a couple of photographs before leaving hurriedly, having heard that fierce dogs were loose. We understand that it is 'the seat of the ancient family of Auchinlech or Affleck of that ilk.'

David Affleck, Sheila's cousin, has extensively explored the history of the earlier Fifeshire Afflecks/Auchinlecks. The story is a colourful one, partly because several found themselves on the wrong side of the popular religious divide in the 17th century and experienced dramatic, not to say dangerous, events. I am sure that sooner or later a link will be found between these Afflecks and Sheila's earliest known Affleck ancestors, but so far a firm connection evades us.

Here, before we start, is a photograph of St Monans church which figures much in this history. (See also below on p 208 a reference to the painting by Sheila's grandfather.)

Early Afflecks

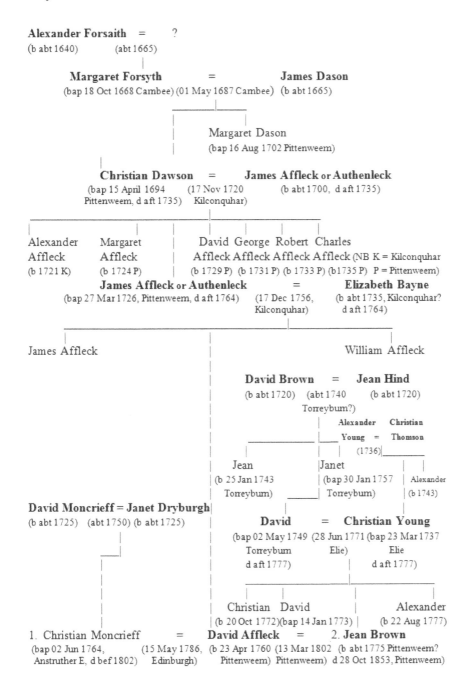

Alexander Forsaith = ?
(b abt 1640)   (abt 1665)

       Margaret Forsyth   =   James Dason
       (bap 18 Oct 1668 Cambee) (01 May 1687 Cambee) (b abt 1665)

                Margaret Dason
                (bap 16 Aug 1702 Pittenweem)

      Christian Dawson   =   James Affleck or Authenleck
      (bap 15 April 1694   (17 Nov 1720   (b abt 1700, d aft 1735)
      Pittenweem, d aft 1735)   Kilconquhar)

Alexander   Margaret   David George Robert Charles
Affleck   Affleck   Affleck Affleck Affleck Affleck (NB K = Kilconquhar
(b 1721 K)   (b 1724 P)   (b 1729 P) (b 1731 P) (b 1733 P) (b1735 P)   P = Pittenweem)
      James Affleck or Authenleck   =   Elizabeth Bayne
      (bap 27 Mar 1726, Pittenweem, d aft 1764)   (17 Dec 1756,   (b abt 1735, Kilconquhar?
                               Kilconquhar)   d aft 1764)

James Affleck   William Affleck

                   David Brown   =   Jean Hind
                   (b abt 1720)   (abt 1740)   (b abt 1720)
                         Torreyburn?)
                               Alexander   Christian
                               Young = Thomson
                                  (1736)
              Jean   Janet
            (b 25 Jan 1743   (bap 30 Jan 1757   Alexander
            Torreyburn)   Torreyburn)   (b 1743)
David Moncrieff = Janet Dryburgh
(b abt 1725)   (abt 1750) (b abt 1725)   David   =   Christian Young
                   (bap 02 May 1749 (28 Jun 1771 (bap 23 Mar 1737
                   Torreyburn   Elie)   Elie
                   d aft 1777)   d aft 1777)

                     Christian   David   Alexander
                   (b 20 Oct 1772)(bap 14 Jan 1773)   (b 22 Aug 1777)
1. Christian Moncrieff   =   David Affleck   =   2. Jean Brown
(bap 02 Jun 1764,   (15 May 1786, (b 23 Apr 1760 (13 Mar 1802 (b abt 1775 Pittenweem?
Anstruther E, d bef 1802)   Edinburgh)   Pittenweem) Pittenweem) d 28 Oct 1853, Pittenweem)

161

We begin with Alexander Forsaith. No more is known of him except that he was the father of Margaret Forsyth, the name of whose mother is not given. In early years this is not unusual. We may assume that the family lived in Carnbee, the home also, we shall see later, of the Butters family.

James Dason (or Dawson) who married Margaret in 1687, may also have been a native of Carnbee, although the fact that both of their children were born at Pittenweem may suggest otherwise.

We may infer from the dates of birth and the naming of the two daughters, Christian and Margaret, that there were other children who either did not survive, or are missing from the parish register. I have already commented about Scottish naming patterns, but it may be that Christian was named after either her maternal or her paternal grandmother, neither of whose names are at present known to us. Margaret's birth, coming as it did more than fifteen years after her parents' marriage, could suggest that she was named after her own mother.

Christian Dawson and James Affleck or Authenleck were married at Kilconquhar on 17 Nov 1720. Here is the entry in the parish register:

> *OPR Kilconquhar, Co. Fife (436/2) Marriages:* '1720 October 16
> James Affleck and Christian Dawson both within this parish being
> Contracted and therefore orderly proclaimed in order to marriage were
> married the seventeenth day of November next'

The apparent confusion over the dates arises from the fact that several weeks had to elapse after the contract was made before the couple could be married. This point can be well illustrated by a quotation from *Tracing your Scottish Ancestry* by Kathleen B Cory:

> *When a couple gave intimation of marriage (Proclamation of Marriage or*
> *Banns) they often had to consign a sum of money as a surety for good*
> *behaviour before the marriage and a guarantee to marry within forty days of*
> *contracting. This sum of money was called a Pawn, Pand or Pledge and most*
> *of it was retrievable on marriage, provided that the bridal couple had behaved*
> *themselves to the satisfaction of the elders of the Kirk and the minister, when*
> *a smaller amount was paid to the poor of the parish.*

James and Christian remained in Kilconquhar until at least 1821, when their first son was born:

OPR Kilconquhar, Co. Fife (436/2) Births/Baptisms
'1721 December 17
> James Affleck and Christian Dawson his wife had a child baptized named
> Alexander. Witnesses Andrew Bridges and Thomas Webster, and born on the
> eleventh day of the same month'

After this they must have moved to Pittenweem, for the remainder of their children we know about were born there.

Their third child, James, was born in 1726:

OPR PITTENWEEM Co Fife (452/1) Births/Baptisms: '1726 March 27th James Affleck and Christina Dason his spouse had a child Baptized Called James. Witn. Jas: and Da: Dason.' [the two witnesses may have been Christian's father and uncle (or brother)]

Perhaps here I should mention again that it is usually easy in Scotland to establish the parentage of a child, such as the son of James and Christina, because, unlike in England, the baptismal register almost invariably names the mother as well as the father, giving her unmarried name. Before I was aware of this, I seemed to be faced with the likelihood of a large number of children born out of wedlock!
For it was customary in Scotland for a married woman to keep her maiden name throughout marriage. Sometimes women were even given their unmarried names in the burial register.

Records of marriages, where the couple came from different parishes, are usually documented in both villages; for example, when James Affleck married Elizabeth Bayne in 1756:

OPR Pittenweem, Co. Fife (452/2) Births/Baptisms/Marriages (mixed)
'1756 December 17th
        James Affleck in this Parish and Elizabeth Bayne in the Parish of
Kilconquer [sic] were contracted and married on Decbr. 17th'

OPR Kilconquhar, Co. Fife (436/2) Marriages
'1756 Novr. 19th.
        James Authenleck in ye parish of Pittenweem & Elizabeth Bayne in this
parish were contracted, regularly proclaimed and married Decr. 17th.'

Note:
1. That in the bride's parish the date of the contract, 19 Nov, is given, but not in the groom's.
2. That the reading of the Banns is also noted in Kilconquhar ('regularly proclaimed').
3. James is given the surname Authenleck.
4. In the Pittenweem parish record Kilconquhar is misspelled.

I have no record of the ancestors of Elizabeth Bayne (although the surname appears many times elsewhere in the family tree) the problem being that a number of women of the same name were born in Fife at about the same time.
James' son David Affleck was married twice. His first wife was Christian Moncrieff, daughter of David Moncrieff and Janet Dryburgh. They were married in Edinburgh:

Anstruther Wester 1786 May 15:
'John Afflect in Pettenweem Parysh & Crisstian Moncrieff in this Parysh were Clandesstenly maried at Edinburgh.'

163

'John' seems to be an error (NB how erratic the spelling is) for 'David' since the Pittenweem register for 1787 gives:

Baptismal entry:OPR Pittenweem,Co.Fife (452/2) Births/Baptisms/Marriages(mixed
> 1787 April 13th
>
> David Auchinlect & Christian Moncrieff had a son born born [sic] on the 13th and baptized on the 15th of April 1787. Childs name James. Witnesses James Auchinlect [child's grandfather?] and James Martin'

Clandestine marriages were quite legal and usually arose because no banns had been called. Presumably this is why the marriage took place in Edinburgh. The circumstances are unclear because no child appears to have been born soon after the marriage - the usual reason for a hasty wedding. As we have seen, the first child arrived 11 months later. The second child came as follows:

The Pittenweem register for 1789 gives:

> 'August 20th/David Auchinlect & Christian Moncrief had a daughter born on the 23d of August 1789 Childs name Jannet. Witnesses James Auchinlect & Alexr. Anderson.'

These two births to David and Christian are the only ones known .

After 1789 we find no further reference to Christian Moncrieff. She must have died for on the 13 March 1802 David married for a second time:

Pittenweem register:
> '1802 March 13th
>
> Baillie David Afflect & Jean Brown both in this Parish were proclaimed on 7th and married on 13th March 1802.'

This marriage too appears to be irregular: note that the marriage took place only six days after the proclamation. Later we shall see why. But first we must look at the ancestry of Jean Brown.

Her grandparents, David Brown and Jean Hind, were probably married at Torreyburn, upstream of the Forth, about 1740. We know of three children: Jean (1743), David (1749) and Janet (1757). All were born at Torreyburn. David, born 2 May 1749 married Christian Young on 28 Jun 1771 at Elie:

OPR ELIE, Co Fife Marriages:
> ' 1771 June 28th   David Brown in the parish of Pittenweem & Christian Young in this parish were contracted June 7th & married the 28th 1771.'

From the baptismal record in 1777 of his son, Alexander, we know David's profession:
OPR PITTENWEEM, Co Fife Births/Baptisms:
> '1777 August 22nd   David Brown, *Inn-keeper* & Christian Young his Spouse had a Child born 22nd and Baptized 31st Called Alexander, Wittness Alexr. Young [the bride's father?] and Peter Hederwick.'

David and Christian had at least three children before Alexander. Christian was born in 1772:

OPR PITTENWEEM, Co Fife Births/Baptisms:

> ' 1772 October 20th   David Brown & Christian Young had a child born 20th October & baptized 25th 1772. The name is Christian. Wittness Alexr. Young & Peter Hederwick.'

Then David:

OPR PITTENWEEM, Co Fife Births/Baptisms:

> '1773 June 14th   David Brown & Christain [sic]Young had a Child born [illegible] and baptized 14th called David. Wittness [rest of entry illegible because of a repair having been carried out.]'

Now, Jean Brown. Here we have a problem because no reference can be found to her birth. It is of course a very common surname in Scotland. I have trawled through Jeans and Janets Brown born in Fife over forty years with no result. There are, however, a number of clues which point strongly towards the present assumption.

First of all her marriage to David Affleck:

Pittenweem register:

Marriage to Jean Brown

> '1802 March 13th
> Baillie David Afflect & Jean Brown both in this Parish were proclaimed on 7th and married on 13th March 1802.'

Secondly, her appearance on the 1851 Census:

1851 census: living High St North Side with son and family

> '..Jean Affleck..Mother..W..76..Farmer's Widow..Fife Pittenweem.'

Next, her burial entry:

Burial reg:

> '1853 Octr. 28th   Mrs David Affleck Senr. widow of Dd.Affleck land labourer died on the 28th Octr. and was buried on the 1st Novr. 1853 aged [blank].   Cause Decay of Nature.'

Finally, the traditional naming pattern is followed: Jean (Hind) was her paternal grandmother.

For the above reasons I think we may conclude that we have the correct ancestor.

It remains to consider the ancestry of Jean Brown's mother, Christian Young, who was baptized at Elie 23 March 1737. She was the daughter of Alexander Young and Christian Thomson, both born about 1716. Their marriage entries are interesting:

OPR ELIE, Co Fife (427/1) Marriages:

'1736 June 22d   Alexr. Young in this Parish & Christian Thomson in the Parish of Newburn were Contracted & after usual Intimation married 22d   June'

OPR NEWBURN, Co Fife (451/2) Marriages:

'1736 June 24th

On May 29th Alexr. Young in the parish of Ely was contracted with Christian
Thomson in this parish & in lieu of pledges gave 14 shill: [Scots?] to ye
poor and after 3 Sabbaths proclamation without Objection were married June
24th.'

It seems reasonable to assume that as the wedding presumably took place in Newburn it is
the 24 June that is the more likely date. Or did the ceremony take place in both parishes?
It is worth noting that we are talking here of Scots shillings. At the time a Scots shilling was
equal to one penny sterling. Fourteen pence was nonetheless quite a sum of money.

Returning now to David Affleck and Christian Moncrieff, we come to the two children of
that marriage, James and Jannet.

Baptismal entry:OPR Pittenweem,Co.Fife (452/2) Births/Baptisms/Marriages(mixed

'1787 April 13th   David Auchinlect & Christian Moncrieff had a son born born
[sic] on the13th and baptized on the 15th of April 1787. Childs name   James.
Witnesses James Auchinlect [child's grandfather?] and James Martin'

[Baptismal entry of OPR Pittenweem]
'August 20th/David Auchinlect & Christian Moncrief had a daughter born on
the 23d of August 1789 Childs name Jannet. Witnesses James Auchinlect
[child's gfandfather?] & Alexr. Anderson'

There is still confusion over the spelling of *Affleck.*
The histories of these two children are not followed up because they are not directly related
to Sheila.

On 13 March 1802 David Affleck and Jean Brown were married in Pittenweem:

Pittenweem register: Marriage to Jean Brown.
'1802 March 13th Baillie David Afflect & Jean Brown both in this Parish were
proclaimed on 7th and married on 13th March 1802.'

As noted above this marriage seems to be irregular and the following gives the clue to the
hasty marriage.

Pittenweem register:
'1802 April 9th   Baillie David Afflect and Jean Brown had a Son born on the
19th of April and baptized on the 2d of May 1802. Childs name --- David'

Two years later Jean had a second child:

[Pittenweem Register]
'1804 August 18th   Baillie David Affleck & Jean Brown had a Son born on the

166

18th and baptized on the 26th of August 1804. Childs name --- Alexander'

And in 1809 a daughter:
[Pittenweem Register]
> '1809 April 15th Baillie David Affleck & Jean Brown had a Daughter born on
> the 15th and baptizes on the 23d of April 1809. Childs name Christian.
> Witnesses David Brown & David Simson.'

We come now to the questions: what was a bailie at beginning of the 19th century and what were his duties?
The answer is not clear and the sources I have consulted are not very explicit. The application of the title in urban circumstances seems to mean 'town councillor' and/or a 'magistrate' with some sort of legal overtones. The term nowadays appears to be more of a courtesy title, the equivalent of the title 'alderman.'
David Affleck was a bailie from at least 1802 to 1809, as is evidenced from the Pittenweem registers. What I find surprising is that he could at that time have remained an officer of the council, having blatantly broken custom by marrying Jean so late in her pregnancy, when normally a couple would have forfeited their 'deposit'
because of bad behaviour.
In fact, David Keir Affleck, Sheila's cousin, shows that the couple were reprimanded:

> 'The second marriage was to a Jean Brown on 13th March 1802 with a son,
> David, born on the 9th April 1802. This clearly was an issue for the Session of
> St Aidens and is recorded as follows:
>
>> Minute of 23/3/1802:
>> Compeared before the meeting, Baillie Affleck delated   for ante-
>> nuptial fornication and having received a rebuke from the Members
>> present, they delay further censure against him on account of some
>> Circumstances [?] till a more numerous meeting of Session.
>> Minute of 1/5/1802
>> The Session agree that Baillie Affleck again be rebuked before the
>> members of the Session and again restored to the Privileges of the
>> Church accordingly after a suitable exhortation, being rebuked he was
>> dismissed [released], and the Session order his wife to be called before
>> them as soon as the state of her health shall permit.
>
> There is no further reference to this matter....'

Because of the above it is perhaps even stranger that he was for some time an elder of the kirk. This has been demonstrated, again by David Keir Affleck:

> '...David Affleck is listed as an elder of the Church from 1819. We can get
>   some indication of life as recorded in the minutes in the following examples:

167

"1792 - agreed a lease for David Affleck for Hungryflat for nine years after separation of crop at a rent of œ3..1..2p[?]

  1803 - to pay a further 12/6p [?] annually

  1826 - listed a a tenant of the Kirk Sessions for Scroggy Faulds and Hungry flat."

He appears to have been a significant elder, as the minutes include the following references:

"August 1819
Respective Quarters for the elders for promoting the Poor.
David Affleck from the Ladywynd to his own house."

September 1824 Appears as a witness as to whether Euphemia Dott had ever asked him for the money due to her (the lady was challenging the treasurer that she had not received the pension he had recorded in the accounts "that credit was taken by him for a pension due to her")

1/12/1834
Appointed by a majority to represent the Kirk Session at future meetings of the inheritors. (There is no record of the voting numbers!)

18/12/34
Appointed along with others by the session to investigate a complaint that a M Jack had put onto his seat a form or stool by which he was elevated 6" above the common level so that Mr Dick who sat behind him had his view of the Preacher completely obstructed. The minute records that the best method of settling this matter was to persuade the Misses Phial to remove from their seat in the church, the cushion which had been the cause of Mr Dick's raising his to the height complained of. Dissent to this solution is also recorded. There is also a reference to a James Affleck in the minute of 15/6/1791 for a meeting of the Session to hear evidence that a James Horsburgh was the father of her [?] child. The extract tells us that:
"Mary further said 'Do you remember James of a fine moonlight night when you came to my house and desired me to go to Mr Finlayson's stacks and you would wait for me at James Affleck's Barn".."upon which James said you were as willing as I was, to which Mary assented." 'Clearly the Barn had [was] a significant location!

David Affleck died in 1846:

Burial register: Pittenweem:
> '1846 August 4th David Affleck, farmer died on the 4th of August 1846, and was buried on the 8th 24 feet West of the East dyke and 31 1/3 feet North from the South dyke. Aged 86. Cause Old Age.'

This a surprisingly accurate setting.
So far as I know, there is no monument to him.

The death of his second wife, Jean, in 1853, is shown above on pp 161 & 165.

The Lumsdens

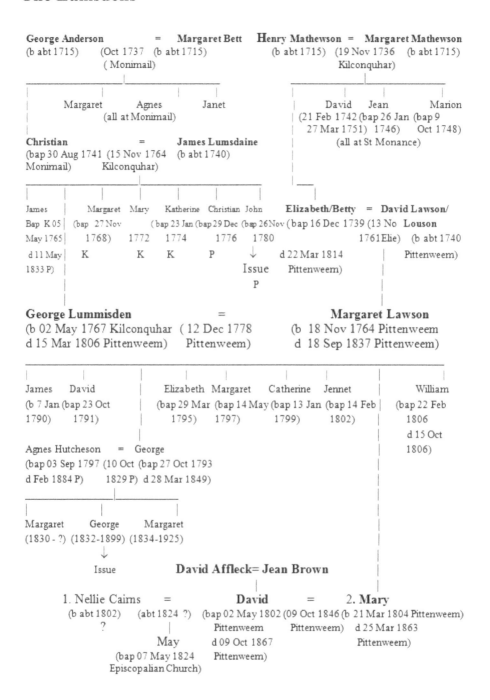

George Anderson   =   Margaret Bett   Henry Mathewson = Margaret Mathewson
(b abt 1715)   (Oct 1737 (b abt 1715)   (b abt 1715) (19 Nov 1736   (b abt 1715)
              (Monimail)   Kilconquhar)

_____   _____

| | | | | | | |
| Margaret   Agnes   Janet | David   Jean   Marion
| (all at Monimail) | (21 Feb 1742 (bap 26 Jan (bap 9
| | 27 Mar 1751) 1746)   Oct 1748)
Christian   =   James Lumsdaine | (all at St Monance)
(bap 30 Aug 1741 (15 Nov 1764 (b abt 1740) |
Monimail)   Kilconquhar)   ___

_____

| | | | | | |
James | Margaret Mary Katherine Christian John Elizabeth/Betty = David Lawson/
Bap K 05| (bap 27 Nov   (bap 23 Jan (bap 29 Dec (bap 26 Nov (bap 16 Dec 1739 (13 No Louson
May 1765| 1768)   1772   1774   1776   1780   1761 Elie) (b abt 1740
d 11 May| K   K   K   P   ↓   d 22 Mar 1814 | Pittenweem)
1833 P) | Issue   Pittenweem) |
| P |
| |
George Lummisden   =   Margaret Lawson
(b 02 May 1767 Kilconquhar (12 Dec 1778 (b 18 Nov 1764 Pittenweem
d 15 Mar 1806 Pittenweem)   Pittenweem)   d 18 Sep 1837 Pittenweem)

_____

| | | | | | | | |
James   David | Elizabeth Margaret Catherine Jennet | William
(b 7 Jan (bap 23 Oct | (bap 29 Mar (bap 14 May (bap 13 Jan (bap 14 Feb | (bap 22 Feb
1790)   1791) | 1795)   1797)   1799)   1802) | 1806
                     | | d 15 Oct
Agnes Hutcheson = George | 1806)
(bap 03 Sep 1797 (10 Oct (bap 27 Oct 1793 |
d Feb 1884 P)   1829 P) d 28 Mar 1849) |

_____ |

| | | |
Margaret George   Margaret |
(1830 - ?) (1832-1899) (1834-1925) |
           ↓ |
         Issue   David Affleck= Jean Brown |
                                  | |
1. Nellie Cairns   =   David   =   2. Mary
  (b abt 1802)   (abt 1824 ?) (bap 02 May 1802 (09 Oct 1846 (b 21 Mar 1804 Pittenweem)
      ? | Pittenweem   Pittenweem) d 25 Mar 1863
                    May   d 09 Oct 1867   Pittenweem)
             (bap 07 May 1824   Pittenweem)
             Episcopalian Church)

OPR MONIMAIL, Co Fife. Marriage Proclamation:
> '1737 Octor 1st   George Anderson and Mary Bett both in this parish were
> contracted. William Broadie caur [ie 'cautioner'] for the man and James Bett
> for ye woman.'

As we have seen previously, the marriage would have taken place up to forty days later. It seems that the couple could not raise the money to guarantee themselves; two men had to act as sponsors, the second being perhaps the bride's father.

Monimail, a small settlement even today, lies in the north of Fifeshire, a few miles south of the Tay, south-west from Dundee. The nearest town is Cupar.

All the children that we know of from this marriage were born at Monimail but the family may have moved before Christian's marriage:

OPR Kilconquhar, Co. Fife (436/2) Marriages
'1764 Octr. 13th
> James Lumsdale [sic] & Christian Anderson both in this parish were
> contracted and Regularly proclaimed and Married November 15th'

I have assumed that *Lumsdale* is a mistake for *Lumsden*, as there is no other obvious candidate and the subsequent naming pattern appears to fit.

Between the births of Katherine and Christian the family moved from Kilconquhar to Pittenweem and it was there that James and George died. James's burial record reveals more information than is usual in parish registers:

Pittenweem Burial Register:
> '1833 May 11th James Lumsden died of Cancer aged 68.'

George, the second son, married Margaret Lawson (see later for details of her ancestry) in 1778:

OPR PITTENWEEM, Co Fife Marriages:
> '1788 December 12th   George Lummisdane and Margaret Lawson both in
> this Parish were contracted on The 29th proclaimed on the30th November &
> 7th of December 1788 and Married on the 12th December1788.'

George was a coal miner:

OPR Pittenweem, Co. Fife (452/2) Deaths
> '1806 March 15th
> George Lumisden, Coalier died on 15th of March 1806'

Margaret and George had a family of nine children, four boys and five girls.
The eldest, James, became a coalminer and the next, David, a lime worker.
George did very much better. He was an apprentice of John Smith, watch and clock maker

in Pittenweem for 7 years from 1 Jan 1806. He was discharged on 4 Jan1813.(FFHJ Vol9 No3). A watch made by him is in the National Museum of Antiquities, Edinburgh. George became prosperous and eventually left a large estate of money, property, domestic goods and commercial stock - all carefully inventoried. Even debts - good doubtful and bad - are listed. Cash in hand and bank assets alone are totalled £839 - a very large sum in 1849. A very long will left his estate to his family.

PITTENWEEM BURIAL RECORDS:
> '1849 March 31st. George Lumsden, watchmaker died of decay of nature aged 55.'

No further details of cause of death are given. 'Decay of Nature' implies that he had declined in health at a relatively early age.

George's second child, also George, followed in his father's footsteps, as is revealed by this entry in the 1851 Census:

1881 Census, PITTENWEEM, High St:

Lumsden	George	Head	M	48	M	Watchmaker	FIFE PITTENWEEM	
do	Ellen	Wife	M	46	F	-	RFW	PAISLEY
do	Mary	Daur	-	8	F	Scholar	FIFE PITTENWEEM	
do	George	Son	-	6	M	do	do	do
do	John	Son		4	M	Scholar	do	do
do	Agnes	Daur		3	F		do	do

The youngest son, William, died as a baby:

PITTENWEEM Deaths:
'1806 Octr 15th William Lumisden aged 9 Months died'

Of the five daughters I have information on two only. Margaret is shown on the 1851 Census as a grocer, unmarried and living near her sister-in-law, Agnes Lumsden (née Hutcheson)
Mary Lumsden became the second wife of David Affleck. She was born in 1804:

Birth
Pittenweem:
'1804 March 21st
> George Lumisden & Margaret Lowsan had a Daughter born on the 21st and
> baptized on the 25th of March 1804. Childs name Mary. Witnesses David Wilson & John Lumsden.'

Both David and Mary were in their forties when they married.

Marriage: OPR Pittenweem, Co. Fife (452/4) Marriages

'1846 October 9th
>David Affleck and Mary Lumsden both residing on this parish, having been regularly proclaimed in order to marriage, and no objections being offered, were married on the 9th October 1846 by the Revd. James Millar, New Street, Canongate, Edinburgh'

I am unclear whether this means they were married in Edinburgh or - more likely - that the Rev James Millar was staying in Pittenweem at the time and performed the ceremony there.

Nearly two years later their only child was born:

Birth entry
Pittenweem Register:
>'1848 May 17th
>David Affleck or Auchinleck, land labourer in Pittenweem and Mary Lumsden his wife had a Son born the 17th May 1848 and baptized on the 11th June by the Revd. John Cooper, Minister of Pittenweem. Childs name David. Witnesses James Peat and William Bayne.'

There is still confusion over David's surname, although Affleck had been the only one used in the marriage register.
James Peat is almost certainly the husband of Christian, the sister of the child's father, and therefore an uncle by marriage. (See below)

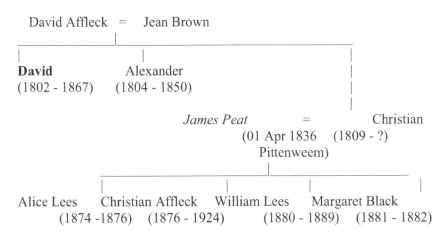

The above chart is included also to illustrate two scourges of later Victorian life:
child death -   out of four children born to James and Christian, one only survived childhood;
consumption - Alexander Affleck's burial notice cites 'Decline' as the cause of death. 'Decline' is generally thought to refer in the nineteenth century to consumption, tuberculosis.

Reaching Back

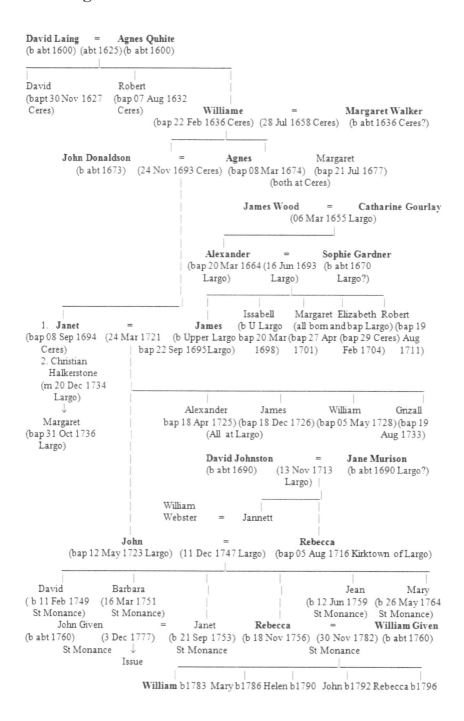

David Laing   =   Agnes Quhite
(b abt 1600) (abt 1625) (b abt 1600)

David   Robert
(bapt 30 Nov 1627   (bap 07 Aug 1632
 Ceres)   Ceres)   Williame   =   Margaret Walker
                                                  (bap 22 Feb 1636 Ceres) (28 Jul 1658 Ceres) (b abt 1636 Ceres?)

John Donaldson   =   Agnes   Margaret
(b abt 1673)   (24 Nov 1693 Ceres) (bap 08 Mar 1674)   (bap 21 Jul 1677)
                                                     (both at Ceres)

                                    James Wood   =   Catharine Gourlay
                                              (06 Mar 1655 Largo)

                          Alexander   =   Sophie Gardner
                          (bap 20 Mar 1664 (16 Jun 1693 (b abt 1670
                              Largo)   Largo)   Largo?)

                                              Issabell   Margaret Elizabeth Robert
     1. Janet   =   James   (b U Largo (all born and bap Largo) (bap 19
(bap 08 Sep 1694 (24 Mar 1721 (b Upper Largo bap 20 Mar (bap 27 Apr (bap 29 Ceres) Aug
  Ceres)   bap 22 Sep 1695 Largo)   1698)   1701)   Feb 1704)   1711)
2. Christian
 Halkerstone
(m 20 Dec 1734
   Largo)
    ↓   Alexander   James   William   Grizall
 Margaret   bap 18 Apr 1725) (bap 18 Dec 1726) (bap 05 May 1728) (bap 19
(bap 31 Oct 1736   (All at Largo)   Aug 1733)
  Largo)
                          David Johnston   =   Jane Murison
                          (b abt 1690)   (13 Nov 1713   (b abt 1690 Largo?)
                                                 Largo) |

                    William
                    Webster   =   Jannett

             John   =   Rebecca
   (bap 12 May 1723 Largo) (11 Dec 1747 Largo) (bap 05 Aug 1716 Kirktown of Largo)

David   Barbara   Jean   Mary
(b 11 Feb 1749   (16 Mar 1751   (b 12 Jun 1759 (b 26 May 1764
 St Monance)   St Monance)   St Monance)   St Monance)
    John Given   =   Janet   Rebecca   =   William Given
(b abt 1760)   (3 Dec 1777) (b 21 Sep 1753) (b 18 Nov 1756) (30 Nov 1782) (b abt 1760)
  St Monance   ↓   St Monance   St Monance
                  Issue

       William b1783 Mary b1786 Helen b1790 John b1792 Rebecca b1796

Ceres is an inland village in Fifeshire, a few miles to the south-east of Cupar.
It is here that we begin this section of the narrative. David Laing and Agnes Quhite were probably born in the village in the early years of the 17th century. The three children that we know of from this marriage were all baptized in this parish:

OPR Ceres Co Fife:
    '1627 Sunday November 30 David law. Child to D[a]vid Laing and Agnes Quite
    bap: witnesses James Ross & Petter Irving'

OPR Ceres, Co Fife:
    '1632 Monday 7 August Baptized Ro[ber]tt umqle Sone to David Lainge &
    Agnes Quhyt witnesses Rot. Bermiett [?] & thomas fforth'

The spelling of Agnes's surname is puzzling until one realizes that the initial 'quh' stands for the 'wh' ('hw') of modern English, concerning the correct pronunciation of which Scots are most particular.

I do not have an extract from the parish register giving details of Williame's baptism but an entry in the IGI confirms its existence.

The significance in this context of 'umqle' (pronounced *umwhile*) is not clear. It should mean 'late' or 'deceased' but clearly that cannot be right. If it implies that the father died before his son was born, how do we explain the birth of another child to the same parents four years later? The simplest answer is perhaps that the minister or his clerk misunderstood what he heard. A certain carelessness in the writing up of the entries is evident. It is known that in some parishes entries were first noted on a piece of paper and written up later. Or forgotten. This is often why, generally speaking, parish registers sometimes seem corrupt or incomplete.

The parentage of Williame's wife, Margaret, is unknown and no more than two children have been found from this marriage:

OPR Ceres, Co Fife:
    '1674 Mar 8 Eodem die Wm Laing and [blank] had a daughter bapt. called
    Agnes. Witnesses Rot. Laing and [illegible]'

'Eodem die' means 'on the same day' (ie relating to another event already mentioned).

OPR Ceres, Co Fife:
    '1677 July 21 William Laing and Mar[gare]t Walker had a child bapt. & called
    Mart.   Witnesses Andrew Bred and [blank]'

The Laing's elder child, Agnes, married a John Donaldson, about whom nothing is known. We are aware of only one child of this marriage, Janet:

OPR Ceres, Co Fife:
> '1694 Septr 8th John donaldsone & Agnes Layng his Spouse had a child bap. called Janet wit. John Donaldsone & John Sim'

Enter the Woods.

James Wood married Catharine Gourlay, about whom we know nothing except that they had one child, Alexander, the record of whose marriage to Sophie Gardner in 1693 is interesting :

OPR LARGO Co Fife:
> '1693 June 16   20 May Alexander Wood and Sophia Gardner both in the congregation were contracted and their pands were consigned that same day, and their marriage was the 16 of June, their given back.'

'Pands' is the money given as surety for good (sexual) behaviour. Their money was returned to them after three weeks of self-denial!
Alexander and Sophie subsequently had at least five children. The eldest is Sheila's ancestor:

OPR LARGO Co Fife:
> 'Alexander Wood in Upper Largo had a child baptized (by the min[iste]r.) called James witnesses were James Cornfoot and David Carmickell both indwellers in over Largo'

'Indwellers' mean 'inhabitants.'

The centre of attention has now moved to Largo. The main settlement (Lower Largo) is on the coast, westwards from Elie, at the head of a bay. Inland lie Kirkton of Largo and Upper Largo. The area is dominated by a hill called Largo Law. This word, found in Scotland and as far south as Derbyshire (Arbor Law), means a rounded hill.

On the 24th March 1721, James Wood married Janet Donaldson. The event was recorded in both parishes:

OPR LARGO Co Fife (443/2) Marriages:
'1721 March the 24th
> Feb: 18th James Wood in this Paroch and Jane Donaldson in the parish of Ceres were contracted, Orderly proclaimed and married at Ceres by Mr   Greenless Minister of the Gospell there March 24th 1721.'

OPR Ceres Co Fife (415/2) Marriages
> '1721 ffebuar 19th James Wood in Largo parish & Janet Donaldson in this were Contracted. Cau[tione]rs   Alexander Wood & John Donaldson.'

The two fathers acted as sureties. The actual date of the marriage is given in the Largo document but not by Mr Greenless of Ceres.

We know of five children of this marriage, but it seems that Janet died either when Grizall was born in 1733 or else soon after, because in 1734 James was married for a second time - to Christian Halkerstone. A child, Margaret, was born in 1736.

The mention of Christian Halkerstone leads to a puzzle. This is the second person of that name that I have on the database. If we refer back to the chart of the Early Afflecks we find that the fourth child of James Affleck and Christian Dawson was called David, born in 1729. This David married twice and his first wife was - Christian Halkerstone, married in 1756. They had a son, John Auckinleck, in 1757. Could this possibly be the same woman who had married James Wood in 1734? It seems very unlikely, although James was certainly still alive in 1736 and she could, probably would, have retained her maiden name. There seems to be little likelihood of getting to the bottom of this mystery.

Of the five children born to James Wood and Janet Donaldson, the first, John, was born in 1723. The last was named Grizall, a popular variant of Grizelda.

John married Rebecca Johnston in 1747:

OPR LARGO Co Fife:
> '1747 December 11th Novr 6th Eodem die John Wood in the Par- ish of St Monance and Rebecca Johnston in this Parish were contracted orderly proclaimed and married at Largo by Mr fferier our Minister December 11th 1747'

OPR ST MONANCE Co Fife (454/2) Marriages.
> '1747 December 11th. John Wood and Rebecca Johnston Contracted Novbr.22nd & after Regular Proclamation Married 11th December 1747.'

John had gone from Largo to live in St Monance.
The expression 'our Minister' seems to imply that a parish clerk had written the entry.

Rebecca was the daughter David Johnston and Jane Murison (a variant of 'Morrison'). She was born in Kirkton of Largo in 1716 and was therefore seven years older than John Wood:

OPR LARGO Co Fife:'1716 August 5th..David Johnston in Kirk town of Largo had a child called Rebecca [bap by Mr Moncieff] the witnesses were James Balbirnie in Largo Mill, David Wilson & David Smyth tennants in the Kirktown and many others'

The only other child of the marriage we know about was Jannett, She married a William Webster and died in 1798.

OPR LARGO Co Fife:

    'Janet Johnstone relict of William Webster [?] in Fluthers 78 east 18 1/2 south best large Do [Mortcloth]'

John and Rebecca had six children:

OPR ST MONANCE Co Fife:

    '1749 Febry 11th. David son of John Wood & Rebecca Johnston Born 11th Baptized Febry 12th.'

OPR ST MONANCE Co Fife.

    '1751 March 16th. Barbara Daur of JohnWood & Rebekah Johnston. Born March 16th & Baptized March 24th 1751.'

OPR ST MONANCE Co Fife:

    [1753]'Janet Daur of James Wood & Rebecca Johnston. Born Septbr the 21st & Baptized Septbr 23d.'

OPR ST MONANCE Co Fife:

    '1756 Novbr 18th. Rebecca Daur of John Wood & Rebecca Johnson Born Novbr. 18th & Baptized Novbr. 24th.'

OPR ST MONANCE, Co Fife:

    '1759 Junr 12th. Jean Daughter of John Wood and Rebecca Johston [sic] his Spouse was born 12th & baptized 17th June 1759.'

OPR ST MONANCE Co Fife:

    '1764 May 26th. Mary Daughter of John Wood & Rebecca Johnston was born on the 26th & Baptized on the 27th day of May 1764.'

At this point the Givens family enter the story; and in a rather an interesting fashion. Rebecca Woods married William Given in 1782 and it seems that before that her elder sister Janet married William's brother, John Given, in 1777. We cannot prove that the two Givens were related but it seems probable.

We have the detail of William's marriage only:

OPR ST MONANCE Co Fife (454/2) Marriages:

    '1782 Novr 30th William Given and Rebecca both in this parish were contracted Novr 16th & after proclamation married Novr 30th 1782.'

We must now turn to the Givens ancestors and their related families.

The Early Given Family and Other Lines

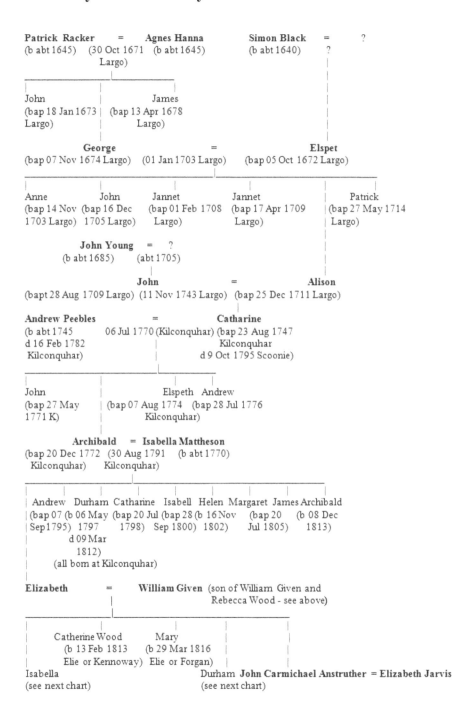

```
Patrick Racker        =      Agnes Hanna            Simon Black      =        ?
(b abt 1645)    (30 Oct 1671  (b abt 1645)           (b abt 1640)    ?
                  Largo)                                             |
_____|_____                                     |
|                 |              |                                  |
John              |           James                                 |
(bap 18 Jan 1673 | (bap 13 Apr 1678                                 |
Largo)           |      Largo)                                      |
           George                      =                  Elspet
(bap 07 Nov 1674 Largo)   (01 Jan 1703 Largo)    (bap 05 Oct 1672 Largo)
_____|_____
|            |           |             |             |            |
Anne        John       Jannet        Jannet          |        Patrick
(bap 14 Nov (bap 16 Dec (bap 01 Feb 1708 (bap 17 Apr 1709 |(bap 27 May 1714
1703 Largo) 1705 Largo)  Largo)         Largo)           | Largo)
                                                          |
       John Young  =   ?                                  |
      (b abt 1685)   (abt 1705)                            |
                   |                                       |
               John               =                    Alison
(bapt 28 Aug 1709 Largo)  (11 Nov 1743 Largo)  (bap 25 Dec 1711 Largo)
                            |
Andrew Peebles        =            Catharine
(b abt 1745      06 Jul 1770 (Kilconquhar) (bap 23 Aug 1747
d 16 Feb 1782            |              Kilconquhar
Kilconquhar)            |          d 9 Oct 1795 Scoonie)
_____|_____
|            |          |      |
John         |       Elspeth  Andrew
(bap 27 May  | (bap 07 Aug 1774  (bap 28 Jul 1776
1771 K)      |       Kilconquhar)
             |
       Archibald  = Isabella Mattheson
(bap 20 Dec 1772  (30 Aug 1791    (b abt 1770)
 Kilconquhar)   Kilconquhar)
_____|_____
|    |     |         |        |       |        |        |       |
| Andrew Durham Catharine Isabell Helen Margaret James Archibald
| (bap 07 (b 06 May (bap 20 Jul (bap 28 (b 16 Nov (bap 20 (b 08 Dec
| Sep1795) 1797    1798)    Sep 1800) 1802)   Jul 1805) 1813)
|        d 09 Mar
|          1812)
|      (all born at Kilconquhar)
|
Elizabeth        =        William Given  (son of William Given and
             |                            Rebecca Wood - see above)
_____|_____
|       |              |           |        |
|  Catherine Wood    Mary          |        |
|    (b 13 Feb 1813  (b 29 Mar 1816 |        |
|    Elie or Kennoway) Elie or Forgan) |     |
Isabella                       Durham  John Carmichael Anstruther = Elizabeth Jarvis
(see next chart)               (see next chart)
```

179

We return to Largo for marriage of Patrick Racker (the name sometimes appears as Raiker or Raker) and Margaret Hanna:

OPR LARG Co Fife:
> '1671 30 of October Patrick Raker and Agnis Hanna were maried being both in this paroch. Witnesses wert John Lundie of Strathkerlie and John Gilchrit [sic].'

Three children are known of this marriage:

OPR LARGO, Co Fife:
> '1683 Jannary 18   Patrick Racker   John W.[itness] John Londie of Stratherlie'

OPR LARGO Co Fife:
> '1674 7 of October [sic] P [= Pater? = son   Patrick Racker F [= Filius? = son] George W[itnesses)   James Racker and James Bell'

The IGI gives November. James may have been the child's uncle.

OPR LARGO, Co Fife:
> '1678 Aprile 13 Patrick Raker had a child baptized called James ye witnesses were James Raker & William hedge'

George married Elspet Black, daughter of Simon (mother unknown):

OPR LARGO Co Fife (443/2) Marriages:
'1703 Jannuar 1
> The same day George Raker and Elspeth Black both in this parish were contracted in order to proclamation and their Marriage, after they were thrice severall dayes orderly proclaimed was solemnized att Largo by the Minr. 1 Jannuar 1703.'

In the past it was not unusual for baptisms to occur on Christmas Day, a holiday on which it would be possible to assemble relatives. Whether this was true of marriages (in Scotland) on the 1st   January, is unclear; it depends for how long 1st January has been celebrated. It should be remembered that Christmas was barely celebrated in Scotland from the late 17th century until the mid 20th century. Christmas was thought of by the Presbyterian Scots to be a Popish superstition. Hogmanay was the time for winter celebrations.

Elspeth's baptism is recorded:

OPR LARGO Co Fife:
> '1672 5 of October   P Simon Black [P = Pater?] F   Elizabeth   [F = Filia?] W[itness]   Mr John Beagrie   W[itness]   David Craig'

180

Of the couple's six children five survived: the first Jannet must have died as a baby, as another child was also named Jannet fifteen months after the previous one.

Alison Racker married John Young in 1743. He, also born in Largo was the son of another John; his mother is unknown. The record of his baptism is interesting:

OPR LARGO Co Fife (443/2) Births:
> 1709 Aug: 28th
> John Young, Sailer in leven had a childe baptized by the Min[iste]r. called
> John, but held up by James Young, he being at Sea, the witnesses were Alan
> Lamont in Leven [....] Anderson also indweller in Leven & many others.'

It is unusual in early 18th parish records to have shown the occupation of common people. We also have the clear picture of the child being presented by a relative, possibly his uncle.

The marriage of John and Alison:

OPR LARGO Co Fife:
> '1743 Novr. 11th. Octr. 15th. The said day John Young and Alison Raiker both
> in this Parish were contracted, orderly proclaimed and married at Largo by Mr
> fferriar our Minister Novr.11th Anno Instanti.[= 'the present year']'

Alison appears to have married late (for that era) and was 36 when her one child, Catharine, was born in 1747.
But she lived to the age of sixty:

OPR KILCONQUHAR Co FIFE [Deaths 1771]:
> 'Alison Raker Spouse to John Young.'

John himself appears to have lived to the ripe old age of ninety:

OPR LARGO Co Fife:
> '1799 Sept 19 John Young in Drumochy 112 east, 30 south, best large M.C.'

There is now a Drummochy Rd running along the sea-shore in Lower Largo and John perhaps died near there. The position of his grave is given and that he was buried in a best large mort cloth - as was now the fashion.

Catharine, who was baptized in Kilconquhar parish, married Andrew Peebles (sometimes written 'Peoples') there in 1770.
Andrew died in 1782:

OPR KILCONQUHAR: ' 1782 Febry 16th Andrew Peebles in the Muirs.'

Catharine died thirteen years later:

OPR KILCONQUHAR, Co FIFE:
'[9 Oct 1795] Catherine Young Relict of Andrew Peebles Died at Scoonnie [sic] and was   buried there.'
'Relict' = 'widow'.

Catharine and Andrew had four children, the second of which, Archibald, married Isabella Mattheson in 1791 at Kilconquhar, where all their subsequent nine children were born. Elizabeth, the eldest married William Given, son of Rebecca Wood and William Given.

But before we come again to them, we should look at Archibald and Isabella's second daughter, Durham.
First, the name: it is a puzzle and is not found in the family as a first name before this time, though it occurs twice more later. It almost certainly began life as the surname of one of the earlier ancestors of this family. An Agnes Durham is found in Fifeshire in 1569 and there are plenty of other examples in Lowland Scotland. The use of such a surname, especially of a female ancestor, is often found as a second forename. The use of a former surname as first name can be found in our families in examples such as Lumsden Affleck and Coulson Defty.

OPR Kilconquhar, Co. Fife (436/3) Baptisms:
'1797 May 6th   Durham, Lawful Daughter of Archibald Peebles and Isabella Matheson his Wife was born on the 6th day of May 1797 and Baptized the 12th of Do.[May] in Colinsburgh Meeting House.'

Secondly, the manner of Durham's death - tragic and unusual:

O.P.R.Kilconquhar, Co. Fife (436/3) Deaths/Burials:
'1812 March 9th Durham Peebles Daughter of Archibald Peebles Died the 9th of March and was Buried the 11th of Do. her Death was Occasioned by an explosion of Gunpowder when on a visit at her Uncle's at Clunie, North from Kirkcaldie.'

I know nothing further about this incident. It may have resulted from a use of explosives in a mine.

Now, Elizabeth and William:

OPR St Monance, Co Fife (454/2) Baptisms
'1783 October 19th
 William son of Willm. Given and Rebecca Wood was born 16th & Baptized 19th October 1783 pd. Do. [sc King's] Duty 3d'

OPR Edinburgh, Co Edinburgh (685/1/54) Marriages:
>'1811 September 7th William Govan, Laborer Parish of Newburn and
>Elizabeth Peebles, Old Church Parish, Daughter of Archd. Peebles, Mason
>Parish of Largo.'

The couple are found with their daughter - another Durham - on the 1841 Census:

1841   Census   [digitised]

Name	Occupation	Approx dob	Where born	Address
William Given	Farmer	1786	Fife, Scotland	Elie House and Farm Steading
Elizabeth Given		1793	do	do
Durham Given		1821	do	do

William died in 1854:

OPR ELIE Co Fife Deaths (1822-1854):
>'1845 December   20th William Given Farmer Elie he departed this [life?] 20th
>December and Buiread [?] from McIntyiers Ston.'

A search in Elie churchyard might reveal McIntyre's Stone!

By the time of Elizabeth's death much later in 1872 Statutory Death Certificates had been compulsory for seventeen years:

Death cert:
'1872 Kilconquhar, Co.Fife (436/25)
>on September 20th (about midnight) at Earlsferry, Kilconquhar Elizabeth
>Given..Aged 78. Widow of William Given, Farmer daur of..Archibald
>Peebles, Grocer, (deceased) and of Isabella Peebles M[aiden]/S[urname]
>Mathieson (deceased) Cause of death..Debility. Not certified. Informant.
>Alexr.Sunter.Son-in-law Earlsferry.'

It can be seen from a comparison between the two death entries how full is the information in the second and how useful it is to family historians. Kilconquhar was presumably the registration centre for Earslferry, which lies immediately to the west of Elie.

We now move on to a consideration of the Jarvis/Jervis/Jervie family. Elizabeth Jarvis became Elizabeth's and William's daughter-in-law.

183

The Taylor, Jarvis, White and Hay Families

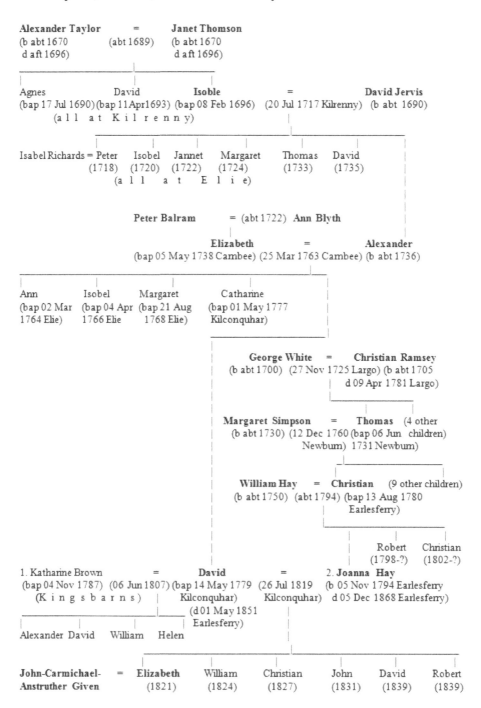

Alexander Taylor　　　=　　　Janet Thomson
(b abt 1670　　　(abt 1689)　(b abt 1670
　d aft 1696)　　　　　　　　　d aft 1696)

Agnes　　　　　David　　　　Isoble　　　　　　=　　　　　David Jervis
(bap 17 Jul 1690)(bap 11Apr1693)(bap 08 Feb 1696)　(20 Jul 1717 Kilrenny)　(b abt 1690)
　　　　(a l l　 a t　 K i l r e n n y)

Isabel Richards = Peter　Isobel　Jannet　Margaret　Thomas　David
　　　　　　(1718)　(1720)　(1722)　(1724)　(1733)　(1735)
　　　　　　(a l l　 a t　 E l i e)

Peter Balram　　　= (abt 1722)　Ann Blyth

Elizabeth　　　　=　　　　Alexander
(bap 05 May 1738 Cambee) (25 Mar 1763 Cambee) (b abt 1736)

Ann　　　　　Isobel　　　Margaret　　　Catharine
(bap 02 Mar　(bap 04 Apr (bap 21 Aug　(bap 01 May 1777
1764 Elie)　1766 Elie　1768 Elie)　Kilconquhar)

George White　=　　Christian Ramsey
(b abt 1700)　(27 Nov 1725 Largo) (b abt 1705
　　　　　　　　　　　　　　　d 09 Apr 1781 Largo)

Margaret Simpson　　=　　Thomas　(4 other
(b abt 1730)　(12 Dec 1760 (bap 06 Jun　children)
　　　　　Newburn)　1731 Newburn)

William Hay　=　Christian　(9 other children)
(b abt 1750)　(abt 1794) (bap 13 Aug 1780
　　　　　　　　　Earlesferry)

Robert　　Christian
(1798-?)　(1802-?)

1. Katharine Brown　　　=　　　David　　　=　2. Joanna Hay
(bap 04 Nov 1787)　(06 Jun 1807)(bap 14 May 1779 (26 Jul 1819 (b 05 Nov 1794 Earlesferry
　(K i n g s b a r n s)　|　Kilconquhar)　Kilconquhar)　d 05 Dec 1868 Earlesferry)
　　　　　　　　　　|____ (d 01 May 1851
　　　　　　　　　　|　Earlesferry)
Alexander David　William　Helen

John-Carmichael-　=　Elizabeth　William　Christian　John　David　Robert
Anstruther Given　　(1821)　(1824)　(1827)　(1831)　(1839)　(1839)

Kilrenny lies a short distance from the coast, north-east of Anstruther and was the home of a well-established branch of the Lumsden family - apparently not related to the Lumsdens already mentioned.

Isoble Taylor, youngest daughter of Alexander and Janet Thompson, was baptized there:

OPR Kilrenny, Co Fife:
>'1696 Feb 8 Alesr. Taylor and Janet Thomson had Isoble witnesses James Taylor and [illegible]'

From the wording of the register it looks as if she was born on this day.
Isoble and David Jervis were married at Kilrenny in 1717:

OPR KILRENNY, Co Fife Marriages/Baptisms (Intermixed):
>'1717 July 20   The same day David Jarves in the parish of [illegible] and Isabel Taylor in this were Contracted and gave half [illegible] to the poor,' [page repaired with tape]

It is a pity we cannot tell where David was born. The couples' children, however, were all baptized at Elie and this may indicate David's parish of origin.
The later illegible part of the entry will have referred to the pands or money given as surety for good behaviour until the wedding.
The first child, Peter, married Isabel Richards; their memorial can be seen in Elie churchyard:

>'...IN MEMORY of ISABELL RICHARDS SPOUSE to PETER JERVIS tenant
In BALMOUNT Who Died MAY 15 1794 Aged 63 years
>Also in MEMORY OF PETER JERVIS Who Died JUNE 26 1806 Aged 76 Years...'

'Balmount' may be a version of 'Belmont.'

Alexander Jervis, born much later, married Elizabeth Balrom in 1763:

OPR CARNBEE, Co Fife Births/Marriages(Intermixed):
>'1763 March the 25th This day allexander Jerves in the Parish of Elie and Elisabeth Balrom in this Parish gave in their named [sic] to be Proclaimed in order to marriage.'

It is the date of Proclamation that is given above. The actual marriage date is recorded in Elie - on the 22 April. Elizabeth had been baptized on the 5th May 1738, daughter of Peter Balram and Ann Blyth.

David, being Sheila's direct ancestor, is the child of Alexander and Elizabeth who most concerns us, but we have first to mention the death and burial of his elder sister, Isobel:

185

OPR KILCONQUHAR:
'1841 June 15th Isobel Jervis died at Earlsferry aged 75 years.'
and:

OPR Elie Co Fife Deaths (427/3) (1824-1854):
'1841 Jun 16 Isable Jarves Daughter of the late Alxender Jarves Earlsferry Depart[ed] this life 16 Jun and is Buired 2 yds South from William Dudngstons Ston.'

It seems Isobel never married. It is unclear why, if she died in Earlesferry, she appears also in the Kilconquhar records.

David Jarvis/Jervis/Jervie, and so on, was married twice.
He married Katharine Brown at Kingsbarns in 1787:

OPR Kingsbarns, Co Fife (441/2) Marriages:
'1807 June 6th   Were married David Jarvis and Katharine Brown both of this parish.'

David, then aged 28, must have moved there from his native Kilconquhar. Kingsbarns is about a mile inland from the coast, after it turns from north-east to north-west, heading towards St Andrews.
Four children came from this marriage: Alexander (1808), David (1809), William (1812) and Helen (1814).
Katharine must have died shortly after Helen was born for by 1819 he is ready to marry again:

OPR KILCONQUHAR, Co FIFE (463/3) Marriages:
'1819 July 26 David Jervis &Joanna Hay both in this Parish were Contracted in order to Marriage the 17th of July & after being three times etc..they were married the 26th July by the Rev [?]'

She is called Joanna here but she was christened slightly differently:

OPR Kilconquhar, Co Fife (436/3) Births.
'1794 November 5th   Johnsie Lawful Daughter of William Hay, Shoemaker in Earlsferry by Christian White his Wife was born on the said day and Baptized the 9th of Do.'
Elsewhere the name is again different.
The time allowed for three proclamations of the Contract (17th - 26th July) is unusually short but there is no evidence that this was a shot-gun wedding!
To find out more about Joanna's antecedents we need to go back a few generations.

George White and Christian Ramsey were married in Largo. No details of their life are available except for Christian's death in 1781:

OPR Largo Co Fife:
'1781 Aprile 9th Christian Ramsey in Drumlochy, 104 east 28 south best large mortcloth' also: '1781 Apr 9   Christian Ramsay best large Do [mortcloth]'

The entry is obscure: is Drumlochy where Christian was living? And what is the reference point for the measurements given?

George and Christian had five children. The family must have moved to Newburn, which may have been George's native parish. Thomas, the third son was born there and married Margaret Simpson:

OPR NEWBURN Co Fife (451/2) Marriages:
'1760 Decr 12 Thomas Whyte in this Parish and Marharet Simpson in the Parish of Cairnbee [sic] gave up their Names in Order to be proclaimed for Marriage. And after three several Sabbaths Proclamation without Objection were married Decr 12 1760 by Mr. James Smith our Minister.'

Thomas and Margaret had ten children and it should be possible to make a few educated guesses about ancestral forenames. In particular, it may be legitimate to assume from the name of the seventh child, John Thompson White, that Margaret Simpson's mother's maiden name was Thompson.
But it was the tenth child, Christian, who was to be Sheila's ancestor. She married William Hay, a shoemaker, (born about 1750) about 1794. William had already been married to a Helen Rumgay. Although we have extensive and sometimes interesting information on her ancestry, for lack of space and because she was not an ancestor, she and her forbears have been omitted from the chart.

There is a mystery over Christian's marriage to William. It is not recorded but is confirmed by Joanna's birth, which was mentioned earlier.
The difficulty is compounded by the fact Christian was only fourteen years and two months old when married. This may not have been unusual at the time but if she was pregnant when married one would have expected some sort of official censure to have been recorded. Perhaps this was an irregular marriage, celebrated in Edinburgh.

We know of two other children born to William and Christian: Robert (1798) and Christian (1802). The latter appears on the 1851 Census:

1851 Census Earlsferry:
1851/436/7/3 'at North side of the Street of Earlsferry, Kilconquhar, Co Fife
[in the household of David Jervie [sic]]

Christina Hay Sister-in-law 50 Pauper   Works out in summer B[orn] Earlesferry, Co Fife'

I am unsure what is meant by 'works out in summer.' Perhaps Christian was not in good health.

Now back to Joanna Hay. We have already seen that she was David Jarvis's second wife and that they were married in Kilconquhar in 1819.   They had six children,   although gaps between later births suggest that there were others whose births are not known to us. David and Robert seem to be twins and, arriving when their mother was forty-five, must have caused quite an upset.

In fact, Robert died in 1841:

ELIE Elie Deaths 1822-54:
    1841 May 2d Robert Jarves son of David Jarves Earlsferry depart [sic] this life 2d May and Buired 1 yd from the South Dyke and 6 yds west from Margret Woods Ston.'

The eldest child, Elizabeth, married John-Carmichael-Anstruther Given in 1847:

Marriage entry (Kilconquhar):

    '1845 June 14th/John Givan Parish of Elie & Elizabeth Jarvis of this Parish were Contracted & after being proclaimed on Three Sundays were married by [blank] on 14th June 1845.'

She died in 1894 at 5 Rankeillor St, Elie, which had become the home of the Afflecks:

Death cert:
    '..9h.15m pm..73 years..[daughter of] David Jervis/Linen Weaver/ (deceased)/ [and] Joan Jervis/MS Hay/(deceased)..Atheroma of Aorta/Angina Pectoris/As certified/by JT Mallach/LRCP VS Ed DPH..'

How John-Carmichael-Anstruther Given acquired his Christian names is not altogether sure. A clue is perhaps provided by his baptismal entry:

Birth entry, Elie
    '1821 Nov 23d   John Carmichael Anstruther Givan 5th child & lawful son to William Givan Labourer Elie House by Elisabeth Peebles his wife was born this day & baptised by the Revd. Mr.J.Clarke.
    Note: Although the following names are registered in other parishes yet the parents requested their insertion here too.' [Here follows an account of the baptisms of John's siblings.]

Now, Elie House was at that time held by an important family - the Carmichael Anstruthers. It appears, therefore, that one of the family may have stood as god-father to John. The other possibility - that a member of the family was the father, not the god-father of the child - seems negated by the assertion that he was 'lawful son…etc'.

John did not use his inflated forename. For example, in the 1851 Census he is shown as 'John Givan, Farmer of 10 acres employing no labour.'

The marriage to Elizabeth as recorded in Elie, shows rather more detail than the Kilconquhar entry shown earlier:

Marriage entry: (Elie)

> ' 1845 May 24th/Contracted in order to marriage John Given, Carpenter residing in Elie, and Elizabeth Jervis residing in the Parish of Kilconquhar they were three several times duly proclaimed in the Parish Church here and no objections offered.Married on the sixteenth day of June by the Rev. George Smith Minister of Tolbooth Parish Edinburgh.'

The mention of the Rev George Smith from Edinburgh explains the blank in the former entry: the writer did not know who the minister was.

John's was an interesting life; he was in turn: 1845 - carpenter; 1851 - farmer of 10 acres employing no labour; 1871 - ploughman; 1876 - salmon fisher; 1907 - coal merchant. Ten children were born form John's marriage to Elizabeth. He lived to a ripe old age and died in 1907, thirteen years after Elizabeth:

Death cert:

> '..Retired Coal Merchant/(Widower of Elizabeth Jervis)/..8h.0m.AM Jubilee Cottage, Earlsferry, Elie../ [father] William Given/Crofter (deceased)/ [mother] Elizbeth Given/MS Peebles (deceased)../Cerebral haemorrhage 15 days/as Certified by JT Mallach/LRCP VS Ed DPH/ [reported by] A.[?] Given/Son. '

The Afflecks in the 19th Century

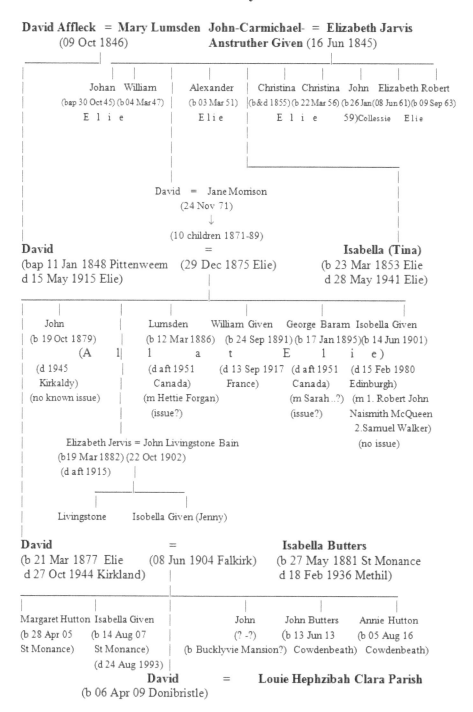

David Affleck and Mary Lumsden had only one child - not surprising as they were both in their forties when they married:

Pittenweem Register:
> '1848 May 17th
> David Affleck or Auchinleck, land labourer in Pittenweem and Mary Lumsden his wife had a Son born the 17th May 1848 and baptized on the 11th June by the Revd. John Cooper, Minister of Pittenweem. Childs name David. Witnesses James Peat and William Bayne.'

Note that the alternative surname, Auchinleck, is still in use.

The family is found on the 1861 Census:

1861/452/2/23 at Mary Street, Pittenweem, Co Fife

'David Affleck   Head   Marr 58   Land Labourer Born Pittenweem, Co Fife
 Mary Affleck   Wife   Marr   57   B Pittenweem,
Co Fife
 David Affleck   Son   12   Scholar   B Pittenweem, Co
Fife'

Mary died two years later:

1863. 45 no22 Pittenweem

Death cert: 'Mary Affleck/(married to David Affleck/Landlabourer)/1863/March/ Twentyfifth/10h.P.M./…[father] George Lumsden/Collier/(Deceased)/[mother] Margaret Lumsden/M.S.Lawson/(Deceased)/Phthisis/2 years//As cert by/Wm Constable/Surgeon/ Pittenweem./David Affleck [signed]/Widower/Present.'
Signed At Pittenweem Alexdr Murray, Registrar.

Phthisis was an alternative name for consumption or tuberculosis.

Her husband died in 1867:

Death Cert:
'..Land labourer (Widower of Mary Lumsden)/1867/October/Ninth/ 0h.30m.P.M./Pittenweem/..65 years/[father] David Affleck/Landlabourer/(Deceased)/[mother] Jane [sc Jean] Affleck/M.S.Brown/(Deceased)/Paralysis 4 Months/..David Affleck [signed]/Son/ Present..'

On the 1851 Census he had been described as a Farmer of 16 acres. He was a Baillie from 1844 to 1845 and 1848/9. He left no will.

In 1851 the family lived High Street (north side), Pittenweem and in 1861, as we have seen, they were in Mary St.

In the year after his father's death, David entered the service of the Hudson's Bay Company. Documents received from the archives in Canada in 1999 confirm this:

NAME: AFFELECK David   PARISH: Pittenweem,   Fife, SCOTLAND ENTERED
*   also AFFLECK   SERVICE:*
1868 at
Stromness, Orkney
DATES born 18 May 1848

*   died 15 May*
1915

Appointments & Service
Outfit Year*:   Position: Post: District: HBCA*
Reference:
* An Outfit year ran from 1 June to 31 May

1868, 25 June-29 August Came out to York Factory on the Prince Rupert
*   C.1/971, 972*
1868-1869   Labourer   General Charges   Northern Dept.   B.239/u/3
*   #6; B.239/g/45*
1869-1873   Labourer   Norway HouseNorway HouseB.239/g/46-48;
B.154/a/68-70; B.154/d/250, 256, 262

1873, 1 June-17 October to Europe on the Prince Rupert

Filename: Affeleck, David (b. 1848 (fl. 1868-1873)   JHB 1997/07 (Revised 1998/03) ;
May/99/mhd

Stromness (Orkney) was the watering stop for ships heading for the New World.

We have no details of the work David carried out at York Factory and Norway House (both on the shores of the Hudson Bay) but no doubt the fur trade formed the basis of his employment.
It is still possible to visit these sites, but only between the months of May and September. Such a journey would involve a flight to Winnipeg and from there north to the Hudson Bay and that is probably not now a practical proposition for Sheila and for me!
Not long after his return from Canada, David married:

Wedding cert [29 Dec 1875]:
        '..David Affleck Station Agent age 27/Isa. Given Domestic
        Servant age 22/ resided Elie...Father David Affleck farmer
        (deceased)/[Mother] Mary nee Lumsden (deceased)'

We have photographs of David in his station-master's uniform, and of him standing on the platform at Elie station. We also have an inscribed plaque (originally attached to a clock) which reads:

'Presented to Mr David Affleck
ALONG WITH A PURSE OF SOVEREIGNS
(and Cake Basket to Mrs Affleck)
BY RESIDENTS & VISITORS OF ELIE AND EARLSFERRY
As a mark of respect for him as Station Master at Elie during 25 Years
JUNE 1899'

The above shows that he must have joined the Railway almost immediately after his return from Canada.

David must have been a very interesting man - self educated, with a mordant wit - a keen observer of humanity. Here are specimens of his letter-writing:

'Elie 1-3-15   Hope the bairns are now better, and yourself, Spouse and Anne Sp..y[?] Tell David that his Uncle G. B. A. has been at Bury[?] learning to shoot   round corners with a bayonet made of a stocking line.

Dear David
                Had a letter from the Sergt. to say he is well but very busy in the dept. there by now over 50 men on the Staff. He expects to be busier still as the casualties lists come in from the Canucks at the front. It will be glory there shortly eggs or young uns. We are well. Deed is fine pleased at the Sergt not being in the fighting line but all the same she is vowing what she would do to the German Wilhelm if she had him. Bow. Wow. I've been engaged in the slicing of the dumpling (Uncle Pa's) Aunty Janes share is £40 which is to be placed jointly along with Bobs on D.P. The rest of the 10 Ravens (Bob included) get £8-1-8. Cousin[?] John will spend his in a day, Willie will keep his & so will Jean.   Douzie ½ an hour Lizzie is all right Bella all depends if Jack Lazy[?] is capable of putting the bit in her mouth. Your Mum will think all these remarks on some of the Givens damned impertinent of me, but I did not begin to study human nature yesterday. I think I forgot to tell you that the custodian of the Hoolet-Ha[?] millions are now Haims[?]   A.M.Cook, Provost Don & D Garland. I am ....ting[?] on in the meantime. If possible I would like to live to hand the share of the dumpling to the Apostle John. If not I may be permitted to to shout down to him from the edge of a cloud. Alleluia slice the dumpling. Alleluia, Amen.
                Your Pater D Affleck

Notes:
bairns = children of David Affleck and Isabella Butters; at that time
Spouse = Isabella Butters
Anne etc = ? possibly Ann Hutton

David = David Affleck (Sheila's father)
GBA = George Baram Affleck
The Sergt = William-Given Affleck
Canucks = Canadians
eggs or young uns = ?
Deed = (presumably) Isabella Given, writer's wife
Uncle Pa = (presumably) David Given, brother of Isabella Given. He had died 20 Nov 1914
Aunty Jane = Jane Morrison, wife of Robert Given
Bob = Robert Given, son of David Given and Jane Morrison
DP = ? Deposit?
The 10 Ravens = the children of John-Carmichael-Anstruther Given (?)

John	=	John Given	)
Willie	=	William Given	)
Jean	=	Jane Given	) all children of the deceased,
Douzie (?)	=	Douglas Given	) David Given.
Lizzie	=	Elizabeth Given)	
Bella	=	Isabella Given	)

Jack Lazie (?)
Hoolet-Ha(?) stupid (?)
Haims(?) under control ?
AMCook (?)
Provost Don (? D Garland (?)

David was to die two months later:

Death cert: '..son of David Affleck, Farmer (deceased) and of Mary Affleck
M.S.Lumsden (deceased)/Cerebral Haemorrhage, 4 days/Rheumatoid
Arthritis, Chronic/as certified by A.L.Pentland Smith M.B.C.M./Robert Given
son of David Given and Jane Morris? or possibly Robert Given /Nephew-in-Law/
Enfield Cottage, Elie.'

'AFFLECK, David, retired Station Agent "Rupertia", Elie, died 18 May 1915, at Elie,
testate. Confirmation granted at Cupar, 19 August to Isabella Given or Affleck,
"Rupertia" aforesaid, his widow, David Affleck, Coal Salesman, 28 Park Street,
Cowdenbeath, and John Affleck, Compositor, 9 North Street, Leven, his sons, Executors
nominated in Will or Deed, dated 12 September 1906, and recorded in Court Books of
Commissariot of Fife, 12 August 1915. Value of Estate £99:9:2.'

He is buried with his wife in Elie churchyard

Here is an obituary published in the *East of Fife Record*

'Obituary
David Affleck
20th May 1915

There will be many in the district, and a good few further afield, who will
regret to learn of the death of Mr David Affleck, which occurred at his
residence, Rupertay *[sic] House, on Tuesday. Mr Affleck had been in failing*

health for some time back, and never rallied from an apoplectic seizure he had on Friday. The deceased, who was 68 years of age, had a varied and interesting career. In his young days, he heard and responded to the call of the west, and leaving for Canada, received an appointment under the Hudson Bay Company. *After a strenuous life out in Canada, Mr Affleck returned to his native land, and in 1873 was appointed station agent in Elie. This post he continued to discharge with ability and success until 1899, when he retired. He then occupied the post of librarian, latterly, his extensive knowledge of old china was turned to good account in the antique business he conducted. His public services include a couple of terms on the Town Council while he was also a member of the Recreation Committee for a number of years. By most, however, he will be remembered for his pawky humour. This last feature was his outstanding characteristic, and many a long evening has been brightened with his reminiscences and jokes. Mr Affleck is survived by a widow, and a grown up family, two of his sons being now with the forces.*

David had named his house 'Rupertia' after the ship that had taken him to Canada (and brought him back).

He and his family are shown on the 1901 Census:

1901 Census Elie:

Sched 68   5 Rankeillor St 1 inh   6 rooms with windows

David Affleck	Head	Mar	52	Retired Station Master	Fifeshire,	Pittenweem
Isabella do	Wife	Mar	47		Do	Elie
David do	Son	S	24	Railway Clerk Worker	Do	Do
John do	Son	S	21	Printer's Apprentice Worker	Do	Do
Elizabeth J do	Daur	S	19		Do	Do
Lumsden do	Son	S	15	Plumber's Do Worker	Do	Do
William G do	Son		9	Scholar	Do	Do
George B do	Son		6	do	Do	Do

John Bain   Boarder   24   House Painter   Own Account
Fifeshire,   Elie
            [NB John Bain mar Elizabeth Jarvis Affleck 22 Oct 1902]

Two doors on are David's father-in-law and niece:

Sched 70   9 Rankeillor St 1 inh   4 rooms with windows

John C[armichael] A[nstruther]	Given	Head	Wid	80	Retired Coal Merchant	Fifeshire ,	Elie
Elizabeth		do	Daur	S	39		
Do	Do						

We have already seen that Isabella Given (also known as 'Tina') was one of ten children born to John C A Given and Elizabeth Jarvis. Some of her siblings turn up in various contexts but only one on whom we have detailed information is David, born 1849, who married Jane Morrison in 1871. He was at one time town postman at Elie but latterly described as a 'coal merchant,' which probably means that he took over his father's business.

David and Jane also had a large family and it is David's death in 1914 which is the one mentioned above in David Affleck's letter.

There are two pointers to a long connection between the Given and Affleck families.

In the first place, one of David Given's and Jane's sons was born and named   David Affleck Given on the 1st November 1875, two months before Isabella Given married David Affleck.

Secondly, in the 1881 Census John-C-A Given was living in the same house in High Street, Elie as David Affleck and his wife, Isabella Given.

Isabella was the fifth child of her parents' marriage and was a domestic servant when she married David Affleck in 1875:

Wedding cert: '..David Affleck Station Agent age 27/Isa. Given Domestic Servant age 22/ resided Elie [taken down by Sheila in 1985]

We have two striking photographs of her. In the second (later) image she is shown holding one of her grandchildren:

In the earlier photgraph she has a formidable aspect and that there were tensions in the family is revealed not only by her husband's letter shown earlier but also by remarks

197

gathered from her granddaughter, Annie, and her own son, David. The latter is said to have remarked of Sheila that she 'was a Given.' This was apparently the result of some show of temper by Sheila when she was about two and a half years old!

She had a very long life and died in 1941:

Death cert:1941
       'Elie, Co. Fife (427/10) on May 28th at The Ramblers,Earlsferry'..Widow of
       David Affleck, Station Master. Daughter of John Carmichael Anstruther   Given,
Farmer (deceased) and of/Elizabeth Given M.S. Jarvis   (deceased)../Cardio-vascular
Degeneration, 10 years/As certified by ../..Robert   McQueen.Son-in-law.'

David Affleck and Isabella Given had seven children, all born at Elie.
Omitting for the moment the first, David - the ancestor of Sheila - we pass to the second,
John, named regularly after his maternal grandfather, John Butters.
He was born in 1879. It was essential now to give the parents' marriage date.

Birth cert (19 Aug 1879):
       '..Son of..David Affleck, Station Agent and of Isabella Affleck M.S. Given.
       Marriage of Parents..1875, December 29th. Elie [9 High St]
       Informant...David Affleck. Father. Present.'

Annie Affleck writes (01 Jun 95):
'...Enclosing a picture of Uncle John my dads [sic] brother, he & his wife
Bessie lived in Leven, he was a printer for the newspaper & lived upstairs
from the office, I used to visit [them] with my Mum [Isabella Butters]'

Sheila's mother [LHC Parish] used to say that he befriended his nephew, John Butters
Affleck, and left him £100.

We have records of his army service (WW1):

Digest

181860 Gunner Affleck, John -   Royal Garrison Artillery
Enlisted 29 Nov 1915. Age on enlistment 37 years 10 months. Date of birth 29 Jan 1878
Birthplace: Elie Fife
Medically examined at Kirkcaldy 22 Nov 1916
Height 5'10"
Weight 198 lb
Chest expanded 42 and quarter"
Physical development good
Slight defects: slight varicose vein on left ..? Protuberance of abdomen.

Terms of Service: Duration of War
Religion: Presbitarian
Occupation: compositor
Date of Discharge: 28 Jun 1918
Cause of Discharge: medically unfit: heart trouble - regurgitation mistral stenosis, aggravated by service during war with Germany.
50% disablement.
Gratuity [not pension] £5[!]

Proceedings on Discharge [extra description] dated 8 Jun 1918, at Dover
complexion: ruddy
eyes: blue
hair: brown
Intended place of residence: 5 North Street, Leven [?] Fife* see below
Being no longer physically fit for War Service.
Military character: good. Well-behaved during his short period with the colours.
Length of service: 2 years 212 days.
*address on another discharge cert shown as 9 North St, Leven, Fifeshire
There is a slight but definite oedema of the legs

John died in 1945 in Kirkaldy.

The third child was Elizabeth Jervis Affleck, clearly named after her maternal grandmother.

Birth Record:
'1882 Elie, Co. Fife (427/7) on March 19th (2.30am) at High Street, Elie
Daughter of David Affleck, Station Agent and of Isabella Affleck M/S Given
Marriage of Parents 1875, December 29th. Elie
Informant   David Affleck. Father. Present.'

Here is a photograph:

Elizabeth married:

    Marriage of John Livingstone Bain and Elizabeth Jervis Affleck
    '1902 Elie, Co. Fife (427/7) on October 22nd. at Rupertia, Elie. After Banns
    according to the Forms of the Established Church of Scotland

    John L. Bain   Aged 25. Painter (Master). Bachelor
                    Usual residence 21 High Street, Elie

| Son of | George Bain, Painter and of |
| | Elizabeth Bain M/S Sutherland |

Elizabeth J. Affleck   Aged 20. Assistant Librarian. Spinster
                 Usual residence Rupertia, Elie

| Daughter of | David Affleck, retired Station Agent and of |
| | Isabella Affleck M/S Given |

| Signed | R.H.Dunlop, Minister of Elie |
| Witnesses | Duncan S. Bain. Maggie Don' |

John L Bain was the lodger who had been with Afflecks at the time of the 1901 Census. The couple had two children.

Lumsden Affleck was born on the 12th March 1886. His name was chosen from the surname of his paternal grandmother, Mary.

It is assumed that Lumsden, together with his two younger brothers, William-Given and George-Baram, emigrated to Canada in the early years of the 20th century but no details are available for Lumsden. For a few months - October 1914 to August 1915 - he receives a monthly allowance of $20 Canadian from William-Given, who was by this time was a serving soldier. We do not know the reasons for starting or stopping this allowance. Lumsden's address at the time is Winnipeg, Manitoba.

William-Given Affleck - the *Given* portion is from his mother's maiden name - was born on 27th September 1891:

Statutory Records.
'...0h 20m AM 5 Rankeillor Street,Elie. [Father] David Affleck, Railway Station-Agent. [Mother] Isabella Affleck, MS Given. [Married] 1875 December 29th Elie. David Affleck, Father, present [at birth]...'

Nothing is known of his early life but that he was employed as a bank clerk in Canada. Margaret Walker writes (Feb 95)

'..[I have] Also three letters from Willie to his brother David, the first in a lovely flowing hand was written in August 1914 from the Bank of Toronto, telling him that he had enlisted, the second from Seaford, Sussex, in April 1917 when he was with the 6th Canadian Reserves & down with bad tonsillitis the third later in April from the Canadian Military Hospital.'

Here are extracts from letters to his family:
1912, 10 August   Writes from the Bank of Toronto at Peterboro, Ontario
             to his brother David. Served three years in the '7th Black Watch

(Territorials)'; elsewhere shown as '7th Royal Huss[ars] 3 yrs, Black Watch Terr[itorials]'

1914, 12 August   Writes to brother David, from the Bank of Toronto, that he intends to enlist. 'I go down to Quebec with the Peterboro [?] boys on Friday..... I just got seven rotten teeth [!]pulled today with the object of making myself eligible.....No doubt Bram being in the "Terriers" will be out [there?] [France]by this time.....'

On 15th December 1997 I received from National Archives of Canada documents relating to the War Service of William Given Affleck. The following is a summary.

William Given Affleck

Summary of Service Record in the Canadian Army: 1914-1917

Army number: 7601

26 August [1914]   Medical Examination at Valcartier - passed fit for overseas service. Described as 6 ft tall, with expanded chest of 37¼ins, complexion 'fair,' eyes 'blue', hair 'light yellow.' Distinguishing features: '2 large vacc marks left upper arm, one small mole over right deltoid.'

22 September [1914]   Attested at Valcartier Camp; trade or calling given as 'clerk'; date and place of birth given as '24 September 1891, Elie, Fifeshire, Scotland'; next of kin given as 'David Affleck'; altered at some later date to 'Mrs David Affleck (mother); [her] address given as 'Rupertia Elie Scotland.' Is willing to be vaccinated and to serve in the Canadian Over-seas Expeditionary Force.

23 September [1914]   Took oath of allegiance to the King

3 October [1914]   His unit (Peterboro Rangers) sailed [for UK]

25 October [1914]   Arrived in England

October [1914]   Started allowance of $20 (Canadian) per month to brother, Lumsden Affleck, 431½ Dudley Ave, Fort Range, Win[nipeg], Man[itoba].

December [1914]   Started work in Record Office

1915

29 January   Transferred to 2nd Battalion at Tidworth [? Probably a paper transaction].

8 February   Promoted to Acting SQMS in London

1 March   Transferred to 9th Battalion at Tidworth [? Probably a paper transaction]

[1 March   His father wrote to his brother, David, saying 'Had a letter
         from the Sergt to say he is well but very busy there[.] by now
      over 50 men on the Staff. He expects to be busier still as the
      casualty lists come in from the Canucks [Canadians] at the
         front....']
1 April   Promoted to Acting Sergeant in London
24 April   Promoted to Staff Sergeant in London
1 August   Stopped allowance to Lumsden Affleck for 'personal reasons'.
         [At some time after this, started assigning pay of $20
      (Canadian) per month to mother.]
1 November   Promoted to SQMS

1916

21 February[?]-   Admitted to 2nd London General Hospital, Chelsea, suffering
February [?]   from tonsillitis

6 or 8 March   Discharged to duty
9 March   Granted a pass in London for 10-16 March 1916
25 March   As a Staff Sergeant, had a medical re-examination in London
6 April   WO 1st Class Superintendent Clerk
[19 July   Wrote to brother David. Was living (billeted?) 'c/o Mrs
               Newsome , 12   Griffiths Rd, Wimbledon']
26 October   'Award: Brought to notice by Sec of State for War. Auth. WO
               Letter RL70 26-10-16.'

1917

24 February   Brought to notice of Secretary of State for War for valuable
               services in connection with thc War
1 March   Returned to Reserve Battalion, Shorncliffe. [This apparently a
               real move]
3 March   Reverted to the ranks [private] on return to unit at Seaford
14 March   Struck off strength to 6 Reserve Battalion
[14 March   Letter to brother David, as from C Company 6th Canadian
         Reserve Battalion, Seaford, Sussex. '.....I have been in the
      Brigade Hospital for 13 days with.....tonsillitis. I.....was just
      ready for draft. The draft left a few days after I was struck
      down......[I] ought to be in France inside a month.']
16 March   Taken on strength 6 Battalion at Seaford
3 April   Admitted to no 14 Canadian Hospital, [Seaford?] Medical
         history shown on admission sheet. Stated inter alia that he was
      'taken sick Sunday (1-4-17) with general malaise. This morning
      wakened up with sore throat - pains in body better he says.
      Family History unimportant. Past illnesses:- has had trouble
      with tonsils before - lanced about 1 yr ago; no other serious

illnesses. Venereal:- Neiser*   infection about 18 mths ago -
healed   [.....]' 'a well nourished young adult' 'moderate drinker
and smoker'; diagnosis: 'acute follicular tonsillitis, quinsy'
[*A Neiser infection does not necessarily imply sexual activity.]

25 April 1917   Transferred to Eastbourne for tonsillectomy
[28 April   Letter to brother David from the Canadian Military Hospital,
                       Eastbourne. Acknowledges David's letter and commiserates
          with his difficulties over the 'Tribunal'. [Part of the letter is
missing and so the details are not quite clear.] Did not think
much of Seaford but '...... [Eastbourne   ] is dandy.......[Bram] is
still at Ripon.....I don't think he will go out [to France?]
again.....[He] was taking a course in musketry, which......means
he will eventually become an instructor......']

2 May   Tonsils extracted
16 May   Discharged to duty
9 June   Made will, benefiting mother
21 June   Arrived at CBD [Canadian Base Details] France
11 July   Left CBD for 1Battalion
13 July   Arrived 1 Battalion
25 July   Joined 2 Battalion
13 September   Killed in action

               [Info from Commonwealth War Graves Commission]
                       Buried as William *Owen* Affleck of the Canadian Army,
               Eastern Ontario Regiment in Plot 1, Row R, Grave 2,
        Communal Cemetery Extension, Aix-Noulette, Pas de Calais,
        France. Aix-Noulette is 13 Kms south of Béthune on the main
        road to Arras. Take the D937 towards Béthune, turn R at the
        church in Aix-Noulette. The cemetery is a few 100 metres on
                       the LHS of the road to Bully-Grenay.]

1921
4 June   Memorial Cross sent to mother[.] Scroll despatched ['The
                       Memorial Cross was the gift of Canada issued as a memento for
        personal loss and sacrifice on the part of widows and mothers
        of Canadian sailors and soldiers who laid down their lives for
        their country during the War. It was silver, suspended on a
        purple ribbon' - information from the Medals Office of the
        Ministry of Defence, London.] 21June 1921 Plaque despatched
        [The plaque was made of bronze - information from the Medals
        Office of the Ministry of Defence, London.]
                       Apparently not eligible for 1914-15 Star, or the VM [Victory
                       Medal] or BWM [British War Medal]

The memorial at ELIE and inside ELIE Church give more details of his army career but not the date of his death

Rank on War Memorial is: 'Sergt-Major 2nd CEF' Pte in the 6th Canadian Reserves.' In other words his *substantive* rank throughout his military career was a private; the promotions were temporary or local.

William Given did not marry and had no children.

On the War Graves Commission memorial *Owen* is shown in error instead of *Given*.

George-Baram Affleck was born on the 17th July 1895 at 5 Rankeillor St, Elie.

The middle name is not easily explainable, as there are no obvious precedents.
Here are three possible reasons:

Annie Affleck writes (1995):

'...I asked my grandmother how to spell Bram's [ie Baram's] name & why she chose it, she said I always liked the name Bram & and just spelled it how it sounds, no other reason..'

Margaret Walker writes (Feb 1995):

'...The name Bram - I used to think it must be an abbreviation of Abraham - perhaps inspired by Abe Lincoln, otherwise that it came from Isabella Given's family.'

Sheila suggests it may really have been 'Durham.' This name is found in the Given family. (See above)

David Keir Affleck writes that the Minutes of Elie Town Council Roll of Honour for 1914 lists George B Affleck, Rankeillor Street as a painter and a private in the 7th Black Watch Territorials.

Below are two photographs: first, George-Baram and Lumsden, taken in 1951 at Walkerville, Ontario, Canada; second, George-Baram with his wife, Sarah and Tom Stevenson 'with his new car,' also taken in Canada in June, 1951.

Isabella Given Affleck, the last child of David Affleck and Tina Given, was born on the 14th June 1901.

She seems to have been quite a character: in 1985, when Sheila and I visited Elie, she was still remembered, five years after her death in Western General Hospital, Edinburgh on the 15th February 1980, as an avid follower of snooker on television. By that time she was a widow, having married twice. The following story is based on an account by Sheila's mother:

She was also known as 'Jenny', according to LHC Parish who described her as a 'Daisy'. She inherited the property at Elie [5 Rankeillor St] and apparently used to go to Methil monthly to collect a cheque from her brother, David. This procedure was carried out grim-faced on both sides. It seems she got hold of all the furniture and books after her brother's death and then sold them to buy a pub for her first husband, McQueen. He was a widower with two sons who were forthwith despatched into an orphanage. Isabella looked after her aged mother until the latter died in 1941 aged 88. It was only then that she married McQueen. She subsequently married Samuel Walker, a transport officer.
Widowed a second time, she lived in Earlsferry.

On the 1st June 1995 her niece Annie wrote:
    '...Aunt Jenny dads [sic] youngest sister lived with grandmother [Isobella Given] & married late in life. At a later date I will tell you about a visit, Pop,   'that [sic] what I always called my dad', took Tom [her husband] and I [sic] to   visit his cousins Bob Givens,& Tina, the last of a big family, it's a story in its'   [sic] self & one I will never forget...'
Unfortunately, she never told us the story!

Death cert:
            'Isabella Given Walker (nee Affleck)/Dist 414 Year 1980 Entry 18/
            Walker/Isabella Given (b 1901 6 mth 14 day) aged 78
        years/Occupation - Widowed Spouses/1)Robert John Naismith
        McQueen - Publican/Samuel Walker - Transport Officer/Died 1980
        February 15th 0510 hrs/Western General Hospital, Edinburgh/
            Residence/The Auld Hoose, Earlsferry/Father David Affleck Station
        Agent (deceased)/Mother Isabella Affleck ms Given
        (deceased).Carcinoma of the breast.'

Here is photo of Sheila outside the house at Earlsferry.

We come now to the eldest son, and Sheila's grandfather, David Affleck.
He was born on the 21st March 1877 at 9 High St Elie, the first child of David Affleck and Isobella Given. While his brothers Lumsden, William-Given and George-Baram moved to Canada, apparently in their twenties, David and his next brother John stayed in Scotland. He became in turn railway clerk, fruiterer, coal-weigher, and accountant. He was also a teacher. He painted the view of St Monance Church now at 7 Porthmeor Rd. He is alleged to have burned his call-up papers for WW1, stating that 'he was not prepared to fight for politicians.'

 It seems appropriate at this point to quote from his descendents. First, his youngest daughter, Annie, writing in 1996:

> '[He] Gave up his job in the railway on marriage, sold all their lovely things and bought tickets to sail to America (Kentucky). [His] Wife changed her mind since all her brothers and father had been drowned at sea when fishing. My Dad was the smartest of anyone we have known, a wonderful sense of humour, also impatient and irritable, above all honourable. Dad was strict and like a stranger, he wanted quiet to write and paint. I never really knew him till after Mum died.'

Next, his granddaughter, Margaret, writing in 1995:

> 'Mum [Isabella Given Affleck]... was confirmed before she married. It wasn't until I sorted through her photos when she died that it struck me that Grandad wasn't in any of the wedding photos & and only recently Dad's brother was able to explain that he would not enter a church. [quoting Anna "He believed religion to be dangerous, keeping people in ignorance and fear, but recognized a power in back of all manifestations."]...'

Finally, his grandson, David Keir Affleck, writing in 1996:

'A very talented man, skilled fiddle player, painter and poet. Would he have achieved more in his working life if the emigration had taken place? [See above for relevance.] The poem *The Sinking Ship* gives us an insight here.
We will never know. However, the heart disease of his wife affected family life from 1916 when Margaret the eldest daughter was taken out of school to care for Anna as a baby. Some of the paintings are in the possession of his heirs, for example Jenny McNaughton [née Affleck] had a painting of a woodland scene in 1996, He did not volunteer for war service and did not agree with the fights of the power groups. The poems *'Tammie'* and *'Wullie'* give us an insight into his thoughts on that disastrous time of the First World War. However, one does not get much of a feeling of family closeness with his brothers and sisters. Louie Affleck [née Parish] described him to me as a difficult man who warmed to her Cockney humour and character with a laugh and a comment that there was a 'Given' in her heart (a reference to his mother's family.) [In fact, LHC Parish confirmed that the remark was made to describe her own daughter, Sheila.]'

Here he is, with his future wife, Isabella Butters, in what looks to be an engagement photograph:

…and finally with John Parish, Anna Stevenson, Louie Parish and Sheila, taken about 1939 at Macduff's Castle, near St Monans.

The Butters

Much of what has been already said about the Afflecks is relevant to the Butters and their family links and lineage. Again, the East Neuk is their homeland since at least the 17th century.

According to George F Black, in *The Surnames of Scotland,* Butters and its variants are found in both Fife and Perthshire and may be connected with Buttergask, the name of a small settlement lying just south of the A9, between Stirling and Perth. Black says that the name is also recorded in Shetland in 1802, but that it is now extinct there. Butter was apparently the name of an old family of Perthshire, and Black cites a number of examples.

The picture below, by an unknown 19th century artist, and entitled *Old Buttar,* may or may not be a portrait of one of Sheila's ancestors.

The Butters Family

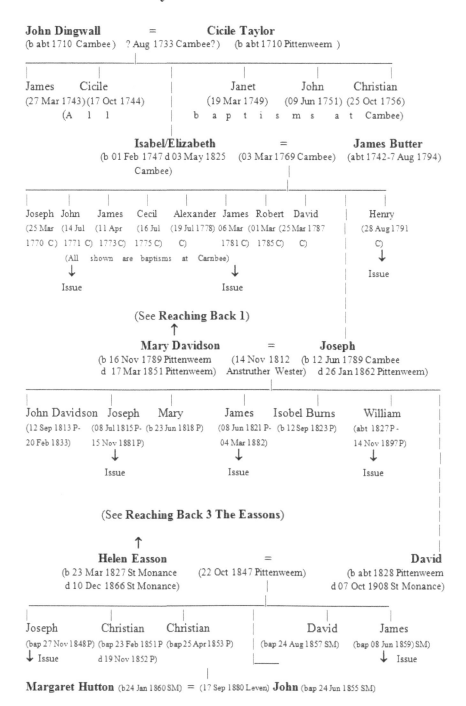

John Dingwall   =   Cicile Taylor
(b abt 1710 Cambee)   ? Aug 1733 Cambee?)   (b abt 1710 Pittenweem)

James	Cicile		Janet	John	Christian
(27 Mar 1743)	(17 Oct 1744)		(19 Mar 1749)	(09 Jun 1751)	(25 Oct 1756)

(A   l   l   b   a   p   t   i   s   m   s   a t   Cambee)

Isabel/Elizabeth   =   James Butter
(b 01 Feb 1747 d 03 May 1825   (03 Mar 1769 Cambee)   (abt 1742-7 Aug 1794)
Cambee)

Joseph	John	James	Cecil	Alexander	James	Robert	David		Henry
(25 Mar	(14 Jul	(11 Apr	(16 Jul	(19 Jul 1778)	06 Mar	(01 Mar	(25 Mar 1787		(28 Aug 1791
1770 C)	1771 C)	1773 C)	1775 C)	C)	1781 C)	1785 C)	C)		C)

(All   shown   are   baptisms   at   Carnbee)

↓   ↓   ↓
Issue   Issue   Issue

(See **Reaching Back 1**)
↑
Mary Davidson   =   Joseph
(b 16 Nov 1789 Pittenweem   (14 Nov 1812   (b 12 Jun 1789 Cambee
d 17 Mar 1851 Pittenweem)   Anstruther Wester)   d 26 Jan 1862 Pittenweem)

John Davidson	Joseph	Mary	James	Isobel Burns	William	
(12 Sep 1813 P-	(08 Jul 1815 P-	(b 23 Jun 1818 P)	(08 Jun 1821 P-	(b 12 Sep 1823 P)	(abt 1827 P-	
20 Feb 1833)	15 Nov 1881 P)		04 Mar 1882)		14 Nov 1897 P)	

↓   ↓   ↓
Issue   Issue   Issue

(See **Reaching Back 3 The Eassons**)

↑
Helen Easson   =   David
(b 23 Mar 1827 St Monance   (22 Oct 1847 Pittenweem)   (b abt 1828 Pittenweem
d 10 Dec 1866 St Monance)   d 07 Oct 1908 St Monance)

Joseph	Christian	Christian		David	James
(bap 27 Nov 1848 P)	(bap 23 Feb 1851 P)	(bap 25 Apr 1853 P)		(bap 24 Aug 1857 SM)	(bap 08 Jun 1859) SM)
↓ Issue		d 19 Nov 1852 P)			↓ Issue

Margaret Hutton (b 24 Jan 1860 SM) = (17 Sep 1880 Leven) **John** (bap 24 Jun 1855 SM)

John Dingwall and Cicile Taylor were married in 1733 but the first child of the marriage we know of was born in 1743. From this fact and the naming pattern of their children we can be fairly certain that there were others before 1743 whose births have not been recorded: one would have expected two other girls before Cicile and perhaps one other boy before James - representing two grandmothers and one grandfather.

As for the marriage between John and Cicile, we have only the first proclamation:

OPR Carnbee Co Fife (413/2) Marriages:
> '1733 July 22   John Dingwal in this Parish and Cicile Taylor in Pittenweem were proclamd. pro 1mo.'

The marriage does not appear on the Pittenweem register, yet that is where it would normally have taken place.

Isabel Dingwall was born and baptized on the same day. Perhaps there were fears for her life:

OPR Carnbee Co Fife:
> '1747 January 29th John Dingual Cicile Taylor had a daughter born and baptized 1st Febry: by name Isabel witt Jo: Thom. Ja. fyall.'

She married James Butter at the age of 22:

OPR CARNBEE Co Fife:
> '1769 March 3d. Jas. Butter & Isabel Digual Both in this parish after Regular proclamation were married the 3d of March.'

We know nothing of James's origins except that his father may have been named Joseph - a deduction made from the fact that James's first son was called by that name.
James and Isabel had a large family, nine of whom were boys, but it is clear that the first Joseph and the first James did not survive into adulthood. John, the second James and Henry, as well as the second Joseph all married and had children; the details are available on the database but because of lack of space they have not been introduced on the chart. Cecil, a form of Cecilia, was at this time more common as a name for girls, presumably owing its origins to the blind saint, Cecilia, patron saint of music.

John Butter(s) became a blacksmith and died in Edinburgh at the age of 81. His body was brought back to Carnbee for burial.
James Butter(s) lived even longer (88) and his death certificate shows that his mother was also known as Elizabeth. (Isabel was originally a Spanish version of Elizabeth.)

Death Cert:
> '1867 Anstruther Easter, Co. Fife (402/20) on December 9th at Anstruther Easter (3.30 pm) James Butter Aged 88. Farm Servant. Married to Elspeth Fleming Son of   James Butter, Church Officer (deceased) and

Elizabeth Butter M/S Dingwall (deceased)/Decay of Nature No Medical Attendant/Informant David Whitehill/N'bour/Present.

This entry shows that James senior had been a church servant - a paid official appointed by the elders of the kirk and the minister to look after the church.

Joseph, Sheila's ancestor, was born in 1789:

OPR Carnbee Co Fife:
> '1789 June 12th James Butter in Carnbee and Isabel Dangwall his wife had a son born the 12th June & baptd before the Congregation the 14th Currt named Joseph.'

Joseph must have retired from the sea, for on his death certificate he is shown as a fisherman.
He became married in 1812 to Mary Davidson (whose ancestry is to be considered later):

OPR Anstruther Wester Co Fife:
> '1812 Novr 14 Joseph Butter & Mary Davidson both of this Parish gave in their names for proclamation previous to Marriage.'

The actual marriage probably took place a few weeks later. Anstruther Easter lies on the coast, on one side of the Dreel Burn, and Anstruther Wester on the other side, a few miles north-east of Pittenweem. Mary and Joseph had seven children, five of whose births are recorded as follows:

OPR Pittenweem, Co Fife (452/2) Births, 1812-1838
> '1813 Septr. 12th   Joseph Butter & Mary Davidson had a son born the 12th and baptized on 19th of Septr. 1813. Childs name John Davidson. Witnesses John Davidson and Thomas Davidson.
>
> 1815 July 8th Joseph Butter and Mary Davidson had a Son born on the 8th & baptized on the 16th of July 1815. Childs name Joseph. Witnesses James Bowman & Thomas Adamson.
>
> 1818 June 23d. Joseph Butter & Mary Davidson had a Daughter born on the 23d. & baptized on the 30th of June 1818 Childs Name Mary. Witnesses   James Adam James Brown
>
> 1821 June 8th   'Joseph Butter & Mary Davidson had a Son born on the 8th and baptized on the 20th of June 1821. Childs name James. Witnesses the Revd. Mr Addie & James Adam.
>
> 1823 September 12th Joseph Butter & Mary Davidson had a Daughter born on

the 12th and baptized 28th September 1823. Childs name Isabel Burns
Witnesses The Revd. Mr.Taylor & David [sic]'

The births of William and David will be discussed a little later on.

It is curious that the first child seems to have been named (as we shall see later) after his *maternal* grandfather; one solution might have been that the John Davidson who was a witness *was* this grandfather. It turns out, however, that the grandfather in question had died on the 15th November 1813. The child seems therefore to have been named in his memory. The witness must have been Mary's brother.
The anomaly continues: the next child is named Joseph, not James. Now, James, the child's paternal grandfather, had been dead for twenty years, so perhaps it seemed appropriate to use the child's father's name instead.
Having used the father's name, it seemed suitable to use the mother's name for the next child, a girl.
In 1821 another boy was born and at last the child's paternal grandfather receives recognition: James
Next comes 'Isobel Burns' Butters and a clue here may be that on 30 June 1776 an Isabel Burns was baptized at Pittenweem, daughter of William Burns and Isabel Davidson. She may be a relation, but no firm connection to Sheila's family has been observed.

Now for William; neither his birth nor baptism is recorded, although it has been assumed in the Family Search records that he was born in 1824. This does not, however, square with the 1881 Census:

1881 Census, West Shore Street, Pittenweem:

'Butter William	Head	M	54	M	Fisherman	Fife	Pittenweem
Butter Betsy	Wife	M	54	F		do	do
Butter William	Son	U	24	M	Fisherman	do	do
Butter Jessie	Daur	U	17	F	Net Mender	do	do
Butter Isabella	Daur	-	14	F	Net Mender	do	do

where a birth year of 1827 is implied.

David's birth too is unrecorded but we have a Census record:

1881 Census St Monance, East End (part of the Gay household.)

'Butter	David	Head	W	54	M	Fisherman	Fife	Pittenweem [therefore dob = c1827]
Easson	Agnes	SisL	U* 51	F		Houskeep+	Fife	St Monance
Butter	James	Son	U	21	M	Fisherman	do	do

[* This is probably incorrect and should read W (= widow). She was the sister of Helen Easson (dec) and had been married to James Mathison, reverting to

215

her maiden name after her husband's death (although his death has not yet been discovered.)]

The 1851 census gives his age as 23 (born 1828)

But his detailed death certificate disagrees with both of these:

Death cert:
> '..(1am) at East Braehead, St Monance/..aged 74 [b1834].Fisherman/
> **Widower of Helen Easson/ [son of] Joseph Butters, Fisherman (deceased) and of Mary Butters M/S Davidson (deceased)**/Cancer of Throat, 3 months/As certified by R.J.Pirie L.R.C.P./James Butters, son/Coalwynd, St Monance.'

The **bold characters** make it clear that we have the right David. However, see below:

'OPR Pittenweem, Co. fife (452/4) Marriages
> 1847 October 22nd David Butter and Helen Easton [sic] both residing in this parish having been regularly proclaimed in order to marriage and no objections being offered were married on the 22d. October 1847 by the Revd. D.L.Foggo, Minister of Abercrombie. [ie, St Monance]'

This last entry seems to rule out the date of 1834 for David's birth, unless he was married at the age of 13 - unlikely in the 19th century.

There has been so much conflicting evidence about the Butters family that I have reviewed the facts several times and have come to accept as correct the ancestry line that I have given above. The Butters story from now on is straightforward but at times tragic.

David Butters married Helen Easson on the 22nd of October 1847. The details are given three paragraphs above. They had five children, as follows:

OPR Pittenweem, Co. fife (452/4) Births
> '1848 Novr. 27th David Butters, Fisherman, Pitenweem and Helen Easton his wife had a Son born on the 27th Novr.1848 and baptized in Decr. following by the Revd. John Cooper, Minister of Pitenweem Childs name Joseph. Witnesses John Eeaston [sic] and Joseph Butter.'

Joseph was conventionally named after his paternal grandfather

The next child, Christian, named after her maternal grandmother, was baptized on the 23rd February 1851 and died on the 19th February 1852, from croup.

Another girl, also named Christian, was born in 1853 and a second son, John, in 1855.

Then came David in 1857 and James in 1859.

Helen, their mother, died in 1866:

Death cert: '11 am..Aged 40. Married to David Butter, Fisherman..[father]John
    Easson, Fisherman (deceased..Christian Easson M/S Duncan deceased)
    /Gastric Fever, 6 weeks/Debility/As certified by John Todd L.R.C.S.
    Edinr./Colinsburgh/   David Butter (his X mark). Widower. (not present).

We will return to Helen and David after reviewing those of their ancestors so far
unmentioned.

Reaching Back (1)

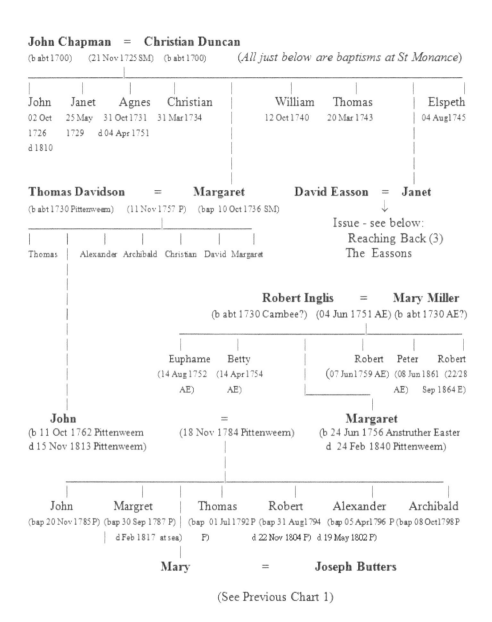

John Chapman = **Christian Duncan**

(b abt 1700)   (21 Nov 1725 SM)   (b abt 1700)   *(All just below are baptisms at St Monance)*

John	Janet	Agnes	Christian		William	Thomas	Elspeth
02 Oct	25 May	31 Oct 1731	31 Mar 1734		12 Oct 1740	20 Mar 1743	04 Aug1745
1726	1729	d 04 Apr 1751					
d 1810							

Thomas Davidson = **Margaret**   **David Easson** = **Janet**

(b abt 1730 Pittenweem)   (11 Nov 1757 P)   (bap 10 Oct 1736 SM)

Issue - see below:
Reaching Back (3)
The Eassons

Thomas	Alexander	Archibald	Christian	David	Margaret

Robert Inglis = **Mary Miller**

(b abt 1730 Carnbee?)   (04 Jun 1751 AE) (b abt 1730 AE?)

Euphame	Betty		Robert	Peter	Robert
(14 Aug 1752	(14 Apr 1754		(07 Jun1759 AE)	(08 Jun1861	(22/28
AE)	AE)			AE)	Sep 1864 E)

John   =   **Margaret**

(b 11 Oct 1762 Pittenweem   (18 Nov 1784 Pittenweem)   (b 24 Jun 1756 Anstruther Easter
d 15 Nov 1813 Pittenweem)   d 24 Feb 1840 Pittenweem)

John	Margret		Thomas	Robert	Alexander	Archibald
(bap 20 Nov 1785 P)	(bap 30 Sep 1787 P)		(bap 01 Jul 1792 P	(bap 31 Aug1 794	(bap 05 Apr1796 P	(bap 08 Oct1798 P
	d Feb 1817 at sea)		P)	d 22 Nov 1804 P)	d 19 May 1802 P)	

Mary   =   **Joseph Butters**

(See Previous Chart 1)

218

The surname Duncan and its variants occur quite frequently in the Butters narrative. It is a common name in Scotland and it is generally not possible to see how the various persons in this story are related.

Here, the marriage between John Chapman and Christian Duncan is simply recorded:

OPR St Monance Co. Fife (454/1) Marriages:
    'John Chapman & Christian Duncan Contrd. married afterward.'

Two of the daughters from this marriage turn out, as we shall see, to be Sheila's ancestors. Burial registers from this period do not generally survive but two of the children of the marriage figure in the St Monance archive for obvious reasons:

ST MONANCE Death Reg:
    '1810 [undated] John Chapman an old man was buried' [aged about 84]
and

ST MONANCE Death Reg:
    '1751 April 4th Agnes Chapman a young woman died' [aged 19]

It seems likely that the first-named Janet must also have died young, some time before 1743. The marriage of the second Janet to David Easson and their descendents will be considered in the next section.

Margaret's marriage was probably celebrated in St Monance but we have only the Pittenweem evidence:

OPR PITTENWEEM, Co Fife (452/2) Births/Marriages intermixed:
    '1757 October 15th Thomas Davidson in this Parish & Margaret Chapman in
    the Parish of St Monance were contracted and married Novbr. 11th'

We know that Thomas Davidson was a fisherman or sailor because:

OPR PITTENWEEM, Co Fife (452/2) Births/Marriages intermixed:
    '1760 July 20th Thomas Davidson and Margaret Chapman his Spouse had their
    Son (b. 18th) baptd. and called Thomas; which child was presented by John
    Chapman the Grandfather who became Sponsor in the *Father's absence at
    Sea.* [my italics] Witnesses Matthew Henderson and Andrew Mason.'

For his second son Thomas was ashore:

OPR PITTENWEEM Co Fife   Births Baptisms:
    '1762 October 17th Thomas Davidson   [&] Margrat Chapman his spouse had
    their son (b 11) baptized and called John witnesses William Mclod [sic]   [or
    Melvel?] & James Hugh'

Thomas was also available for the baptisms of his next four children; but for Margaret:

OPR PITTENWEEM (452/2) Births/Marriages intermixed:
'1780 May 5th Thomas Davidson & Margt Chapman had a Child born 5th May & baptized the 7th called Margaret. The father being absent at sea James Anderson stood Sponsor Witnesses John Nicholson & Willm. Melvill.'

James Anderson is probably a younger brother of the baby's grandfather.

We turn for a moment to the Inglis family
'Inglis' and its variants mean 'English' and as a name is found in mediaeval documents. Thus the fact that an 18th century ancestor holds the name does not imply immediate English parentage. Here is the entry for the marriage of Robert Inglis and Mary Miller:

OPR ANSTRUTHER EASTER, Co Fife:
'1751 June 4th. May 4th Robert Ingles in the parish of Carnbee and Mary Miller in this Parish contracted Mar: June 4th.'

Their first child was named Euphame, presumably after Mary Miller's mother. This was at the time quite a popular name for a girl in Scotland. The origin is a fourth century martyr and saint, Euphemia.

Here is the relevant entry for the birth of their second daughter:

OPR Anstruther Easter, Co. Fife (402/2) Births/Baptisms
'1754 Born 28 Bapt. 30th April Parents Names: Robt.Ingles [sic], Land labourer Mary Miller A Daughter: Betty Witnesses: Archibd. Brown, Slater John Hodge, Baxter'

'Baxter' means baker.

There are two sons named Robert in the family and we assume that the first died when young. It should be mentioned, however, that parents have been known to give two children the same name when the first is still living. Although this is quite rare, one can never be absolutely certain, without a death or burial entry, that the first has died before the birth of the second.

We now catch up with the Davidsons because Margaret Inglis and John were married in 1784:

OPR PITTENWEEM Co Fife:
'1784 Novr 18th John Davidson, Sailor in this Parish & Margreat [sic] Inglis were Contracted on the 12th Proclaimed on the 14th & Married 18th Novr 1784.'

John had followed in his father's footsteps.

Of John and Mary's children at least one was drowned at sea:

PITTENWEEM Deaths 452/2:
'1817 Feby 8th On Saturday 8th of Feby instant A Boat called the Paton belonging to this place sailed from Inverkeithing in a gale of wind and has never been heard at this date the 17th Feby the Crew were four in Number viz. John West **Thomas Davidson** Alexr. Grieve & James Watt Jnr.'

There were at least two other tragedies in the family:

PITTENWEEM Deaths:
'1802 May 19th John Davidson had a Son called Archibald who died of a Croup'

and

PITTENWEEM Deaths:
'1804 Novr 22d Alex. Davidson Son of John Davidson'   [aged eight]

It will be noted that John and Margaret named their first two children after themselves; the pattern then proceeds more conventionally. The last two boys are named after brothers of their paternal grandfather.

We have already seen that Margaret Davidson married Joseph Butters.

It is time to wind back the clock again.

Reaching Back (2)

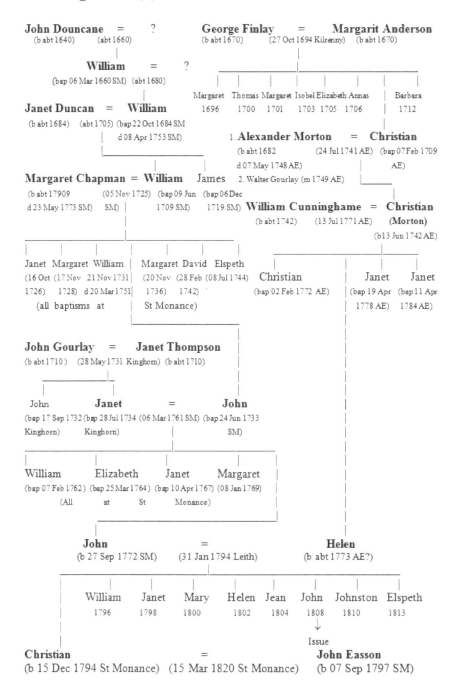

The spelling of the first *Douncane* probably illustrates the manner John spoke his name;

from hereon the usual *Duncan* is found. His wife is unknown.
The baptism of William, John's son, is recorded but his mother is not named:

OPR ST MONANCE, Co Fife:
      '1660 March 6 The qlk day John Douncane had a child baptized called
      William...[illegible]' [*qlk* = 'which']

The next William may have married a cousin but the wedding is not found in the archives.
His baptism is recorded:

OPR St Monance Co Fife:
      '1684 Octr 22   Wm Duncan in St monants had a child baptized Called Wm
      various witnesses being pnt.'

as is his death:

ST MONANCE Death Reg:
      '1753 April 8th Willm. Duncan an Old Man died' [59 - is this the same person?]

William and Janet had two sons (recorded) and the elder was yet another William:

OPR St Monance Co Fife:
      '1709 January 9th William son of William Duncan & Janet Duncan Baptized
      January 9th.'

This William a Margaret Chapman:

OPR St Monance Co Fife:
      '1725 Novbr 5th Wm Duncan & Margt Chapman. Contrd Octb5 10th. Married
      Novbr 5th 1725.'

We may have a record of Margaret's death, if she retained her unmarried name:

ST MONANCE Death Reg:
 '1773 May 23th [sic] Margaret Chapman an old woman died'

Margaret gave birth to seven children; her eldest son, William's, death is recorded:

ST MONANCE   Death Reg:
      '1751 March 20th William Duncan a young Married [man] died'

The next child, John, was born in 1733:

OPR St Monance Co Fife:

'1733 June 24th John son of William Duncan & Margt.Chapman Baptized
June 24th'

John married Janet Gourlay, whose parents came from Kinghorn, a town lying on the coast
between Kirkaldy and Burntisland and thus some distance from St Monance.

Baptism. OPR KINGHORN, Co Fife (439/3) Births/Baptisms:
'1734 Julie 28   Janet daur lawll [lawful?]to John Gourlay and Janet thomson in
this parish was baptized. witnesses John Hoggan. William Bruce'

Marriage. OPR KINGHORN, Co Fife (439/3) Marriages:
' 1731 May 9th John Gourlay in this parish and Janet Thomson in the Parish of
Kirkaldie being Contracted were this day proclaimed in order to marriage pro pro
[?], May 16 pro 2do and May 23d pro 3tio and were married the 28th   May after
witnesses James Gourlay and Robert Greig.'

The marriage between John and Janet is shown in the St Monance register but not at
Kinghorn, where it probably took place:

OPR St Monance Co.Fife ((454/1) Marriages:
1761 March 5th John Duncan and Janet Gourlay were contracted
..[illegible]..February & after regular proclamation married March 6th 1761.'

John Duncan is the last of five children known from this marriage:

OPR St Monance, Co Fife (545/2) Baptisms
'1772 Octbr. 4th John son of John Duncan & Janet Gourley Born 27th Septbr.
& Baptized 4th Octobr. 1772'

John married Helen Cunninghame. To see her ancestors we have to scroll back once more
to the final years of the seventeenth century.

George Finlay and Margarit Anderson were married on the 27th October 1694 at Kilrenny.
Now, Kilrenny has already appeared in the narrative - it is where some of the Lumsden
family lived in the 19th century. It lies a few miles inland from the Firth of Forth, northeast
of Anstruther Easter. The marriage is also recorded in the register at Crail, the next town up
the coast

The couple's first child, Margaret, was baptized at Kilrenny:

OPR St Monance, Co Fife (545/2) Baptisms:OPR Kilrenny, Co Fife:
'1696 Feb 1 George Finlaw and Margaret Anderson had Margaret. Witnesses
Thomas Finlaw and Robert [illegible]

A daughter, born in 1706, was called Annas, according to the IGI. This may be a dialect form of Anna, or may be an error in transcription.

Most of the children were a baptized at Anstruther Easter, including the next but youngest, Christian:

OPR ANSTRUTHER EASTER Co Fife (402/2) Baptisms:
>'1709 ffeb 8 George ffinlay and Margaret Anderson had a laull [lawful?]
>daughter bap: called Christian the wit: John Kemp and Alexander paton.[?]'

Christian married an Alexander Morton in 1741:

Marriage. OPR AE,   Co Fife (402/2) Marriages:
>'1741 July 25 Alexr. Morton & Christian Finlay both in this Parish contracted.'

We know that William was 59 when he married because when he died seven years later his age was given:

OPR Anstruther Easter, Co Fife (402/2) Deaths:
>'1748 May 7 Alexr Morton, Landlabourer. Aged 66 of old Age.'

There was one child from this marriage:

Baptism. OPR AE, Co Fife (402/2) Births/Baptisms:
>'1742 Born 13 Bap 18 June To Alexr. Morton, Land Labourer and Christian
>Finlay a daughter Christian. Witnesses David Murray, Gardner & John
>Turben, Land Lab.'

There is a slight mystery here. For the time, Christian Finlay, at the age of 32 married quite late, and to a much older man. The birth of their daughter nearly a year later does not seem to have required a speedy wedding; (as a matter of fact, their actual marriage, as opposed to a contract, is not recorded.) Perhaps Christian had had a previous marriage at an earlier age.
She certainly had a *later* marriage:

OPR ANSTRUTHER E Co Fife (402/2) Marriages:
>'1749 Augt 19 Walter Gourlay in ye Parish of Carnbee & Christian Finlay in
>this Parish contracted. Married Septr. 2d.'

and in Carnbee

OPR CARNBEE Co Fife (413/2) Marriages:
>'1749 August 20th Walter Gourlay in this parish and Christian Finely [sic] in
>Anstruther East'r parish were proclaimed and Married 2d. Septr.'

There were apparently no children from this second marriage.

Christian Morton married William Cunninghame:

Marriage. OPR AE, Co Fife (402/2) Marriages:
'1771 June 15
     William Cuninghame [underlined] in the parish of Carnbie &
     Christian Morton in this Parish Contracted. Married July --th.'
The actual date has an ink blot over it but it could be the 13th.
William and Christian had four recorded children. Here are details of the first, third and
fourth:

Baptism. OPR AE, Co Fife (402/2) Births/Baptisms:
     '1772 Born Jan 31 Bapt Feby 2 To William Cunningham, Labourer and
     Christian Morton a Daugtr. Christian Witnesses James Pitbladdo, Labourer
     and James Robertson Weaver.'

Baptism. OPR AE, Co Fife (402/2) Births/Baptisms:
     '1778 April 16[th] Janet daughter to William Cuningham, Labourer and Christian
     Morton born 16th April and Baptized 19th.'

Baptism. OPR AE, Co Fife (402/2) Births/Baptisms:
     '1784 April 11   William Cuningham and Christian Morton Spouses had a
     Daughter baptized Born the 9th Cur[ren]t and named Janet.'

The first Janet almost certainly died young.

As for the second daughter, Helen, we have a problem in that there is no record of her birth
or baptism. Mrs Corkerton comments:

     'There is only 1 baptism listed for November 1772 and 2 for December 1772.
     There are only 14 listed between January and 11th April 1773 and thereafter
     none until 6th June when there are approximately 2 entries a month. The
     register appears to be more regularly kept from February 1774 onwards, which
     may explain why there is no entry for Helen circa 1773.'

There is, however, record of a marriage between Helen Cunningham and John Duncan:

OPR ST MONANCE, Co Fife:
     '1794 Jan. 31st. John Duncan in this parish and Helen Cunningham in the parish
of [blank] were married at Leith by the revd. Mr Johnson Minr. there   Jan 31st.'

The fact that the marriage took place in Leith may indicate a clandestine marriage - usually
meaning that the banns had not been called in the appropriate parishes. It appears that the
result was usually a fine imposed by the elders who would then accept the marriage as
legal. John and Helen had a very large family. The first daughter, Christian, is Sheila's
ancestor and here are birth details:

OPR St Monance, Co Fife (454/2) Baptisms:

'1794 Decr 21st Christian, daughter of John Duncan and Helen Cunninghame was born Decr15th and baptized Dec 21th [sic]'

Christian married into the Easson family, to which we must now turn.

Reaching Back (3) The Eassons

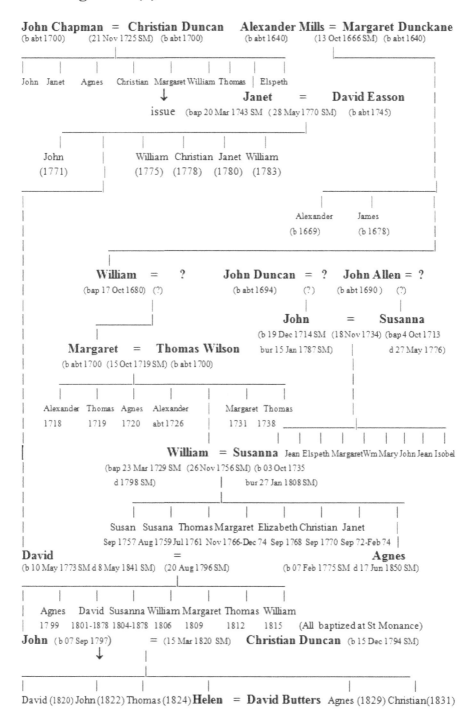

John Chapman = **Christian Duncan** **Alexander Mills** = **Margaret Dunckane**
(b abt 1700)   (21 Nov 1725 SM) (b abt 1700)   (b abt 1640)   (13 Oct 1666 SM) (b abt 1640)

John   Janet   Agnes   Christian Margaret William Thomas   Elspeth

↓   **Janet**   =   **David Easson**

issue (bap 20 Mar 1743 SM (28 May 1770 SM)   (b abt 1745)

John   William Christian Janet   William
(1771)   (1775)   (1778)   (1780)   (1783)

Alexander   James
(b 1669)   (b 1678)

William = ?   **John Duncan** = ? **John Allen** = ?
(bap 17 Oct 1680) (?)   (b abt 1694)   (?)   (b abt 1690)   (?)

John   =   **Susanna**
(b 19 Dec 1714 SM (18 Nov 1734) (bap 4 Oct 1713
bur 15 Jan 1787 SM)   d 27 May 1776)

Margaret = **Thomas Wilson**
(b abt 1700 (15 Oct 1719 SM) (b abt 1700)

Alexander Thomas Agnes Alexander   Margaret Thomas
1718   1719   1720 abt 1726   1731   1738

William = **Susanna** Jean Elspeth Margaret Wm Mary John Jean Isobel
(bap 23 Mar 1729 SM (26 Nov 1756 SM) (b 03 Oct 1735
d 1798 SM)   bur 27 Jan 1808 SM)

Susan Susana Thomas Margaret Elizabeth Christian Janet
Sep 1757 Aug 1759 Jul 1761 Nov 1766-Dec 74 Sep 1768 Sep 1770 Sep 72-Feb 74

David   =   **Agnes**
(b 10 May 1773 SM d 8 May 1841 SM) (20 Aug 1796 SM)   (b 07 Feb 1775 SM d 17 Jun 1850 SM)

Agnes David Susanna William Margaret Thomas William
1799 1801-1878 1804-1878 1806   1809   1812   1815   (All baptized at St Monance)

John (b 07 Sep 1797)   = (15 Mar 1820 SM) **Christian Duncan** (b 15 Dec 1794 SM)
↓

David (1820) John (1822) Thomas (1824) **Helen** = **David Butters** Agnes (1829) Christian(1831)

We have already come across the Chapmans (see **Reaching Back 1**) and here we meet them again showing another direct line to the Butters.

John Chapman and Christian Duncan married in St Monance on the 21st of November 1725:

OPR St Monance Co. Fife (454/1) Marriages:
        'John Chapman & Christian Duncan Contrd. married afterward.'

Christian's family were probably related in some way to the Duncans we have already met and those we shall come across later (who also came from St Monance.)

John and Christian had a large family and a few provide extra information; for example, the eldest son, whose death is recorded:

ST MONANCE Death Reg:
        '1810 [undated] John Chapman an old man was buried' [aged 84].

The next child, Janet, must have died young, because another of the same name was born 14 years years later.
Certainly the third child, Agnes, did not reach full maturity:

ST MONANCE Death Reg:
        '1751 April 4th Agnes Chapman a young woman died' [aged 20]

For Margaret Chapman's link to the Butters see **Reaching Back (1).**

Thomas and Jannet Chapman were twins:

  OPR St Monance, Co Fife (454/2) Baptisms
        '1743 March 20th Thomas & Janet Children of John Chapman & Christ.
        Duncan Baptized March 20th 1743'

Janet became the wife of David Easson:

OPR ST MONANCE, Co Fife:
        '1770 May 28th. David Easson & Janet Chapman, both in this Parish of St
        Monance were contracted 26th May 1770 and after due Proclamation were
        married 28th May.'

She died in 1811:

ST MONANCE Death Reg:
        '1811 May Janet Chapman an old woman was buried' [aged 68]

Janet and David had six known children. Omitting for now David, the second child, they were:

OPR St Monance, Co Fife (454/2) Baptisms
'1771 March 16th John son of David Easson & Jannet Chapman Born 16th [sic] March & Baptized 16th [sic] March 1771'

OPR St Monance, Co Fife (454/2) Baptisms
'1775 Augt 6th William Son of David Esson [sic] & Janet Chapman born 3th and Baptized 6th Augt. 1775'

who died two years later:

St Monance Parish Register:
1777 Decemr 4th William Easson a child died Small pox'

Next:

Christian, baptized 24 May 1778. She must have been a worry to her parents. She produced an illegitimate child, baptized Christian on the 17 May 1795. She had already been accused of 'uncleanness' in 1792. In 1798 she was again called to account at another Sessions meeting. Was this for the birth of another child?   It must therefore have seemed to the parish that justice finally caught up with her:

St Monance Burial Records:
'1800 [no date] Christian Easson a young woman died in Child Bed.'

Janet, the next child, was baptized on the 25th October 1780, but:

OPR St Monance
'1781 June 23th [sic] died Janet Easson a Child small pox'

Finally, a second William, baptized on the 20th July 1783, seems to have survived into adulthood.

Now we must return to the mid 17th century to pick up a few more threads.

Another Duncan from St Monance appears:

OPR ST MONANCE.Co.FIFE (454/1) Marriages
'1666 October 13 Alex Miln [Mills?] and Margaret Dunckane bote in this   perish was contracted and promising to observe good order and to accomplish   sd. marriage witin ye ordinaire time consigned'

The couple have three children recorded:

OPR ST MONANCE, Co Fife:
'1669 August 15 Alexr.Mill in Stmonance had a child baptized Alexander   Several witnesses p[rese]nt.'

Next:

OPR ST MONANCE Co Fife:
'1678 March 31 Alexander Mill had a child bapized on ye 31 March called James'

Finally:

OPR St Monance Co Fife
'1680 October 17 Alexander Mill had a son baptized before the congregation called William.'

The name of William Mills' wife is not recorded but the marriage of what seems to be his only child is shown:

OPR ST MONANCE Co FIFE (454/1) Marriages:
'1719 October 15th   Thos Wilson & Margt. Mill married.'

In 1763 Margaret died and was buried in St Monance

OPR ST MONANCE
'1763 Feby 8 For the best Mortcloth to Margaret Mill [sic] spouse to Thomas Willison [sic]   4s. 0'

Mortcloths were used in Scotland (and elsewhere) for the burial of the dead, instead of coffins. The parish had several of these for hire, and that is the figure shown above, except that the sum is shown as Scots shillings, worth about 4d   in English money of the time (ie about 2p in today's currency. The same mortcloth was used many times.
Some people did not use the parish mortcloth for burial. Prosperous and important families may have had their own family mortcloth, some trades paid into charitable funds with their own mortcloth. In parishes where mortcloth dues are the only evidence of burial, such cases might have gone unrecorded. Sometimes there was no charge for use of the parish mortcloth, particularly if the family were poor.
It seems that there were grades of mort cloth: New, Plush, Best and Children.

Margaret had borne at least seven children. Here are some of them, starting with the second:

OPR St Monance Co Fife (454/2) Births/Baptisms:
' 1719 Septbr. 1st Thomas son of Walter Wilson & Margt Mill Baptiz'd Septbr. 1st 1719.'

The showing of 'Walter' as the father is almost certainly a scribal error.

Here is the death of Agnes:

ST MONANCE Death Reg:
'1786 June 18th Agnes Wilson an aged woman was buried'

and Margaret:

ST MONANCE Death Reg:
[1806] 'Margaret   Wilson an old woman was buried'

and Thomas:

OPR St Monance
'1789 Decemr. 14thThomas Wilson a middle aged man was buried
3d' [I think this must be in English currency]

William Wilson, the fourth son, was baptized in 1729:

OPR St Monance Co Fife:
'1729 March 23rd William son of Thomas Wilson & Margt. Mill. Baptized
March 23rd 1729.'

William married Susanna Duncan (yet another Duncan) in 1756:

OPR St Monace Co Fife:
'1756 Novbr 26th William Wilson & Susan Duncan both in this parish
Contracted October 30th & after Regular proclamation Married Novbr 26th
1756.'

Susanna was one of nine children born to John Duncan and Susanna Allen.

OPR ELIE Co Fife:
'1735 Octr 3d Susanna lawfull Daughter to John Duncan and Susanna   Allan
his spouse (born 3d) was baptized Octr 6th. Witnesses William Duncan,   John
Allen.[grandfather?]'

I have no explanation for her being baptized at Elie (the next town to the west along the
coast.)
The next girl died aged five:

ST MONANCE Death Reg:
>   '1752 June 21st Jean Duncan a Girl died'

William also died young:

ST MONANCE Deaths Reg:
>   '1749 Janry 22 William Duncan a Child Died smallpox'

Susanna Duncan herself survived into old age:

ST MONANCE Death Reg:
>   '1808 Jany 23d Susanna Duncan an old woman was buried'

Dealing briefly with Susanna's forebears, her father, John Duncan, had married Susanna Allen:

OPR St Monance Co Fife:
>   '1734 Novbr 18th John Duncan & Susan Allan Contrd Octbr 6th Married Novbr 18th 1734.'

John's baptism is recorded and his father's name; but not his mother's:

OPR St Monance Co Fife:
>   '1714 December 19th John son of John Duncan in St Monance Baptized December 19th.'

He died in 1787:

ST MONANCE Death Reg:
>   '1787 Jany 15th John Ducan [sic] an old man was buried' [aged 73].

Susanna's baptism is also recorded and her father's name, but not her mother's:

OPR St Monance Co Fife:
>   '1713 Octbr 4th Susanna Daughter of John Allan fisher in St Monance Baptized Octbr 4th.'

She died in 1776:

ST MONANCE Death Reg:
>   '1776 May 27th Susanna Allan an aged woman died' [aged 63]

Now for the children of   William Wilson and Susanna Duncan.
Two of their children died young:

St Monance Parish Burial Register:
>   '1774 Decr 15   Margt. Wilson a child   2s.0' [mortcloth]

and

OPR ST Monance, Co Fife (454/2) Baptisms
>   '1772 Septembr 2d   Janet daughter of William Willson [sic] & Susanna
>   Duncan Born 2nd Septembr. & Baptized 3d. Septembr. 1772'

Two years later:

St Monance Parish Register:
>   '1774 Feb 22th [sic] died Janet Wilson a child'

If it seems strange that William and Susanna gave two consecutive children similar names (Susan/Susana), almost certainly the first child died young.

The last child, Agnes, was born in 1775:

OPR St Monance, Co Fife (454/2) Baptisms
>   '1775 Febry 9th Agnes daughter of William Wilson and Susanna Duncan was
>   born 7th Febry   and baptized 9th Febry 1775'

She married David Easson:

OPR ST MONANCE, Co Fife (454) Marriages:
>   '1796 Augt. 20th   David Easson, Junior and Agnes Wilson both in this parish
>   were contracted and married 20th Augt. 1796. because he was going
>   immediately to sea, and therefore were three times proclaimed before the
>   Congregation and married after Sermon being upon the Saturday before the
>   Sacrament.'

A hasty marriage, but not for the usual reason!

David and Agnes had eight children, the eldest of which, John, will call for our attention shortly.
Of the other seven, here is some information.

We have details (taken from Monumental Inscriptions East Fifeshire (9/1.56) by John Fowler Mitchell) of the gravestone in St Monance churchyard which tells about David and his family:

David Eason mariner here 31.12 1878 (78), w[ife] Mary Peattie ....56; 8 ch[ildren].
Ann b. 7 1842 (10m); Agnes E. 14.4.1889 (57); Rose E. 18.3.1896   (68); Elspeth
E...4.1898 (58); Mary E. 26.11.1903 (59)

The information is not complete and rather confusing and I have edited it here and there to
make it clearer.

Susanna:
Death cert:
>   '1878 St. Monance, Co. Fife (454/9) on June 29th (4am) at St Monance
>   Susan Easson   Aged 72. Single Daughter of   David Easson, Seaman
>   (deceased) and of Agnes Easson M/S Wilson (deceased)
>   Cause of death Unknown. No medical attendant Informant John Robertson. St
>   Monance. Grandson [? She was single] Not present'

The first William must have died as a child.

Now for John (a fisherman.) He married Christian Duncan. (See **Reaching Back 2**.)

OPR St Monance Co Fife:
>   '1820 March 19th (contracted 18th) John Eason and Christian Duncan both in
>   this Parish were after due proclamation married 19th ditto by the Rev Mr   Robert
Swan.'

The reason for *this* hasty marriage must have been obvious at the time - Christian was
pregnant with her first child, David who was baptized on the 6th of September 1820.
David was a fisherman and he lived until 1888. Three of his six children died young.
and here is the inscription on his tombstone:

St Monance Churchyard
>   David Easson 29.4.1888 (67), w[ife]. Janet Scott da[ughter] Christina 5.6.1850
>   (23m[onths]). s[on] Philip 26.9.1855 (4m[onths]), s[on] David 17.10.1855 (3
>   [months])

John, the next son, was also a fisherman had   five sons who followed in their father's
footsteps.

David's first daughter was Helen:

St Monance Parish Register:
>   '1827 Born March 23rd 1827 Helen, daughter of John Eason [sic] and
>   Christian Duncan and baptized 31st ditto by the Rev. Robert Swan'

At this point we rejoin the Butters family with the marriage of Helen Easson and David Butters:

'OPR Pittenweem, Co. fife (452/4)
> Marriages 1847 October 22nd David Butter and Helen Easton [sic] both residing in this parish having been regularly proclaimed in order to marriage and no objections being offered were married on the 22d. October 1847 by the Revd. D.L.Foggo, Minister of Abercrombie. [sc "St Monance"]'

Here again, from the first chart, are Helen and David with the next generation:

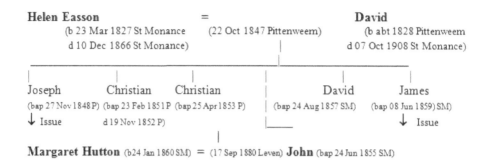

Before we move over to the ancestors of Margaret Hutton, a few words about John Butters. The fourth child of Helen Easson and David Butters and baptized at St Monance, he became a fisherman like his father and his elder brother, Joseph.

In 1880 he married Margaret Hutton:

Marriage of John Butters and Margaret Hutton:
> '1880 Scoonie, Co Fife (456/15) on September 17th at Leven. after Banns according to the Forms of the United Presbyterian Church. John Butters... Aged 24. Fisherman. Bachelor Usual residence St Monance. Son of David   Butters, Fisherman and of Helen Butters M[aiden].S[urname] Easson   (deceased) Margaret Hutton.. Aged 20. Spinster Usual res. St   Monance..[daughter] of William Hutton Lab[ourer]   Brewery (dec) Witnesses   James Kerr and Christian Gay'

It is not clear why Margaret's mother, Isabella Forgan, is not shown.
A few months later the couple appear on the 1881 Census:

1881 Census, St Monance, West End, immediately after Isabella Hutton (Forgan):

'Butter   John   Head   M   25   M   [where born] Fife   ST MONANCE
   do   Margaret Wife   M   21   F   do   do

Then there appears a daughter:

Statistical Records: Birth of Isabella Butters
        '1881 St Monance, Co Fife on 27th May at West End, St Monance. Daughter
        of John Butters, Fisherman, Margaret Butters MS Hutton Marriage of parents
        1880, September 17th Leven. Informant   John Butters. Father.

  Tragedy then struck the family. First John's granddaughter Annie's account, as passed on
by Margaret Isobel Walker:

        '...John Butters, he and his brother [?] were fisherman, they drowned, the boat
        lost in the Bay of Biscay, [?] [Location now known to be incorrect - see   below]
when my Mum [Isabella Butters] was 2 months old. My grandmother   started a shop
with the insurance money and was able to educate her daughter   at the Wade
Academy* as a teacher [*Margaret Walker: "That's in Anstruther I
        think."]...'..however she only taught one term, she had trouble with bad heart
        condition. At the age of 23 Isabella Butters married David Affleck of Elie, the
        next small town to my mother's fishing village.....Dad left the railway, sold all
        his belongings & bought tickets to sail to America, Mum backed down at the
        last minute, she feared the water since her Dad and all [?] his brothers
        drowned...'

This story of Sheila's grandfather's buying tickets for America was news to us.
Sheila's mother had heard that he had drowned in the Wash. This proved to be nearer the
truth.
Finally in 2004 a letter from Jennifer, Sheila's cousin, confirmed that John Butters was
drowned on the return journey from Yarmouth on the 20th of November 1883. The event
was reported in *East of Fife Record* of the   23rd of November 1883 ending: 'The
unfortunate man....never came to the surface.'

Here is a picture of him:

The Huttons and Related Families

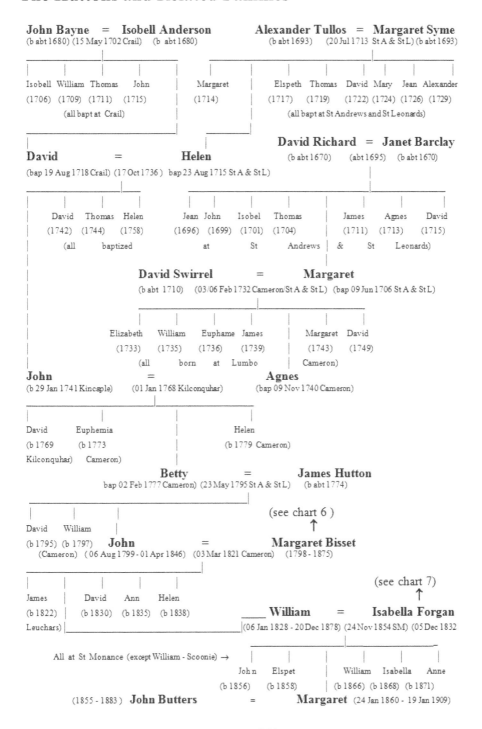

John Bayne = Isobell Anderson
(b abt 1680) (15 May 1702 Crail) (b abt 1680)

Alexander Tullos = Margaret Syme
(b abt 1693)   (20 Jul 1713 St A & St L) (b abt 1693)

Isobell   William   Thomas   John
(1706)   (1709)   (1711)   (1715)
(all bapt at Crail)

Margaret
(1714)

Elspeth   Thomas   David   Mary   Jean   Alexander
(1717)   (1719)   (1722)   (1724)   (1726)   (1729)
(all bapt at St Andrews and St Leonards)

David
(bap 19 Aug 1718 Crail)

=
(17 Oct 1736)

Helen
bap 23 Aug 1715 St A & St L)

David Richard = Janet Barclay
(b abt 1670)   (abt 1695)   (b abt 1670)

David   Thomas   Helen
(1742)   (1744)   (1758)
(all   baptized

Jean   John   Isobel   Thomas
(1696)   (1699)   (1701)   (1704)
at   St   Andrews

James   Agnes   David
(1711)   (1713)   (1715)
&   St   Leonards)

David Swirrel   =   Margaret
(b abt 1710)   (03/06 Feb 1732 Cameron/St A & St L)   (bap 09 Jun 1706 St A & St L)

Elizabeth   William   Euphame   James
(1733)   (1735)   (1736)   (1739)
(all   born   at   Lumbo

Margaret   David
(1743)   (1749)
Cameron)

John
(b 29 Jan 1741 Kincaple)

=
(01 Jan 1768 Kilconquhar)

Agnes
(bap 09 Nov 1740 Cameron)

David   Euphemia
(b 1769)   (b 1773
Kilconquhar)   Cameron)

Helen
(b 1779 Cameron)

Betty   =   James Hutton
bap 02 Feb 1777 Cameron) (23 May 1795 St A & St L)   (b abt 1774)

(see chart 6)
↑

David   William
(b 1795) (b 1797)   **John**   =   **Margaret Bisset**
(Cameron) (06 Aug 1799 - 01 Apr 1846) (03 Mar 1821 Cameron)   (1798 - 1875)

(see chart 7)
↑

James   David   Ann   Helen
(b 1822)   (b 1830) (b 1835) (b 1838)
Leuchars)

William   =   **Isabella Forgan**
(06 Jan 1828 - 20 Dec 1878) (24 Nov 1854 SM) (05 Dec 1832

All at St Monance (except William - Scoonie) →

John   Elspet
(b 1856)   (b 1858)

William   Isabella   Anne
(b 1866) (b 1868) (b 1871)

(1855 - 1883) **John Butters**   =   **Margaret** (24 Jan 1860 - 19 Jan 1909)

239

We begin with John Bayne and Isobel Anderson:

OPR Crail Co Fife:
> '1702 Contracted April 14th John Baynes & Isobell Andersone mar: May 15.'

Of their five known children, all were baptized regularly, David being apparently the last:

OPR Crail Co Fife (471/1) Births/Baptisms:
> '1718 August 19   John Bayne & Isobell Anderson his sp[ouse]: had a child baptized David wit[nesses] John Ross & Thomas Richie.'

The dates of the first and last baptisms being 1706 and 1718, there are almost certainly several unrecorded.

In 1736 David Bayne married Helen Tullos:

OPR St Andrews & St Leonards Co Fife:
> '1736 Octr 13 Contracted David Bayns and Helen Tullus both in this Parish who Consigned ten shillings as their pledges to Mr Wilson. Married 13th   Octr.'

There is no indication that the pledge of ten (Scots) shillings was returned after the marriage.

Helen was the second daughter of Alexander Tullos and Margaret Syme who were married in 1713:

OPR St Andrews & St Leonards Co Fife.
> Kirk Session Minutes Meeting 23 JUL 1713 'Marriages.Reported that [......] this day Alexander Tullus and Margaret Syme were married.'

Helen's baptism is recorded:

OPR ST Andrews and St Leonards Co Fife:
> '1715 Aug 23 Alex. Tullos in Kencaple & Margaret Syme his wife had a child bap called Helen wit[nesses]John Millar and John …[illegible].'

Kincaple is a hamlet a few miles in from the coast at St Andrews . St Leonards church is in South Street, a separate church from the cathedral of St Andrews; the latter fell into disuse after the Reformation and is now in ruins.

Helen had seven brothers and sisters, all born between 1714 and 1729.

At least four children came from the marriage of David and Helen. John was the eldest and Sheila's ancestor:

O.P.R. St Andrews and St Leonards, Co. Fife (453/3) Births/Baptisms
'1741 January 29th John son to David Bayns in Kincaple & Helen Tullos   his
spouse was born on the 29th of January 1741, and baptized on the first of
February immediately thereafter by Mr McCormick. Witnesses Alexr. Tullos
& William Hutton'.

Now we must introduce the Richard and Swirrel families.
David Richards and Janet Barclay were both born about 1670 and married about 1695.
There is a reference to David in the marriage entry of his daughter, Margaret, to the effect
that he is 'late deacon of the weavers in this city [St Andrews].' This has no connection
with church matters. The deacon in this context was the president or another chief official
of the trade guild of weavers. What we cannot say for certain is: which trade of weavers?
Several other baptismal entries of David Richards' other seven children refer to his trade as
'weaver' but none is more specific.
The full entry for Margaret's baptism in the St Andrews register goes as follows:

OPR ST Andrews, Co Fife (453/12) Marriages.
'1732 ffebruary 3rd Contracted David Swirrels in Cameron parish and
Margaret Richard Daughter to David Richard late Deacon of the Weavers in
this City who gave twenty shilling and the said David Richard and John Baxter
became Cautioners for their pledges. The twenty shilling Given by David   Gooll
to John Gardner. The Man gave in a testificate from Cameron which   was
Sustained.'

St Andrews had long been a cathedral city.
Who David Gool was and why he gave the money to John Gardner is not clear, but
evidently David Swirrels brought a certificate (of good conduct) from Cameron, where the
marriage is also recorded:

OPR Cameron, Co Fife (412/1) Marriages:
'1732 Febry 6th   Eodem die David Swirles in this parish and Margaret Richard
in the parish of St Andrews were proclaimed in order to marriage before this
Congregation pro jmo [?].'

There was for a considerable time a mystery about the exact location of 'Bowlong' where
the the IGI stated the Swirrel family lived. The name could not be found. Finally, Mrs
Corkerton examined the entries and deciphered the marriage details of James Hutton and
Betty Bayne (qv below) as LUMBO (489148) which, with the nearby BALLONE, lies just
inside the ST A & St L parish.

David and Margaret had seven children; number five was named Agnes:

OPR CAMERON, Co Fife (412/1) Births/Baptisms.
    '1740 Novr 9th Eodem die David Swirrles and Margaret Richard his spouse had a
child Baptized called Agness before the Congregation.'

Agnes married John Bayne (see above):

OPR Kilconquhar, Co Fife (436/2) Marriages:
    '1767 Novr. 28th   John Bayne and Agnes Swirrels both in this parish were
    Contracted and Regularly proclaimed and [married?] Jany 1st 1768.'

Four children are known to have been born to John and Agnes and there may have been
others whose births are unrecorded.
The third child is shown thus:

[02 Feb 1777] OPR Cameron Co Fife:
    'Quo die ['on which day'] John Bayne and Agnes Swirrels had their lawful
    Daughter Betty Baptized before the Congregation.'

It is now that the Huttons first make their appearance in this narrative:

OPR ST Andrews and St Leonards Co Fife:
    '1795 May 23rd Were contracted James Hutton & Betty Bain both in Lumbo
    of this Parish proclaimed & Married.'

James and Betty are known to have had at least three sons, whose baptisms are reported:

Baptism. OPR Cameron, Co Fife (412/1) Births/Baptisms:
    '1795 Octr 28th David son of James Hutton and Elizabeth Baynes in Bowlong
    Born 28th Octr   and Bapt 1st Novr.'

Baptism. OPR Cameron, Co Fife (412/1) Births/Baptisms:
    1797 Febry 27th   William Son of James Hutton and Eliz: Baynes was born 27th
    Febry and baptized 5th March.'

Baptism   OPR Cameron Co Fife:
    '1799 Augt 6th John son of James Hutton and Elizabeth Baynes in
    Wilkiston.   Born 6th Augt and Baptized 11th before the Congregation.'

It seems possible that some time after this last birth either or both of the parents died.

Wilkiston is a farm lying about a mile to the north-west of Cameron Reservoir
(MR 450121).

John Hutton married Margaret Bisset:

OPR Leuchars, Co.Fife (445/2):
> Marriage Proclamations '1821 Feby 17th This day John Hutton, of this Parish & Margt.Bisset in the Parish of Cameron were contracted in order to Marriage.'

(Leuchars is about five miles north-west of St Andrews, across the River Eden)

and note also:

OPR Cameron, Co. Fife (412/2) Marriages and Proclamations
> '1821 Feb 18 This day John Hutton, of the parish of Leuchars, and Margaret Bizzet of this parish were contracted in order to marriage and having been regularly proclaimed were Married 3rd March.'

Cameron has figured large in the recent pages of the narrative. Sheila and I visited the area in the 1980s and found the church in a farmyard. There is a graveyard with a number of Bissets and Swirrels. The parish is now sparsely populated but the church is still functioning, albeit in conjunction with St Leonards in St Andrews.

The ancestors of Margaret Bisset will appear in the next section.

The five children of John and Margaret that we know about were baptized in different paishes, which indicates that the family moved quite frequently. James and William were born in Leuchars, David in Kilrenny and the two girls in Carnbee. As John was an agricultural labourer (see the reporting of William's death) he would have sought work where he could find it.
(Incidentally, with the recently discussed families we have moved from the career of fisherman to that of worker on the land.)
Here are the details of William's baptism:

OPR Cameron Co Fife:
> '1828 Jany 6th William son of John Hutton & Margaret Bisset was born on the 6th Jany and baptized the 3d Feby.'

The delay between William's birth and his baptism is unexplained.
William grew up to marry Isabella Forgan, whose family will also be examined later.

OPR. Parish of St Monance, County of Fife. Births/Baptisms:
> '11th Nov 1854/Hutton & Forgan/William Hutton in the parish of Kilrenny and Isabella Forgan in this parish were contracted in order to Marriage: and after proclamation in the Church here, on the 12th and 19th were married on 24th of the same month by the Rev Mr Foggs.'

John, William's father, died quite young in 1846:

OPR Anstruther Easter Co Fife (402/4) Deaths/Burials:
> '1846 April 1   Died John Hutton aged [blank] years, Labourer and was interred on the 4th inst. in East Anstruther Church Yard'

Margaret, John's widow, died much later:

Death Certificate:
> '1875 Anstruther Easter, Co. Fife (402/1) on January 13th (10pm) at Card's Wynd, Anstruther Easter Margaret Hutton Aged 74, Widow of John Hutton, Labourer (General) Daughter of John [sc George?] Bisset, Collier (deceased) and of Margaret Bisset M/S Crawford (deceased). Cause of death Old age. No Medical Attendant. Informant William Hutton. Son. Present'

Note that this death took place after the beginning of Statutory Registration in Scotland (1855). The information given is now more extensive (though not always more accurate.)

William and Isabella had six children. Margaret is obviously the one that mostly interests us but several of the others married and had families. We are now drawn in to more recent history where personal reminiscences can be found.

The children's details are as follows.

John, born in 1856, became a fisherman and married a Jane Guthrie, who bore him two children. He died in 1900.

Elspeth, born in 1858, married James Kerr.

We will leave Margaret for the moment and move on to William. Born in 1866, he is remembered in 1995 by Annie Affleck, Sheila's aunt:

> '...Just remembered Willie Hutton the youngest brother didn't go to sea and was still selling fish from a barrow when I was little, the poor old guy was a drunk...'

Nevertheless, he seems to have survived until after 1920. His wife was named Anne.

Isabella was born in 1868 and the last daughter, Anne, in 1871.
The latter is also remembered by Annie Affleck in 1997:

> 'My grandmother's sister, Ann Hutton, whom I am named for [after], lived with us, off and on, till she died. John [John Butters Affleck] was always her favourite, & when I grew up, [I] was given her brooch, which I gave to Jennifer [Jennifer Kenny Affleck], when she was grown...'

Now for Margaret.
She was on the 24 of January 1860 and married John Butters when she was 20:

'1880 Scoonie, Co Fife (456/15)
        on September 17th at Leven. after Banns according to the Forms of the United
        Presbyterian Church. John Butters... Aged 24. Fisherman. Bachelor/Usual
        residence St Monance. Son of..David Butters, Fisherman and of/Helen Butters
        M.S. Easson (deceased)   Margaret Hutton.. Aged 20. Spinster/Usual res.St
        Monance..of William Hutton Lab.. Brewery (dec) Witnesses *James Kerr and
        Christian Gay'

* husband of Margaret Hutton's sister, Elspeth.

They had one child only, Isabella:

Stat Records:
        Birth of Isabella Butters'1881 St Monance, Co Fife on 27th May at West End, St
Monance .Daughter of John Butters, Fisherman, Margaret Butters MS Huttom Marriage of
parents 1880, September 17th   Leven Informant   John Butters. Father.

I have already related the tragedy of John Butters' drowning.

Annie Affleck writes (1995):
  '..[after her husband was drowned] Grandmother collected the insurance &
started a business in the house behind the "old kirk" at the top of the brae.
The big shop window was still there when we were on holiday in 1977[?]...'

Margaret Miles writes (1995):
'...I also have an old business card ':

Annie Affleck again:

'... My grandmother started a shop with the insurance money and was able to educate her daughter at the Wade Academy* as a teacher [*Margaret Walker: "That's in Anstruther I think."]...

'..however she only taught one term, she had trouble with bad heart condition. At the age of 23 Isabella Butters married David Affleck of Elie, the next small town to my mother's fishing village...

...Dad left the railway, sold all his belongings & bought tickets to sail to America, Mum backed down at the last minute, she feared the water since her Dad and all [?] his brothers drowned...'

This story of S's grandfather's buying tickets for America is news to Sheila.

1901 Census:
St Monance   Sched 128 West End

Isabella   Hutton [MS Forgan] Head   W   68   Fife, St Monance
Margaret Butters Daur   W   41 Shopkeeper, Grocer   Own acct   do   do
Isabella Butters   Daur *   S   19   do   do
                [*actually the granddaughter of Isabella Hutton]

Isabella Forgan died 5 years after the Census

'1906 St Monance, Co Fife (454/18) on 29th July at West End, St Monance
Isabella Hutton   Aged 71. Widow of William Hutton, Labourer
Daughter of   William Forgan, Sailor (deceased) and of
                          Elspeth Forgan M/S Fyall (deceased)
Cause of death   Senility   As certified by R.J. Pirie L.R.C.P.
Informant   David Affleck, Intimate Friend [? could be son-in-law]
                          West End, St Monance

We now turn to the ancestors of Margaret Bisset.

The Bisset Family

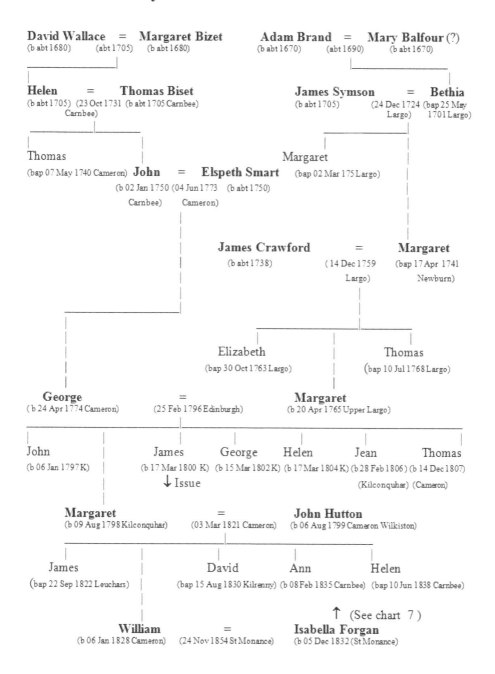

David Wallace = **Margaret Bizet**
(b abt 1680) (abt 1705) (b abt 1680)

Adam Brand = **Mary Balfour** (?)
(b abt 1670) (abt 1690) (b abt 1670)

Helen = **Thomas Biset**
(b abt 1705) (23 Oct 1731 (b abt 1705 Carnbee)
Carnbee)

James Symson = **Bethia**
(b abt 1705) (24 Dec 1724 (bap 25 May
Largo) 1701 Largo)

Thomas
(bap 07 May 1740 Cameron) **John** = **Elspeth Smart**
(b 02 Jan 1750 (04 Jun 1773 (b abt 1750)
Carnbee) Cameron)

Margaret
(bap 02 Mar 175 Largo)

James Crawford = **Margaret**
(b abt 1738) (14 Dec 1759 (bap 17 Apr 1741
Largo) Newburn)

Elizabeth
(bap 30 Oct 1763 Largo)

Thomas
(bap 10 Jul 1768 Largo)

George = **Margaret**
(b 24 Apr 1774 Cameron) (25 Feb 1796 Edinburgh) (b 20 Apr 1765 Upper Largo)

John
(b 06 Jan 1797 K)

James
(b 17 Mar 1800 K)

George
(b 15 Mar 1802 K)

Helen
(b 17 Mar 1804 K)

Jean
(b 28 Feb 1806)

Thomas
(b 14 Dec 1807)
(Kilconquhar) (Cameron)

↓ Issue

Margaret = **John Hutton**
(b 09 Aug 1798 Kilconquhar) (03 Mar 1821 Cameron) (b 06 Aug 1799 Cameron Wilkiston)

James
(bap 22 Sep 1822 Leuchars)

David
(bap 15 Aug 1830 Kilrenny)

Ann
(b 08 Feb 1835 Carnbee)

Helen
(bap 10 Jun 1838 Carnbee)

↑ (See chart 7)

William = **Isabella Forgan**
(b 06 Jan 1828 Cameron) (24 Nov 1854 St Monance) (b 05 Dec 1832 (St Monance)

The name Bisset appears in several forms but no connection with the French composer must be assumed.

David Wallace and Helen Bizet must have married about 1680. This is a conjecture from the *probable* date of birth of Helen, their daughter, who married a Thomas Biset or Besot or Bissat in 1731. Even here there is a problem because of disagreement between the sources. It is not clear whether the marriage was at Ceres or Carnbee, nor in which month. This is the Carnbee entry:

OPR Carnbee, Co Fife (413/2) Marriages:
> '1731 21st 9br [September?October?November?] Thomas Bissat in this parish and Helen Wallace in Ceress were proclaimed pro.uno.[for the first time]mar.23d.'

Then there is the question: did Helen marry a cousin?
Fortunately the complications do not continue into the next generation. The birth of the second son of Thomas and Helen is recorded:

OPR Carnbee, Co Fife (413/2) Births/Baptisms
> '1750 Janry ii Thomas Biset & Helen Wallace had a son born and Baptized 16th by name John. witt: William Bruce and William Bisset.

as well as his marriage to Elspeth Smart (whose parentage is unknown):

OPR Cameron Co Fife:
> '1773 May 9th Quo die John Bisset & Elspeth Smart both in this Parish were Contracted in order to Marriage gave a shilling to the poor and were Married June 4th.'

There is the record of only one child to John and Elspeth:

OPR Cameron Co Fife:
> '1774 April 24   Quo die John Bisset & Elspeth Smart his spouse had a child Baptized called George before the Congregation.'

This seems to be the first son, but it is possible that there was an earlier boy, born perhaps before the parents' marriage, in which case George could have been the name of Elspeth's father.

George married Margaret Crawford and before details of this are given, Margaret's ancestors will be described.

I think it very probable that Adam Brand's wife was called Mary Balfour and that they had seven children. Only Bethia (or, Bessie) however, is certain; she was born on the 25th of May   1701 in Largo.

She married a James Symson:

OPR LARGO Co Fife:

>'1724 Decr 24th. Aug: 30th James Symson and Bessie Brand both in this   Parish
>were contracted their pands consigned orderly proclaimed and married   at
Largo by Mr fferrar our Minister Decer 24th 1724.'

Bethia lived to a good age, dying on the 10th of May 1772:

OPR LARGO Co Fife: 'Bessie Brand, best Do [Mortcloth]'

Bethia and James had two girls called Margaret, which implies that the first died young:

OPR Largo, Co Fife (443/2) Births/Baptisms:

>'1735 March 2d. The said day James Symson and Bessie Brand his spouse in
>Halftown Moortown had a Child baptized by the said Mr.fferiar called
>Margaret Witnesses were Adam and James Brands at Baldestard and many
>others.'

OPR NEWBURN, Co Fife (451/2) Births/Baptisms.

>'1741 Aprile 13th   Margaret daughter to Jases Symson & his spouse Bethia
>Brand subtenants in the parish of Largo was baptized by Mr Smith Minister
>here Witnesses James Wilson Tenant in Newburn Easter
>and Thomas Foulis Tenant in Menhirpie   [Monturpie?].'

It has not proved possible to find the locations mentioned (except Menhirpie). Many have presumably now been absorbed into larger places.

The second Margaret married James Crawford (provenance unknown):

OPR Largo, Co Fife (443/3) Marriages:

>'1759 Novembr.24th.   James Crawford and Margaret Simson both in this
>Parish were contracted, and being regularly proclaimed were married the 14th
>Decr thereafter.'

James died in 1808:

OPR LARGO Co Fife:

>'1808 Jany 18 Jas Crawford, Lundin Mill, 110 East 11 South best large Do
>[Mortcloth]'

The figures given are presumably the measurements, given in feet, from a specified point; but from where? We know from details of his children (see below) that in 1765 he was a day labourer and that in 1796 he was a carrier.

If the meaning of 'carrier' is similar to that I knew of in the 1940s in Berkshire, he would have on a regular basis visited the nearest town and made purchases on behalf of his neighbours and delivered them to the purchasers' homes.

Margaret died in 1793:

OPR Largo Co FIFE:
'Margaret Simpson Spouse to James Crawfurd Upper Drummochy[?] 41 east 12 south best do [mortcloth]'

We know of three children born to James and Margaret.

Elizabeth was baptized   the 30th October 1763 in Largo. Her burial is also recorded:

OPR LARGO Co Fife:
'1817 Augt 30 Betty Crawford 2nd [class] large do [Mortcloth]'

Thomas, the third child, was born in 1768 and there seems to be a duplication, unless the first entry refers to the death and the second to the burial:

OPR LARGO, Co Fife:
'1848 Feb 2 Thomas Crawford'   and
'1848 Feb 2 Thomas Crawford, Largo, 75E, 73½N'

Margaret, the middle child, was born in 1765:

OPR Largo Co Fife:
'1765 October 20th Was born Margaret daughter to James Crawford day Labourer in Upper Largo and Margaret Simson his Spouse and baptized the 24th of Ditto. In presence of the Congregation.'

We have now caught up again with George Bisset, whom Margaret Crawford married in 1796:

OPR Edinburgh Co Edinburgh:
'1796 February 25th George Bisset, Labourer Tron [Dron?) kirk parish and Margaret Crawford same parish Daughter of James Crawford, Carrier from Largo in Fife.' ['Tron' may be a corruption of 'Cameron']

I have no explanation for this wedding in Edinburgh, unless it is another irregular marriage.

The names of the children of George and Margaret conform nicely to the traditional pattern, except for Jean, the origin of which may relate to the mother of either James Crawford or Elspeth Smart.

Here are the details of these children:

OPRb/Kilconquhar 436/Book 3
> '12 January 1797   John Lawful Son of George Bisset Collier in Largo by Margaret Crawford his Wife was born the 6th day of January 1797 and Baptized the 12th of Do in Colinsburgh Meeting House.'

OPR Kilconquhar Co Fife:
> '1798 August 9th Margaret, Lawful Daughter of George Bisset by Margaret Crawford his Wife was born the 9th of August 1789 and Baptd 22d.'

OPRb/Kilconquhar 436/Book 3
> 17th March 1800   James Son to George Bisset Collier in Largon [sic] and Margaret Crawford his wife was born the 17th of March 1800 and Baptised the 19th of Do.'

OPRb/Kilconquhar 436/Book 3
> '15th March 1802   George Third Son and fourth child of George Bisset and Margaret Crawfurd his wife was born the 15th day of March and baptd. the 20th of Do.'

OPRb/Kilconquhar 436/Book 3
> '17 March 1804   Helen, second daughter and fifth child of George Bisset and Margaret Crawford his wife was born the 17th day of March and Bapt the 22d of do,'

OPRb/Kilconquhar436/Book3
> Sixth child of George Bisset Coallier in Largonard [?] and Margaret Crawford his wife was born the 28th day of February [1806] and Baptized the 6th of March.'

OPRb/Cameron 412/Book 1/Frame 228
> '14 Decr 1807   George Bisset and Margaret Crawford had a child (born this day) baptized and named Thomas.'

This information on the whole confirms the order of births of the children.
We also learn that George was a coal miner.
It is intriguing to speculate that Thomas was baptized on the day of his birth because he was not expected to live.
The insertion of 'lawful' before 'child' in the case of the first two children is probably formulaic.
Colinsburgh is a few miles north of Kilconquhar; 'Meeting House' presumably implies a non-conformist establishment.

It is of course the second child, Margaret, in whom we are principally interested but we know that her younger brother, James, married and had children. He is described as a farmer of 52 acres in the 1851 Census for Cameron. He married Margaret Fernie in 1824 and they had five children: George, John (a joiner), Janet, James and Helen.

Returning to Margaret, we will remember that she married John Hutton on the third of March 1821 in Cameron and that John's ancestors were discussed earlier.

To complete this side of the family we now turn to the Forgans.

The Forgans

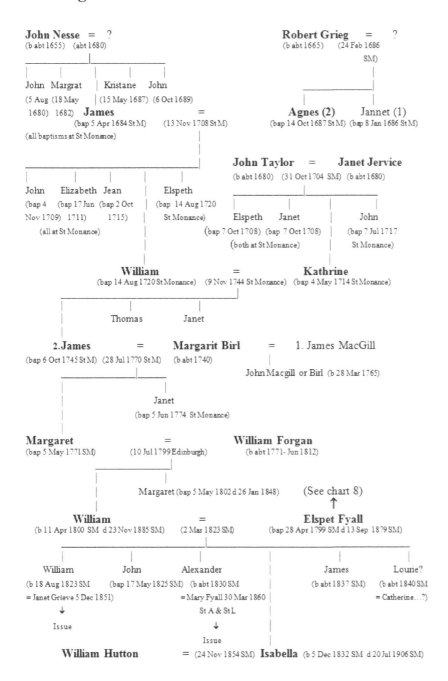

John Nesse = ?
(b abt 1655)   (abt 1680)

Robert Grieg   =   ?
(b abt 1665)   (24 Feb 1686
                        SM)

John   Margrat | Kristane   John
(5 Aug   (18 May | (15 May 1687)   (6 Oct 1689)
 1680)   1682)   **James**   =
          (bap 5 Apr 1684 St M)   (13 Nov 1708 St M)
(all baptisms at St Monance)

Agnes (2)   Jannet (1)
(bap 14 Oct 1687 St M)   (bap 8 Jan 1686 St M)

John Taylor   =   Janet Jervice
(b abt 1680)   (31 Oct 1704 SM)   (b abt 1680)

John   Elizabeth   Jean   Elspeth
(bap 4   (bap 17 Jun   (bap 2 Oct   (bap 14 Aug 1720
Nov 1709)   1711)   1715)   St Monance)
   (all at St Monance)

Elspeth   Janet | John
(bap 7 Oct 1708)   (bap 7 Oct 1708) | (bap 7 Jul 1717
(both at St Monance)   St Monance)

William   =   **Kathrine**
(bap 14 Aug 1720 St Monance)   (9 Nov 1744 St Monance)   (bap 4 May 1714 St Monance)

Thomas   Janet

2.James   =   **Margarit Birl**   =   1. James MacGill
(bap 6 Oct 1745 St M)   (28 Jul 1770 St M)   (b abt 1740)

John Macgill or Birl (b 28 Mar 1765)

Janet
(bap 5 Jun 1774 St Monance)

Margaret   =   **William Forgan**
(bap 5 May 1771 SM)   (10 Jul 1799 Edinburgh)   (b abt 1771- Jun 1812)

Margaret (bap 5 May 1802 d 26 Jan 1848)   (See chart 8)
                                                                    ↑
William   =   **Elspet Fyall**
(b 11 Apr 1800 SM d 23 Nov 1885 SM)   (2 Mar 1823 SM)   (bap 28 Apr 1799 SM d 13 Sep 1879 SM)

William   John   Alexander   James   Lourie?
(b 18 Aug 1823 SM   (bap 17 May 1825 SM)   (b abt 1830 SM   (b abt 1837 SM)   (b abt 1840 SM
= Janet Grieve 5 Dec 1851)   = Mary Fyall 30 Mar 1860   = Catherine…?)
↓   St A & St L
Issue   ↓
                               Issue
William Hutton   =   (24 Nov 1854 SM) **Isabella** (b 5 Dec 1832 SM d 20 Jul 1906 SM)

The Forgans appear only towards the end of this section. We have no knowledge of their early history relating to Sheila's family.

Essentially this part of the narrative is centred around St Monance, and that is where our first members of the Nesse and Grieg families came from.

We have baptismal details of all five of the Nesse children:

OPR ST MONANCE, Co Fife:
> '1680 Aut 5 John Nesse had a son baptized called John befo witnesses'

OPR ST MONANCE, Co Fife:
> '1682 May 18 the same day [as the previous entry] John Ness had a daughter baptized befor witnesses called Margrat'

OPR ST MONANCE, Co Fife:
> '1684 Aprile 5 Jo. Nesse in Sandrigs had a son baptized Called James various witnesses being present'

OPR ST MONANCE, Co Fife:
> '1687 May 15 Jo. Nesse in ye Sandrigs had a child baptized Called Kristane before divers witnesses'

OPR ST MONANCE, Co Fife:
> '1689 Octr 6 John Ness in Sandrigs had a Child Baptized called John before Witnesses'

There is a Sandyrigs Wood lying about a mile and a half to the north-west of St Monance and this probably the location mentioned in the last three entries shown above.

It is assumed that the first John died some time before the birth of the second.

The appearance of the surname *Grieg,* especially with this spelling, inevitably calls to mind the nineteenth century Norwegian composer of the same name. It is known that Edvard Hagerup Grieg's paternal great-grandfather, Alexander, came from Scotland, where the name is frequently found in the seventeenth and eighteenth centuries, especially in Aberdeenshire. But *Grieg/Greig* was also known in other areas, for example in Angus and in Fifeshire. Although no link to Sheila's ancestors is established, it is, therefore, just possible that the families were related.

Only two children are reported as born to Robert and his unknown wife: Jannet and Agnes:

OPR ST MONANCE Co Fife:
> '1686 Jary 8 Rot.Griegg at ye miln of Abercrombie had a child bapt: before divers witnesses' [Child's name?]

and

OPRb/St Monance, Co Fife 454/Book1/
     '14 Octr 1687   Rot. Greig at ye miln of Abercrombie had a child bapt called
     Agnes before witnesses'

If the date for Robert's marriage shown on the IGI is accepted, then clearly Jannet was illegitimate.
Abercrombie is a small village about three quarters of a mile to the north of St Monance, with Sandyrigs Wood (the home of the Nesses) lying close by. From the baptismal record of both his daughters it is clear that he was a miller for the area.
I cannot explain the apparent absence of Jannet's name from the register and its appearance on the IGI. Perhaps this is an error of transcription.

The marriage of Agnes with James Nesse is recorded with a correction:

OPRm/St Monance 454/Book 2/
     '13 Novr 1708   James Greig & Agnes Ness married Novr 13 N.B. The man's
     Name is Ness - the woman's Greig per mistake'

All five of their children appear on the baptismal register, the last two (twins?) together:

OPR ST MONANCE, Co Fife:
     '1709 Novebr 4th John son of James Ness and Agnes Grieg Baptized Novebr
     4th 1709'

OPR ST MONANCE, Co Fife:
     '1711 June 17th Elizabeth daur of James Ness & Agnes Grieg Baptized June
     17th'

OPR ST MONANCE, Co Fife:
     '1715 October 2nd Jean daur of James Ness and Agnes Grieg in Stmonance
     Baptized October 2nd 1715'

OPR ST MONANCE, Co Fife:
     '1720 August 14th Willm. & Elspeth Son & Daur of James Ness & Agnes
     Grieg Baptized August 14th 1720'

William married Kathrine Taylor:

OPRm/St Monance 454/Book 2/
     '9th Novr 1744   Wm Ness & Kat Taylor Contracted 20th Octbr. married 9th
     Novbr'

Kathrine was the daughter of John Taylor and Janet Jervice. They were married on the 31st of October 1704. Although the name of the bride apparently does not appear on the register in 1704, she is shown as the mother of several children. No other candidate is available.

We have already come across the name Jervice in the Affleck section of the narrative as Jarvis/Jervis/Jervie, although these families seem based in Elie, just along the coast from St Monance.

Kathrine was the third of four children, whose baptismal details I do not have. Kathrine and William had three children that we know of:

OPR St Monance, Co Fife (454/2) Baptisms
'1745 October 6th James son of William ness & Katharine Taylor Baptized October 6th 1745'

The second child died as a baby:

ST MONANCE Death Reg:
'1749 January 23d Thomas Ness a Child died smallpox'

James married Margarit Birl (ancestry unknown):

OPR ST Monance Co Fife (454/1) Marriages:
'1770 July 28th James Ness in Carnbee Parish & Margaret Birl in this Parish contracted 28th July & after due proclamation married.'

The wording makes it unclear whether they were proclaimed or married on the 28th of July.

Margaret had already borne at least one child, perhaps illegitimate. She and James had two daughters we know of:

OPR ST Monance, Co Fife (454/2) Baptisms
'1771 May 5th Margaret Daughter of James Ness & Margaret Birl was born 3 May & Baptized 5th May 1771'

and Janet, baptized the 5th June 1774. As with other marriages, one suspects that there were other children.

It is here that the Forgans enter the story, for in 1799 Margaret Ness married William Forgan:

OPR St Monance,Co Fife(454/2)Marriages
'1799 July 10th William Forgan and Margt. Ness both in this parish were irregularly and Clandestinely married at Edinburgh by John Wilson July 10th 1799 and declared married by the Revd. Mr [...?]'

Definitely muddied waters here somewhere! Why else would the couple have fled the parish to be married in Edinburgh? Perhaps it was known in St Monance that they had been misbehaving. Be that as it may, the new William Forgan was born a bare nine months later:

OPR St Monance, Co Fife (454/2) Baptisms
> '1800 May 10th William son of William Forgan & Margaret Ness was born
> April 11th & Baptized 10th May 1800'

The naming of William the younger indicates either that his grandfather was also a William or that there had been other (illegitimate?) children before. Given that Margaret Ness was 28 when she married, it seems that the latter explanation may be the more likely.
William had a sister, Margaret, born in 1802, who died at the age of forty-five:
There may have been other siblings.

OPR St Monance
> '1848 January 26th Margaret Forgan, aged 45 years, died 26th January. Buried
> at the east end of the Church'

I should be surprised if this means she was buried *inside* the church!
William himself married Elspet Fyall (of whom more in the following section.)

There are some problems involving the children of William and Elizabeth:

1. The first son, William appears erroneously on the IGI as the son
of William Forgan and Elspet Duncan. I think this is an error because:
(a) I can find no marriage between a William Forgan and an Elspet Duncan
(b) the name William is correct for the naming pattern. It is
true that no William appears on the 1851 census with the rest of the family
but he would probably be married by then (perhaps in 1850 to Janet Doctor of
Crail.)
But
It is also possible that this was an illegitimate child and that Elspet Duncan
was the true mother.
2. There is no record of the births of Alexander, James and Lourie Forgan, who
all appear on the 1851 census. The first two, however, fit the naming pattern.
3. *Lourie* probably means *Laurie.*

I conclude that the tree shown at the beginning of this section is substantially correct.

Elspet died in 1879:

Death of Elpseth Forgan:
> '1879 St Monance, Co. Fife (454/32) on September 13th (7am) at Shore, St
> Monance Elspeth Forgan   Aged 80. Married to William Forgan, Seaman
> Daughter of John Fyall, fisherman (deceased) and of Elspeth Fyall M/S Hutt
> (deceased) Cause of death Natural Decay /As certified by John Kennedy
> M.D.Informant   William Forgan. Widower. Present'
(Reminder - we are now into the time of statutory registration.)

257

William is shown on the 1881 Census with Lourie and an unknown William Forgan:

1881 Census St Monance, Narrow Wynd:

'Forgan   William* Head   W   80   M   Retired Tailor [! sc 'Sailor'] Fife St Monance
  do   Lowrie   Son   U   35   M   Ag Labourer   do   do
  do   William   U   19   M

Nearby comes another son, Alexander Forgan with two of his children:

1881 Census, St Monance, Narrow Wynd:
'Forgan   Alexander   Head   W   45   M   Fisherman   Fife St Monance
Forgan   Elspet   Daur   U   21   F   -   do   do
Forgan   William   Son   U   19   M   Fisherman   do   do   '

William* died four years later:

Death of William Forgan
        '1885 St Monance, Co. Fife (454/38) on November 23rd (3am) at East End St
        Monance William Forgan   Aged 85. Seaman. Widower of Elspeth Fyall
        Son of William Forgan, Seaman (deceased) and of Margaret Forgan M/S Ness
        (deceased) Cause of death   Debility/As certified by Amerie[sic]E.Flaxman
        L.S.A. Lond Informant James Forgan. Son'

The marriage of Isabella Forgan and William Hutton took place on the 24th of November
1854 at Monance:

        '11th Nov 1854/Hutton & Forgan/William Hutton in the parish of Kilrenny and
        Isabella Forgan in this parish were contracted in order to Marriage: and after
        proclamation in the Church here, on the 12th and 19th were married on 24th of
        the same month by the Rev Mr Foggs.'

Now we pick up the story of the Fyalls and their antecedents.

The Fyals

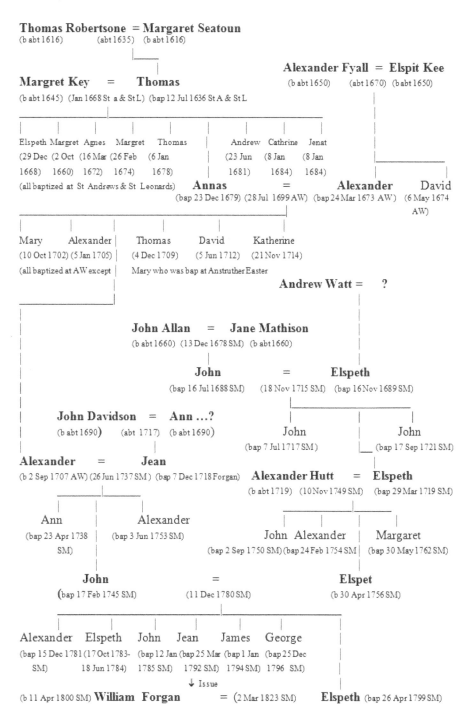

Thomas Robertsone = Margaret Seatoun
(b abt 1616)   (abt 1635)   (b abt 1616)

Alexander Fyall = Elspit Kee
(b abt 1650)   (abt 1670) (b abt 1650)

Margret Key   =   Thomas
(b abt 1645)   (Jan 1668 St a & St L)   (bap 12 Jul 1636 St A & St L)

Elspeth	Margret	Agnes	Margret	Thomas		Andrew	Cathrine	Jenat	
(29 Dec	(2 Oct	(16 Mar	(26 Feb	(6 Jan		(23 Jun	(8 Jan	(8 Jan	
1668)	1660)	1672)	1674)	1678)		1681)	1684)	1684)	

(all baptized at St Andrews & St Leonards)

Annas   =   Alexander   David
(bap 23 Dec 1679) (28 Jul 1699 AW) (bap 24 Mar 1673 AW) (6 May 1674 AW)

Mary	Alexander		Thomas	David	Katherine
(10 Oct 1702)	(5 Jan 1705)		(4 Dec 1709)	(5 Jun 1712)	(21 Nov 1714)

(all baptized at AW except Mary who was bap at Anstruther Easter)

Andrew Watt =   ?

John Allan   =   Jane Mathison
(b abt 1660)   (13 Dec 1678 SM)   (b abt 1660)

John   =   Elspeth
(bap 16 Jul 1688 SM)   (18 Nov 1715 SM)   (bap 16 Nov 1689 SM)

John Davidson   =   Ann ...?
(b abt 1690)   (abt 1717)   (b abt 1690)

	John		John
	(bap 7 Jul 1717 SM)		(bap 17 Sep 1721 SM)

Alexander   =   Jean
(b 2 Sep 1707 AW) (26 Jun 1737 SM) (bap 7 Dec 1718 Forgan)

Alexander Hutt   =   Elspeth
(b abt 1719)   (10 Nov 1749 SM)   (bap 29 Mar 1719 SM)

Ann		Alexander
(bap 23 Apr 1738 SM)		(bap 3 Jun 1753 SM)

John	Alexander		Margaret
(bap 2 Sep 1750 SM)	(bap 24 Feb 1754 SM)		(bap 30 May 1762 SM)

John   =   Elspet
(bap 17 Feb 1745 SM)   (11 Dec 1780 SM)   (b 30 Apr 1756 SM)

Alexander	Elspeth	John	Jean	James	George
(bap 15 Dec 1781 SM)	(17 Oct 1783- 18 Jun 1784)	(bap 12 Jan 1785 SM)	(bap 25 Mar 1792 SM)	(bap 1 Jan 1794 SM)	(bap 25 Dec 1796 SM)

↓ Issue

(b 11 Apr 1800 SM) **William Forgan   =   ** (2 Mar 1823 SM)   **Elspeth** (bap 26 Apr 1799 SM)

The geographical centre in this section starts in the north-east of the Kingdom of Fife, in St Andrews but gradually settles down to the St Monance area, via the Anstruthers, both Easter and Wester.

Although we do not have a marriage entry for Thomas Robertsone and Margaret Seatoun it seems likely that Thomas was their only son:

OPR ST ANDREWS and ST LEONARDS, Co Fife:
    '1636 July 12th Umqll Thomas Ro[ber]tsone and Margaret Seatoun had a Son callid Thomas witnesses George Martyne, George Wishart and James Rotsone younger'.

since we know that *Umqll* means 'late' or 'deceased'.

Thomas junior, on the other hand, had nine children with his wife Elspit Key, about nothing more is known, except perhaps her birthplace, Kingsbarns, a few miles south-east along the coast from St Andrews:

OPRm/St Andrews & St Leonards 453/Book 4/Fr 1860:
    '9 January 1668   Contracted in Kingsbarns Thomas Robertsone in this parish with Mary Kay in ye parish and Maryed ye -- '

The marriage date is not given.
The baptism of their first child gives a location for the family but so far I have been unable to find the place:

OPR St ANDREWS and St LEONARDS, Co Fife:
    '1668 Dec 29 Thomas Robertsone in Swinkstone and Margret Kay a Daughter bap: Elspeth witness Allen and thomas Robertsones'

Only the baptism of the second child specifies *Swinkstone* but all th   e other children were baptized within the parish. The final two are identified as twins:

OPR ST ANDREWS and ST LEONARDS, Co Fife:
    '1684 Jan 8 Thomas Robertsone and Margaret Kaye had twa daughters   bap: being twins one of ym called Cathrine and ye other Jenat witnes David   Carstairs and Robert Russell'

We come now to Annas and this raises two problems.

OPRb/St Andrews & St Leonards 453/Book 1/Frame 422:
    '23 Decr 1679... [Also] Thomas Robertsone and Margaret Day [sc Key] a daughter bapd Annas witness Robert Russell and John Robertsone'

Now, *Annas* or *Annes*, is generally thought to be a variant of *Agnes*. But an Agnes had already baptized in 1672. Is it to be assumed that the first Agnes died, or has a new name

260

been used? Secondly, is the surname *Day* to be construed as a mistake (by either the minister or the transcriber) as an error for *Key* or *Kay*? I have decided to accept the latter explanation because no reference can be found to a *Robertson/Day* marriage. As to *Annas/Agnes*, this problem cannot now be solved.

We now encounter the first Fyall but we know of Alexander and his wife Elspit Kee through the baptisms of their sons, Alexander and David:

OPR Anstruther Wester, Co Fife:
> '1673 March 24th Alexr. ffyall and Elspit Kee had a man child baptized called Alexr. witnesses John fferie Wm Broun & Alexr. ffyall'

OPR Anstruther Wester, Co Fife:
> '1674 May 4th Alexander ffyall and Elizabeth kea had a child baptized called David. Witnesses David Wilsone & David Williamsone'

Elspit/Elizabeth - the two names are interchangeable - may have been related to her in-law Margret Key. In other words, perhaps Elspit and Margret were sisters or cousins.

Annas and Alexander were married at Astruther Wester in 1699 and had six children. The baptism of their first child, Mary, shows that the first Alexander was still alive:

OPR Anstruther Easter, Co Fife:
> '1702 Octob: 10 Alexander ffyall and Anna Robertson in Anstruther Wester had a Laull [?[daughter bap called Mary: The wit: Alexander ffyall elder and James Red'

Their first son was born in 1705 and named Alexander but he must have died because a second child of that name was baptized in 1707:

OPRb/AnstrutherWester,Co Fife/403
> Septr 7th 1707 Alexr Fyall and Anna Robertson his Spouse had a Child born on ye 2nd day of this instant and baptized ye above named day called Alexr before these witnesses Alexr Fyall and David[?]Young'

The grandfather is still alive. I think we can conclude by this time that the original *Annas* was a mis-spelling for *Anna*.

Alexander Fyall married Jean Davidson on the 26th June 1737. Curiously, the bride's name is not mentioned on the IGI but her name may be safely inferred from the naming pattern of her grandchildren.
Forgan parish seems to have been rather lax in its documentation for Jean's mother's name is also missing from the record. Again the naming pattern of the following generation seems to give the clue.
Forgan parish, which now seems to exist only as a civil parish, lies on the south bank of the Tay, opposite Dundee.

Alexander and Jean are known to have had three children but as they were born between 1738 and 1753 it seems certain that some are missing from the records.
We have details of the baptism of the second child:

OPR St Monance, Co Fife (454/2) Baptisms
> '1745 February 17th John son of Alexr.Fyal & Jean Davidson Baptized February 17th'

John Fyal married Elspeth Hutt:

OPR St Monance Co Fife:
> '1780 December 11th John Fyal and Elspeth Hutt both in this parish were Contracted 9th and after due proclamation mar[rie]d December 11th being under Sailing orders was three times proclaimed on Sabbath 10th.'

Here is a snapshot of the times. Did Elspeth think she was pregnant? (No baby was born until a year later.) Certainly the proclamation *three times* on the day (a Sunday) after the Contract and a day before the Ceremony seems unusual. On the other hand, the extreme dangers of seafaring at that time meant that the opportunity of marriage had to be grasped whenever possible.

To catch up with Elspeth Hutt's ancestry we return to the 17th century.

First, Andrew Watt. His marriage is unrecorded and only offspring known was baptized on the 16th of November 1689 at St Monance. Elspeth, his daughter, married John Allan on the 18th November 1715. John himself was the son of John Allan and Jane Mathison:

OPR ST MONANCE, Co Fife:
> '1688 July ye 16 John Allan in St monnance had a Child Baptized Called John Before divers Witnesses'

His parents had been married on the 24th of December 1686 at St Monance.

As far as we know, John and Elspeth had only three children:

OPR ST MONANCE, Co Fife:
> '1717 July 7th John Son of John Allan & Elspeth Watt in Stmonance Baptized July 7th 1717'

This child must have died early because another was baptized with the same name in 1721:

OPR ST MONANCE,Co Fife:
> '1721 Septbr. 17th John Son of John Allan Elspeth Watt Baptized Septbr. 17th 1721'

Between these two Johns a girl, Elspeth, was born on the 29th of March 1719. She married Alexander Hutt on the 10th of November 1749 in St Monance (shown also on the IGI as 'Alexander Hull' - almost certainly a misreading.)

We know that Alexander and Elspeth had four children - there may have been more: John in 1750, Alexander in 1754, Elspeth in 1756 and Margaret in 1762.

It was Elspeth who married John Fyall, thereby becoming Sheila's ancestor. It was *her* daughter, another Elspeth, who married William Forgan, (see Chart 7) the father of Isabella (se Chart 5) who herself became the mother of Margaret Hutton, (see Chart 6) wife of the ill-fated John Butters (see Chart 1).

This has been a complex narrative but reference to the various charts should help to disentangle the plot.

Here we leave the Scottish side of Sheila's ancestry.

The Parishes

It is a paradox that, whereas I and other researchers have encountered great difficulty in establishing firm genealogical lines for the Parishes in the 19th century, work on their earlier ancestors has proved to be relatively straightforward. The story goes like this:

Sheila's mother, Louie Hephzibah Clara Parish, a lady with a lucid memory and a fruitful imagination, seems to have had no firm knowledge of her Parish ancestors before her grandfather, Charles Henry, who died in 1914, when she was five years old. Him she endowed with a number of stories which are so eccentric that they are probably true - except that many of them almost certainly refer to an earlier person, possibly her great-grandfather, George.

The main problem concerns the native county of Charles Henry/George. Louie was convinced that the family came from Ilfracombe, north Devon. She recounted a number of stories, the gist of them being that Charles or George had come to London during the 19th century, working his way as a journeyman plasterer. But when I investigated this version at the West Devon Record Office, Plymouth, about 1985, I discovered that historically there had been few if any persons named Parish in Ilfracombe in post-mediaeval times.

I finally decided that Louie had misheard; I found that some Parishes were living in the 19th century in Ilsington, near Newton Abbot, south Devon. A further complication emerged because in the late 19th century the Parishes found themselves in *Islington,* north London, inviting confusion or disassociation from Ilsington. A final cause for misunderstanding lies in the fact that in one of the 19th Census documents 'Islington' is mistakenly written for 'Ilsington'!

Further work at the Record Office in Plymouth established quite easily a descent from an ancestor named Friswid Downynge, married in Ilsington in July 1560 to John Ford and therefore born about 1535, around the time that parish registration was inaugurated, during the reign of Henry VIII. It is from there that we start.

Early Ancestors of the Parishes at Ilsington (1)

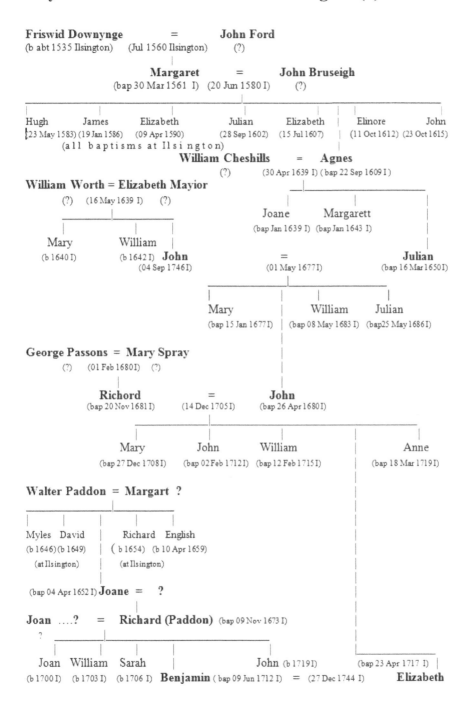

Friswid Downynge   =   John Ford
(b abt 1535 Ilsington) (Jul 1560 Ilsington) (?)

Margaret   =   John Bruseigh
(bap 30 Mar 1561 I) (20 Jun 1580 I) (?)

Hugh   James   Elizabeth   Julian   Elizabeth   Elinore   John
(23 May 1583) (19 Jan 1586) (09 Apr 1590) (28 Sep 1602) (15 Jul 1607) (11 Oct 1612) (23 Oct 1615)
(all baptisms at Ilsington)

William Cheshills   =   Agnes
(?)   (30 Apr 1639 I) (bap 22 Sep 1609 I)

William Worth = Elizabeth Mayior
(?)   (16 May 1639 I)   (?)

Joane   Margarett
(bap Jan 1639 I) (bap Jan 1643 I)

Mary   William
(b 1640 I)   (b 1642 I) **John**   =   **Julian**
            (04 Sep 1746 I) (01 May 1677 I) (bap 16 Mar 1650 I)

Mary   William Julian
(bap 15 Jan 1677 I) (bap 08 May 1683 I) (bap 25 May 1686 I)

George Passons = Mary Spray
(?)   (01 Feb 1680 I)   (?)

Richord   =   John
(bap 20 Nov 1681 I) (14 Dec 1705 I) (bap 26 Apr 1680 I)

Mary   John   William   Anne
(bap 27 Dec 1708 I) (bap 02 Feb 1712 I) (bap 12 Feb 1715 I) (bap 18 Mar 1719 I)

Walter Paddon = Margart ?

Myles David   Richard English
(b 1646) (b 1649)   (b 1654) (b 10 Apr 1659)
(at Ilsington)   (at Ilsington)

(bap 04 Apr 1652 I) **Joane** = ?

Joan ....? = Richard (Paddon) (bap 09 Nov 1673 I)
?

Joan William Sarah   John (b 1719 I)   (bap 23 Apr 1717 I)
(b 1700 I) (b 1703 I) (b 1706 I) **Benjamin** (bap 09 Jun 1712 I) = (27 Dec 1744 I)   **Elizabeth**

The two hundred years covered by this chart, from the institution in 1538 of parochial registration through thirteen reigns (plus the Commonwealth) from Henry VIII to George II, saw great changes.

In the same year that Thomas Cromwell ordered the institution of parish registers, holy relicts were being destroyed and monasteries sacked; rivals for Henry's throne were beheaded; heretics were burned at the stake and the Pope signed a Bull of Excommunication against Henry.

Thereafter, ancestors of the Parishes in Ilsington lived successively through the defeat of the Armada, the execution of Charles I, the English Civil War, the establishment of the Protestant Succession and the defeat of Bonnie Prince Charlie at Culloden.

Friswide Downynge, born about 1535, would not have been greatly affected by the momentous events taking place towards the end of Henry VIII's reign but her name raises an interesting story. The chronicler Holinshed (1529-1580), as part of a projected history of the world, wrote the following:

> *About this time [c 714], there was a maid in Oxford named Friswide, daughter to a certeine duke of noble man called Didanus, with whome one Algar a prince in these parties fell in loue and would have rauished hir, but God the revenger of sinnes was at hand (as the storie saith.) For when Algar followed the maid that fled before him, she getting into the towne, the gate was shut against him, and his sight also was suddenlie taken from him. But the maid by hir praiers pacified Gods wrath towards him, so that his sight was again restored to him. But*
> *[...]hether this be a fable or true tale, heereof grew the report, that the kinges of the realme long times after were afraid to enter into the citie of Oxford, so easilie is the mind of man turned to superstition (as saith Polydor.)*

It is certainly a fact that the name Friswide was popular as a Christian name in the late mediaeval times - over 120 baptisms are recorded on the IGI for the 16th and 17th centuries in Oxfordshire, for instance. For the whole of Great Britain the total exceeds 1800. In Ilsington the last (Friswood) appears in 1569 and as the surname is Forde she may be related to John Ford, who married our Friswide in 1562. An earlier Friswide is surnamed Laskie, a name which will appear in our next chart.

Two names, Julian (Bruseigh) and Richord (Passons), are shown in the parish register as female and these names (along with others) were in the 18th century were commonly given to both girls and boys.

'English' as a first name (English Paddon) is curious but not unique. The name is found quite frequently in southern Britain in the 17th and 18th centuries, mostly in Devon and Cornwall but also in the Home Counties.

The *surname* (as Inglis) is understandable in Scotland, perhaps to make a point about one's nationality; but as a first name, even in Cornwall, it seems eccentric.

266

Furthermore 'English Tredigo' as found in the register at Gerrans in 1781 is an inconsistency. I am still searching for an explanation of this puzzle.

Richard Paddon, the son of English Paddon's elder sister, Joane, seems to have taken his mother's name. Was he illegitimate? or was his unknown father another Paddon?

Some 25 years ago, when I was checking the marriage of William Worth and Elizabeth Mayior in the Ilsington Parish Registers, I came across a curious entry made in 1639. I subsequently discovered elsewhere other references to the event but below is the transcript I made at the time, with a few minor later emendations:

> *To the everlasting Prayse of God; in the memory*
> *of a most wonderfull Deliverance*

> *Over the west Gate of the Churchyard here in Ilsington there was a Room anciently built, about ten feet from yᵉ ground: sixteene feet in Length and twelve feet in breadth: the east and west side walls were about ten feet in*
> *hight: the covering was of slatt or shingle stones layd uppon fayre timber rafters about twelve feet in length.*
> *This room was lately converted to a schoolhouse whither there usually came neere to the numbᵣ of 30 scholler boyes:*
> *But September 17 being Tuesday Aᵒ 1639: the morning was wet [..?] wᵗʰ other exorations [= entreaties] [..?] kept some at home. Others to the number of seventeen were together at schoole wᵗʰ their schoolemaster neare upon eleven of the clock at wᶜʰ time the scholars ready to <u>dept</u> for dinner: a woman passed under neath and Lett the Gate being heavy fall too as formerly it had done: before shee was gone to a [..?] house about six yards from the place: part of the south stone wall wᶜʰ bore the Timber work of the Roofe slidd away: soe that the whole Roofe spead abroad, drove out both side walls east and west; and fell donne upon the flower of the Roome, not one stick stone or Pinn of the whole structure remaining where it was formerly placed:*
> *The schoole doore, wᶜʰ opened to the inside, was shutt when the house began to fall:*
> *Fower of the skollerboyes fell donne into the churchyard wᵗʰ the east side and escaped wᵗʰ little hurt One ran into the Chymny where he continued safe Some were stricken downe wᵗʰ Timber and stones wᶜʰ fell from over their heads*
> *The timber locked one boy fast in the middle of the room and when it was lifted up he Rose up and ran away; and wʰ was yet more wonderfull; another sweet child (called Humpry Degon) fell out wᵗʰ the east side wall into the rubbish so that no pt of his body or clothe appeared; there he lay for quarter of an hower spare or more; At length perceiving that child to be wanting a stricter search was made among the Lomber wᶜʰ fell into the Roome then seeking among the Rubbish wᶜʰ fell into the street; He was there happily found, and was taken up for dead in the Judgment of all that beheld Him*

But heat was not utterly gone, the Child recovered Life, is healthy and well and free from any Greife.

In this Accident and special demonstration of Gods Providence and Goodnesse in delivering from imminent Danger twelve had their heads cut and   broken: so that they Bless for it to mind them of the Danger they were in; but God wth their guard of Angels surrounded them soe that not a bone was broken nor a joynt displaced ; their wounds healed; and there is not any of them any wayes enfeebled from doing its [?] propper office as in former Times.

At the writing hereof they are all in health and soe living to Praise God for their Deliverance:

Here is a photograph of the modern replacement of the West Gate at Ilsington church:

Early Ancestors of the Parishes at Ilsington (2)

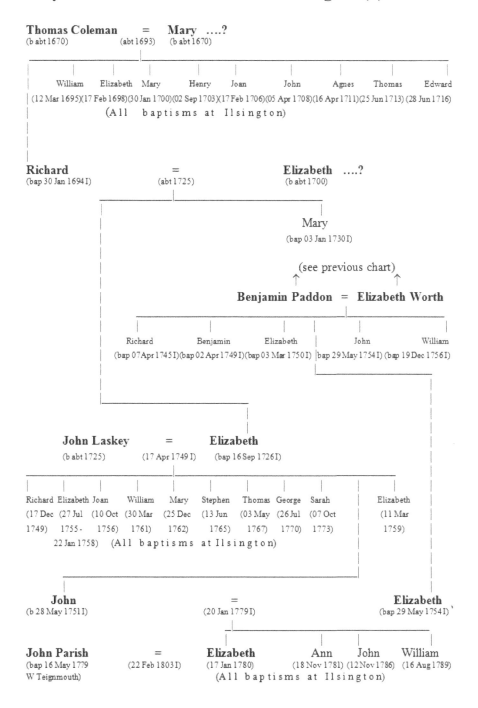

Thomas Coleman   =   Mary ....?
(b abt 1670)   (abt 1693)   (b abt 1670)

William	Elizabeth	Mary	Henry	Joan	John	Agnes	Thomas	Edward
(12 Mar 1695)	(17 Feb 1698)	(30 Jan 1700)	(02 Sep 1703)	(17 Feb 1706)	(05 Apr 1708)	(16 Apr 1711)	(25 Jun 1713)	(28 Jun 1716)

(All   baptisms   at   Ilsington)

Richard   =   Elizabeth ....?
(bap 30 Jan 1694 I)   (abt 1725)   (b abt 1700)

Mary
(bap 03 Jan 1730 I)

(see previous chart)

Benjamin Paddon = Elizabeth Worth

Richard	Benjamin	Elizabeth	John	William
(bap 07 Apr 1745 I)	(bap 02 Apr 1749 I)	(bap 03 Mar 1750 I)	(bap 29 May 1754 I)	(bap 19 Dec 1756 I)

John Laskey   =   Elizabeth
(b abt 1725)   (17 Apr 1749 I)   (bap 16 Sep 1726 I)

Richard	Elizabeth	Joan	William	Mary	Stephen	Thomas	George	Sarah	Elizabeth
(17 Dec 1749)	(27 Jul 1755- 22 Jan 1758)	(10 Oct 1756)	(30 Mar 1761)	(25 Dec 1762)	(13 Jun 1765)	(03 May 1767)	(26 Jul 1770)	(07 Oct 1773)	(11 Mar 1759)

(All   baptisms   at Ilsington)

John   =   Elizabeth
(b 28 May 1751 I)   (20 Jan 1779 I)   (bap 29 May 1754 I) '

John Parish	=	Elizabeth	Ann	John	William
(bap 16 May 1779 W Teignmouth)	(22 Feb 1803 I)	(17 Jan 1780)	(18 Nov 1781)	(12 Nov 1786)	(16 Aug 1789)

(All   baptisms   at   Ilsington)

As on the previous chart, the surnames of some early female spouses are unknown. This is usually because no record of a marriage has been discovered; the first name of the spouse has only been revealed on the IGI at the time of the baptism of her children. As distinct from the Scottish charts, the first names of previous generations cannot be safely deduced, as no set naming pattern was habitually followed. Furthermore, the model would be distorted if a baptism has not been recorded.

The ancestors of Benjamin Paddon and Elizabeth Worth and their marriage appear in detail on the previous chart.

The first Parish (John) appears only at the end of the chart and even this is a little speculative.   No firm and suitable ancestor for John Parish is evident from the IGI: there are several other candidates from neighbouring parishes, none secure.

But despite some earlier doubts, it seems to me that John Parish is almost certainly the ancestor of Sheila's mother and is the Parish who moved from Devon to London.

He first appears as the husband of Elizabeth Laskey, having come from the nearby parish of West Teignmouth, and is apparently found in London on the earliest (1841) Census, together with his family:

1841 Census:
HO 107/684/11
Cumberland Market, Marylebone, Middlesex:

Jno	Parish	60	Plasterer	no[t born in County]	
Jno	Parish	35	Plasterer	no[	do]
George	Parish	20	Plasterer	no[	do]
Wm[?]	Parish	[?]	[?]	[?]	[?]

John has also been found on the 1851 Census for St Marylebone Workhouse:

HO 107/1497
John Parish	Inmate	married	74	Plasterer	Devon	Plymouth

It seems likely that suggesting first West Teignmouth as his birthplace, he would have then given Plymouth as a better-known place.

Except in the case of children, ages in the 1841 Census were given to the nearest -5 or -0 and therefore a person born in 1779 could be reasonably shown in 1841 as being 60. In the 1851 and later Censuses ages were given as accurately as known.   In 1851 John would have been 72 - shown with acceptable divergence as 74.

In 1841 John junior would have been 38 and George 24, both ages reasonably consistent with the Census record.

As for William Parish, whose details are not recorded in the 1841 Census, he may be a son to John and Elizabeth Parish (née Laskey), who was baptized at St Edmund's Church, Exeter on 20 Dec 1818.

The Parishes in London

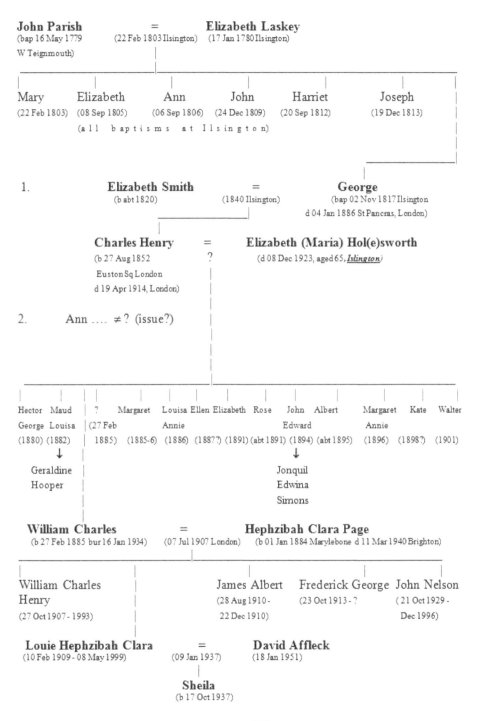

John Parish   =   **Elizabeth Laskey**
(bap 16 May 1779   (22 Feb 1803 Ilsington)   (17 Jan 1780 Ilsington)
W Teignmouth)

Mary	Elizabeth	Ann	John	Harriet	Joseph
(22 Feb 1803)	(08 Sep 1805)	(06 Sep 1806)	(24 Dec 1809)	(20 Sep 1812)	(19 Dec 1813)

(a l l   b a p t i s m s   a t   I l s i n g t o n)

1.   **Elizabeth Smith**   =   **George**
        (b abt 1820)   (1840 Ilsington)   (bap 02 Nov 1817 Ilsington
                                         d 04 Jan 1886 St Pancras, London)

        Charles Henry   =   **Elizabeth (Maria) Hol(e)sworth**
         (b 27 Aug 1852   ?   (d 08 Dec 1923, aged 65, *Islington*)
         Euston Sq London
         d 19 Apr 1914, London)

2.   Ann .... ≠ ? (issue?)

Hector George	Maud Louisa	?	Margaret (27 Feb	Louisa Annie	Ellen	Elizabeth	Rose	John Edward	Albert	Margaret Annie	Kate	Walter
(1880)	(1882)		1885)	(1885-6)	(1886)	(1887?)	(1891)	(abt 1891)	(1894)	(abt 1895)	(1896)	(1898?)	(1901)

    ↓   ↓

Geraldine   Jonquil
Hooper   Edwina
                                           Simons

William Charles   =   **Hephzibah Clara Page**
   (b 27 Feb 1885 bur 16 Jan 1934)   (07 Jul 1907 London)   (b 01 Jan 1884 Marylebone d 11 Mar 1940 Brighton)

William Charles Henry		James Albert	Frederick George	John Nelson
(27 Oct 1907 - 1993)		(28 Aug 1910 - 22 Dec 1910)	(23 Oct 1913 - ?	(21 Oct 1929 - Dec 1996)

Louie Hephzibah Clara   =   **David Affleck**
(10 Feb 1909 - 08 May 1999)   (09 Jan 1937)   (18 Jan 1951)

                       Sheila
                      (b 17 Oct 1937)

We now come to the most difficult, not to say contentious, section of the present story: the Parishes in 19th century London. I will return later to the evidence of Louie Parish; but there are a number of outstanding problems concerning George Parish:

First of all, there seem to have been several of the same name who were also plasterers living in north London in the mid-nineteenth century. Disposing of several of them, as potential candidates, because of age and origin, was fairly straightforward.
But the following entries raise doubts:

1851 Census Parish of St Pancras, Borough of Marylebone folio 771

Schedule 166   15 Mary St

Sarah Parish	H	Wid	67	Formery Lace Worker	Middlesex
Ellen Parish	Daur	U	24	Lace Worker	Devonshire Exeter
George Parish	Son	U	33	Plasterer	Middx
Charles	Son	U	22	Do	Do

[11 more people - 2 families - in the house]

[The Exeter birth for Ellen is interesting and might just support the previously known evidence.]

[The location of Mary St is at present unknown. It can hardly be the one in Islington since the Schedule states it is in the Borough of Marylebone.]

1861 Census
RG09/102/2/4/Pancras/Tottenham Court/St Johns/St Pancras/Marylebone

(London Street runs SE from Praed St, opposite Paddington Station)

PARISH, George	Head	M	M	41	Plasterer	St Pancras Middlesex
PARISH, Mary D [or A]	Wife	M	F	41		Bermondsey Middlesex
PARISH, George	Son	U	M	10		St Marylebone Middlesex
PARISH, Charles	Son		M			St Pancras Middlesex

These Censuses surely cannot both refer to the same family. 'Charles' in the 1861 Census might possibly be 'Charles Henry' born in 1852 and the age of 'George' senior in the same Census is acceptable (see above chart). But who is 'Mary D [or A]'?
And the address does not seem consistent with other entries.

Secondly, there is a profusion of wives. Already above we have two candidates. When Charles Henry was born in 1852 his mother was shown as Elizabeth Parish née Smith.

But the 1881 Census shows a different wife:

1881 London, St Pancras fiche ref 0200 82 25 1341 044
14 Drummond St

| George Parish | Head | U [?] | | 60 | M | Plasterer | MID Pancras |
| Ann Parish Wife | M [?] | | | 56 | F | | MID Pancras |

[The George Parish whose suicide is recorded was in Jan 1886 aged 69 (date of birth c1817).This age more or less agrees with the 1851 Census but is wrong for the 1881 Census, unless 60 means 60+. And unmarried?!]

272

Were the women shown above successively wives of one George Parish? Very unlikely.

At this point, however, reference should be made to the recognized notion that in mid-nineteenth century London fewer than half the working-class couples living together were in fact married. My own grandfather and grandmother Defty lived for nearly fifty as man and wife but were never in fact married - in their case because my grandfather was already had a lawful wife. In other cases there were doubtless many reasons for co-habitation but they are not particularly relevant to our discussion except to emphasise the possibility that our George may have moved from one partner to another, possibly because of the death of a previous one.

Turning now to the more positive evidence, we have first the birth certificate of Charles Henry:

'Twenty-seventh[?] August 1852 /39 Drummond Crescent/Charles Henry/Boy/
George Parish/Elizabeth Parish formerly Smith/Plasterer/E Parish Mother 39
Drummond Crescent Euston Square/Twenty-eighth September 1852/'

The 1881 Census address (14 Drummond St) is consistent with the birth of Charles Henry (39 Drummond Crescent). Until about 1893, Drummond Street ran in front of Euston Station and joined Drummond Crescent. That end of Drummond Street is now called Doric Way.

We *may* have confirmation of the marriage between George and Elizabeth.
The latest IGI shows this entry:

Husband

George PARISH   Pedigree

Birth:	1817	Ilsington, Devon, England
Christening:	02 NOV 1817	Ilsington, Devon, England
Marriage:	1840	Ilsington, Devon, England
Death:	04 JAN 1886	St Pancras London, , Devon, England
Burial:		

Wife

Elizabeth SMITH   Pedigree

Birth:	1820	Ilsington, Devon, England
Christening:		
Marriage:	1840	Ilsington, Devon, England
Death:		
Burial:		

Children

        None

273

The snag is that this entry has been submitted by a member of the Mormon Church and is not observably supported by official evidence. I would be inclined to suspect that this information is based on my own but for the fact that no children are reported. Unfortunately also the place of the marriage does not square with the 1841 Census on p 270 above. On the other hand, the date of George's death is correctly given.

Going back to the memories of Louie Hephzibah Clara Parish, we have the following:

- The Parish family came from Devon in the nineteenth century, specifically from Ilfracombe (but none found on the IGI - prefer Ilsington);
- They were plasterers/'mosaic artists' - ie laying of decorated floors;
- Charles Henry Parish worked his way to London, encountering a number of adventures. (He was actually born in London. It may have been his father, George, or grandfather, John, or both, who made the journey;)
- Louie remembered the outbreak of WW1 (at the age of 5);
- Although it is doubtful that she actually remembered the event she said that Charles Henry Parish was killed by a passing train. She was emphatic that it was not a case of suicide (see below);
- Louie correctly remembered many of the names of her father's brothers and sisters as well as those of their offspring.

Louie did not speak of the death of her great-grandfather Parish (see below). Although I knew of his suicide when talking to her, I refrained from referring to George. I am not even sure that she knew about him and I suspected that she would have denied he had taken his own life. I wish now that I had broached the subject if only to have obtained some sort of reaction.

Now for the death of George Parish. In this section particularly I am pleased to acknowledge the work of Geraldine Hooper, Sheila's second cousin. They are related in that William Parish, Sheila's grandfather, was the younger brother of Maud Louisa Parish, the grandmother of Geraldine, who has persevered in unearthing the facts surrounding the lives of Charles Henry Parish, his father, George and his grandfather, John. Geraldine has also been involved in our unsuccessful search for the ancestors of Elizabeth Holsworth(y). (See below.)

Here is the stark account of George's end:

Death cert: '4th Jan 1886, 46 Werrington Street/
George Parish/Male/69 years/Plasterer/Found Dead Syncope Haemorrhage.
Wounds in throat with razor.
Suicide unsound Mind/Certificate received from George Danford Norman Coroner for Middlesex.
Inquest held 6th January 1886/Eighth January 1886'

I tried for some years to get a report on the inquest, but it was Geraldine who eventually found a contemporary report in the local newspaper *The Guardian and Reporter* dated Jan. 9, 1886:

SAD CASE OF SUICIDE THROUGH
WANT

Dr Danford Thomas held an inquest on Wednesday at Crowndale Hall, touching the death of George Parish, aged 69, by trade a plasterer, living at No.46 Werrington-street, Oakley-square. Annie Parish, the widow, deposed that her husband had done no work for four years, owing to his suffering from dyspepsia and rheumatism. He had had outdoor relief from the parish for eighteen months; and they then offered him the infirmary, but this he had refused, and said he would sooner cut his throat than go into the workhouse. She told him on Monday she should be compelled to go to the workhouse, and he agreed that they both should go, and he would go the next morning and see Mr Moon, the relieving officer, to make arrangements for their removal. She then went out, and on her return at five o'clock she found him face downwards in a pool of blood, and the empty razor-case on the table. Dr. John Thompson, 70, Oakley-square, stated that he found the deceased as described, with an open razor close to him. He was dead and there was a wound in the throat, evidently self-inflicted, which commenced just past the left ear, reaching almost to the right, and completely severing the jugular vein, causing him to bleed to death. The jury returned the verdict of suicide when temporarily insane through dread of the workhouse.

We have already come across the Victorian workhouse in connection with Sarah Hammond (née Knight) and the frightful conditions of the Andover Workhouse; the terrible account above emphasises the fear which the working classes had of even the thought of entry into a workhouse.

The workhouse in question must have been the one which used to exist in the Euston Road almost opposite the present Quaker headquarters. Louie Affleck mentioned it to me several times, recollecting the old men who in her childhood used to sit on benches outside in the sun. Although she never referred to George Parish it is just possible that she had heard something of the story.

Geraldine Hooper tells me that George is buried at St Pancras cemetery, East Finchley, with unrelated people in a public grave no. 117, section T10.

There is probably now very little chance of being one hundred per sure that we have the correct ancestry of Charles Henry Parish; in particular, the parentage of Elizabeth Smith, if she was his mother, appears irretrievable.

Passing to the next generation we find more problems.

First, the surname of Elizabeth Holsworth. It appears as such generally, but on some of her children's birth certificates it is shown as 'Holesworth' - probably a clerical error. Then, 'Maria'. This appears once only: as a second christian name on her death certificate. Is it authentic? Probably not, if only because on the same certificate the person shown as present at her death, (her son, Albert?) erroneously gives her husband as Charles *William* Parish.

Next, it is frustrating that no record exists of a marriage between Elizabeth and Charles Henry because the certificate would have shown the names of her parents. At one time I thought that these were Henry John Holdsworth and Elizabeth Matilda Dolton and traced the two families to the early 19th century in Hampshire. There were, however, so many alternatives and consequent complications that, in consultation with Geraldine Hooper, I have had to admit defeat and leave the question open.

Finally, to make matters worse, Louie Parish used to maintain that Elizabeth's maiden name had been 'Page,' not 'Holsworthy.' She did, however, admit that she was probably confusing Elizabeth with Elizabeth's daughter-in-law, Hephzibah Clara Page. (See below.)

Louie Parish used to say that Charles Henry and Elizabeth had twenty children. I have managed to track down fourteen, including an unnamed child alleged to have been the twin of William Parish, Louie's father. These are named in the chart shown on p 271.

The 1881 Census shows Charles, Elizabeth and their first child, Hector, living in Netley Street, Marylebone. By 1891 the family has much increased; by 1901 three more children have arrived and there is only Walter to come. The family is now living at Denmark Rd in Islington.

1891 Census (RG12/118

St Pancras
Seaton Street (now Seaton Place?)

23 Seaton St

Charles	Parish	Head	M	40	Plasterer	Employed	London,	St Pancras
Elizabeth	do	Wife	M	30			do	do
Hector G	do	Son		11	Scholar		do	do
Maude L	do	Daur		9	do		do	do
Albert H	do	Son		7	do		do	do
William	do	Son		6	do		do	do
Louisa A	do	Daur		4			do	do
Nellie A	do	Daur		2			do	do
Elizabeth M	do	Daur		2 months			do	do

1901 Census:

15 Denmark Road

Charles Parish		Head	M	49	Plaster [sic]	Worker	St Pancras
Elisa	do	Wife	M	49 [? actually 41]			St Pancras
[Hector] George	do	Son	S	22	Coal Porter	Worker	St Pancras
Lizzie	do	Daur	S	16			St Pancras
Nellie	do	Daur	S	14			St Pancras
William	do	Son	S	17	Coal Boy	Worker	St Pancras
Rose	do	Daur		10			St Pancras
John	do	Son		7			St Pancras
Maggie	do	Daur		5			St Pancras
Kate	do	Daur		3			St Pancras

Names *in italics* appear on both Censuses.
By 1901 Maude and Albert appear to have left home, but it is possible that 'Lizzie' in the 1901 Census refers to Maud Louise.

276

I have not been able to obtain birth certificates for all the children.

As stated above, a marriage certificate for Charles and Elizabeth has also not been found. Louie Parish had an explanation for this: she maintained that Elizabeth was a Quaker and that simple promises were all that was required and that the Quaker Headquarters in the Euston Road might have a record of the marriage. I checked but there is none.
(For further comments on this subject, see below the chapter on *The Pages*.)

We must now deal with the tragedy of Charles Henry's death. Louie Parish told us that he had been killed by a train, having wandered somehow on to the track of the City and South London Railway. She sometimes spoke as if she remembered this incident but she was only five years old at the time. On the other hand, she does seem to have remembered the outbreak of the Great War, which occurred only a few months after Charles's death. She was most adamant that it was not a case of suicide.

This mystery was only finally settled recently when Geraldine Hooper unearthed the official reports.

First, here are the details found on the death certificate:

REGISTRATION DISTRICT LONDON CITY 1914 DEATH in the sub-district of ST. SEPULCHRE AND ALL HALLOWS in the COUNTY OF LONDON

No	When and Where died	Name and Surname	Sex	Age	Occupation	Cause of Death	Signature, Description and residence of Informant	When registered	Signature of registrar
240	Nineteenth April 1914 in ambulance on way to Saint Bartholomew's Hospital	Charles Henry Parish	Male	61 years	Plasterer of 31 Denmark Grove Barnsbury Road N	Shock, fractures of skull and ribs with other injuries by motor engine on City & South London Railway at Angel Station jury unable to determine how or why he came upon the railway	Certificate received from FJWaldo Coroner for London Inquest held 23 April 1914 P.M.	Twenty fourth April 1914	Annie J Kemm Registrar

In the following document, which gives evidence by Elizabeth her son, William, and a doctor it should be remembered that the stilted style of the narratives is the result of question and answer sessions.

Inquest touching the death of Charles Henry Parish, held at the Coroner's Court, Golden Lane, Barbican, in the parish of St Giles, Cripple gate, in the City of London, on Thursday 23rd April 1914, by Frederick Joseph Waldo Esq.

Deposition of Witnesses

Elizabeth Parish, 31 Denmark Grove
I am:- the wife
I identify the body now lying dead as that of my husband Charles Henry Parish, his age was 61 years and he was a plasterer, not done much work for 2 or 3 years. He used to work at Maple[s]. He was not healthy. He had pains in his feet and back. He had been

out of work since last November 1913. He lived with me. He had been in St. Mary's Infirmary, Islington for 6 or 7 weeks and had been home only one week. The pains in his feet he had had for years. He left home Sunday 19th April at 12:30 p.m. He said he felt pretty well. He was in good spirits. He said he was discharged from the Infirmary, I saw no difference in him. He was merely going out for a walk. Generally my boys take him but they had gone. I next heard from the police. I cannot account for his death and [he] had never attempted [to take] his life. He was not in want. My children helped. He had met with a cut head 20 years ago, he got over that. He seemed all right in his mind. I did not sleep with him - he slept fairly well - went to bed early. I cannot account for his death. He had no brothers or sisters alive - no insanity in the family. He seemed perfectly sane.

William Charles Parish deposed:
I am a Motor Driver and live at 31 Denmark Grove, 3rd [?] son of decd. I was with father Sat. night and   gave coppers. [?] At 11 till 12 next day he seemed all right. He had no trouble. He never wanted. We kept him. He had the pains in his feet. He had never attempted his life - sober man. I next heard he had been found on the railway at Islington and I saw his dead body here at this mortuary. I cannot account for his death. He had no delusions - no mental trouble. If anything he was very sharp. We made no appointment to meet him. Euston was his native place.
[Question] By Jury:
He made no complaint about his feet - he was more cheerful than ever that morning.
[Question] By Coroner:
Usually we went out together. My father knew that we went to Club Row [Animal market] If he was coming up to meet us he could come from the Angel station.

Ronald Ward deposed:
I am fully qualified and regd. H.S. at St. [Bartholomew's ?]
At 3:15 last Sunday I saw decd. quite recently dead and still warm. I made P.M. (see Report).   He had several corns on his feet and old scars on his shins. The injuries [presumably not those just mentioned] might be produced by an engine as suggested by evidence. No sign of poison. He died of his injuries - and shock from injury to brain.
[Question] By Jury:
He may have been struck full in the chest by engine and pushed along until he fell into pit.

A police constable's   General Report, which must have predated the Inquest, goes as follows:

Decd. was discharged from St Marys Infirmary Highgate on Saturday April 13th. where he had
been an inmate about 6 weeks suffering from bad & tender feet. He was a plasterer by trade but had had no regular employment for years. On Sunday April 19th. He left home about 12.30 pm. in his usual health & spirits, had no quarrel or words with any one. At about 2.20 pm. the same day Timothy Marfell the driver of a motor engine on the City and South London Railway on approaching the Angel Station going south & about 17 yards from the commencement of the platform i.e. 17 yards inside the tunnel he reported he felt his engine strike something. After the train had left the station a search was made & decd. was found lying in the pit between the metals in a line with the platform. A further search was made inside the tunnel where the driver had reported striking some object & distinct marks were discovered shewing decd. must have gone into the tunnel & laid himself down between the metals. The approaching train must have dragged decd. along the wooden gangway until the pit was reached when he dropped into it. There is not sufficient clearance between the gangway (between the metals) & the front of the engine to clear a persons [sic] body. Officials were summoned also the police & decd. was taken to St. Barts' Hospital where he

[was] examined by D^r. Ward who pronounced life extinct. The body was then conveyed to the Mortuary.

Dec^d. Had never been heard to threaten to take his life but his wife states he was sometimes depressed & suffered from general debility. The dec^d. possessed a ticket entitling him to travel either to the Bank or Euston.

There would have been a reluctance to say that Charles had taken his own life - which is why the death certificate gives no opinion as to the cause of death - because at that time there was still a stigma attached to suicide. He was buried in a public grave in Islington Cemetery: BG 15922. This indicates that no plot was purchased by the family and that other, unrelated, bodies are buried in the same grave. It has usually been common to add on the certificate that when a person took his own life 'the balance of his mind was disturbed' but no such comment seems to have been made in this case, indicating perhaps a real doubt as to the cause of death.

Elizabeth survived her husband by nearly ten years, dying in 1923:
Death cert of Elizabeth Holdsworth:

'Eigth [sic: modern transcribing error?] December 1923,   23 Richard Street Finsbury/Elizabeth Maria Parish/female/65 years/widow of Charles William [sic] PARISH Plasterer Journeyman/1. Asthma Bronchitis 2 years 2. Cardiac failure 2 days. Pulmonary congestion. 5 days. No PM. Certified by D.F.O Donoghue MB/ A.H Parish son Present at Death. 100 Wynford Road Islington/Tenth December 1923/H.M Comfort/'

The dedication reads: 'In loving memory of our dear mother Elizabeth Parish died December 8th 1923 age 63 years "At Rest"....'

(Death cert and cemetery book both give her age as 65.)

Later was added: '..also of Bill her son died Jan 12th 1934..'

This was William Charles, Louie's father. (See below.)

Louie used to say that her grandmother Elizabeth spoke with a 'country accent.' It is not clear quite what was meant by this except that she seems not to have been brought up in London. Here is photo of her, undated, supplied by Geraldine Hooper.

I have avoided the task of detailing all the descendents of Charles Parish and Elizabeth Holdsworthy. The resultant chart would be enormous and would in any case need constant revision.

The Page Family

After the Afflecks, the Butters and the Parishes, we come finally to the Pages, the family of Sheila's grandmother, Hephzibah Clara, who became the wife of William Parish.

There are two starting points: in the counties of Bedfordshire and Essex. Louie Parish was aware of both of these origins but the information she passed on to us was rather confused: she was quite clear that her grandmother Page had been born Lucy Mullin(g)s in Sible Hedingham; on the other hand she used to speak of James Page as coming sometimes from Essex (Marks Tey) and sometimes from Bedford(shire). However, the 1891 Census, which shows the whole Page family living at 27 Warren St, St Pancras, notes that James Page was born in Bedfordshire and I have decided that this represents the more likely option.

The Bedfordshire Connection

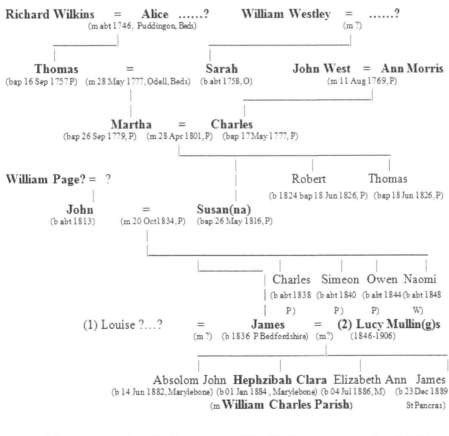

(NB Puddington = modern Podington;   W = Wollaston;   O = Odell.)

The earliest revealed members of this branch of the Page family seem to have come from the farthest north-west corner of Bedfordshire, Puddington and Odell, bordering the county of Northamptonshire. The two parishes are adjoining, Odell being the more southerly. This is still very much a rural, agricultural area.

As is quite common in early parish registers, the full name of the wife is often not recorded. Nothing much is known of the lives of these ancestors until we come to the nineteenth century, the parish records giving only the barest details.

1841 Census, HO107/8/12/13

Parish of Podington [sc Puddington] Bedfordshire:

John	Page	26		Ag Lab	Yes [born in county?]
Susan	Do	28			Yes
James	Do	6			Yes
Charles	Do	3			Yes
Simeon	Do	6 months			Yes
/William	Page	60		Ag Lab	Yes
Mary	Do	7			Yes
/					

In this first Census we have mention of the earliest known Page, William.

The forward slash indicates a change of household (within the same dwelling?) and so it looks as though William Page was John's father and that the 7-year old Mary (James's daughter?) was looking after him. Another possibility is that Mary was in fact William's own daughter.

1851 Census,   HO107/1743/187 Page 35,GSU

Wollaston, Hinwick End 155 (Northamptonshire)

John	Page	Head	Marr	39	Ag Lab	Beds	Poddington
Susan	do	Wife	Marr	38	Labs wife	Beds	do
James	do	Son	U	16	Ag Lab	do	do
Charles	do	Son	U	13	Ag Lab	Northampton	Wollaston
Simeon	do	Son	U	10		do	do
Owen	do	Son	-	7		do	do
Naomi	do	Daur	-	3		do	do

This is clearly the same family, which has now moved a few miles into Northants. John's age has been adjusted, his father, William, has presumably died and daughter Mary is elsewhere. Two more children have been born. An unusual name pattern has also emerged and this will be discussed later.

Turning now to the 1861 Census we find that there is no possible entry for James but the 1871 Census is informative:
1871 Census, Finsbury   RG 10 351 page 62

13 Old Compton St

James Page	Head	Married	34	Blacksmith	Bedford
Louisa do	Wife	Married	24		Berkshire

Here we are on firm ground. For the first time James is shown as a blacksmith. This we have known for some time, because Louie Parish had long maintained that he had a blacksmith shop at 1 Ridinghouse Lane, near the present BBC building, but long gone. She also said that he worked for the Army in what is now called Regents Park Barracks, Albany St. In the nineteenth century this was a cavalry barracks.
Louisa, shown as his wife, is so far unidentified. There is temptation to assume she is the 'Lucy' shown later, but this is unlikely.

James Page is not found on the 1881 Census but in 1891 he is shown with his whole family:

Census Return 1891. 20 St Pancras Fiche no 3
Schedule 479

'27 Warren St 1 inh house

James Page	Head	36 [sic]	Blacksmith	Employed	Bedfordshire
Harry Page	Son	15	Grinder's boy	Employed	London City
Lucy Page	Wife U [sic]	43			Headingham....?
[Absolom] John Page	Son	8		Scholar	Marylebone
[Hephzibah] Clara Page	Daur	6			do
Elizabeth [Ann] Page	Daur	4			do
James Page	Son	1			St Pancras

There are two anomalies here:
 In the first place, James, when asked for his age, apparently gave the year of his birth.
 Next, Lucy describes herself as 'unmarried.' Or perhaps James said so to the enumerator. Or perhaps the 'U' has become displaced from the previous line.
As we shall see later, Harry, whom James presumably adopted, was Lucy's child by another man.

James died in 1901, before the Census took place:

Death Cert: RD Pancras.   SD Kentish Town.   County of London

'127 /Second / James/ Male/ Blacksmith Cystisis /R.E.Lloyd
      /January / Page /64   (Journeyman) /Haematuria /Assistant Resident
      /1901   of   /Exhaustion / medical
      /St Pancras/   /12 Warren Street/   /Certified
      /Infirmary /   /St Pancras/   / by officer
                                                          R.E.Lloyd/Highgate
                                                          / Infirmary'

Louie Parish said she was told by her mother (Hephzibah) that James Page had a bad temper and that this was why he died of a stroke.

Another piece of information Louie gave to me was that James had been in the Crimean War (1853-1856). This is possible but I can find no documentary evidence to support it. One explanation may be that as a blacksmith he had been enrolled to serve with the cavalry. (He did subsequently work in Regents Park Barracks. See above.)

Early Essex and Suffolk Ancestors

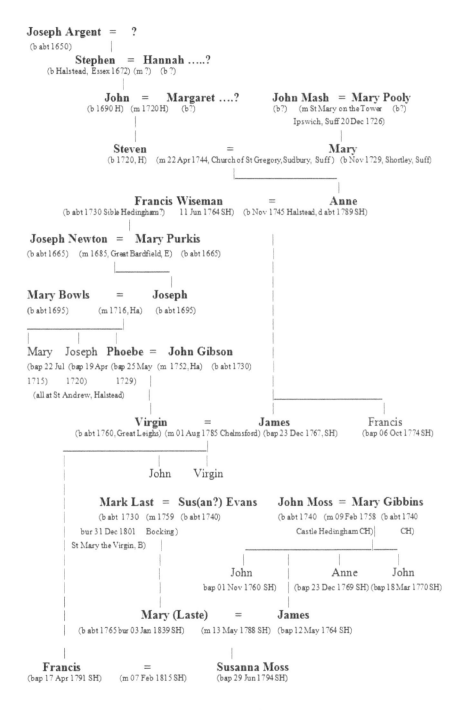

Joseph Argent = ?
(b abt 1650)

Stephen = **Hannah .....?**
(b Halstead, Essex 1672) (m ?) (b ?)

John = **Margaret ....?**   **John Mash** = **Mary Pooly**
(b 1690 H) (m 1720 H) (b?)   (b?) (m St Mary on the Tower (b?)
                                                          Ipswich, Suff 20 Dec 1726)

Steven   =   **Mary**
(b 1720, H) (m 22 Apr 1744, Church of St Gregory, Sudbury, Suff) (b Nov 1729, Shortley, Suff)

Francis Wiseman   =   **Anne**
(b abt 1730 Sible Hedingham?) 11 Jun 1764 SH) (b Nov 1745 Halstead, d abt 1789 SH)

Joseph Newton = **Mary Purkis**
(b abt 1665) (m 1685, Great Bardfield, E) (b abt 1665)

Mary Bowls   =   **Joseph**
(b abt 1695)   (m 1716, Ha) (b abt 1695)

Mary   **Joseph**   **Phoebe** = **John Gibson**
(bap 22 Jul (bap 19 Apr (bap 25 May (m 1752, Ha) (b abt 1730)
1715)   1720)   1729)
  (all at St Andrew, Halstead)

Virgin   =   **James**   **Francis**
(b abt 1760, Great Leighs) (m 01 Aug 1785 Chelmsford) (bap 23 Dec 1767, SH) (bap 06 Oct 1774 SH)

John   Virgin

Mark Last = **Sus(an?) Evans**   **John Moss** = **Mary Gibbins**
(b abt 1730 (m 1759 (b abt 1740)   (b abt 1740 (m 09 Feb 1758 (b abt 1740
bur 31 Dec 1801 Bocking)   Castle Hedingham CH)| CH)
St Mary the Virgin, B)

                                       John   **Anne**   **John**
                                  bap 01 Nov 1760 SH) (bap 23 Dec 1769 SH) (bap 18 Mar 1770 SH)

Mary (Laste)   =   **James**
(b abt 1765 bur 03 Jan 1839 SH)   (m 13 May 1788 SH) (bap 12 May 1764 SH)

Francis   =   **Susanna Moss**
(bap 17 Apr 1791 SH)   (m 07 Feb 1815 SH)   (bap 29 Jun 1794 SH)

This section chronicles the families living in Essex and the south of Suffolk from the seventeenth century to the nineteenth. There are two main areas of provenance: to the west of Essex - centred around Sible Hedingham: Castle Hedingham, Great Bardfield, Great Leighs, Chelmsford, Halstead, Bocking with Sudbury to the north; and to the east, including Ipswich and Shotley (Shortley). The distances concerned do not preclude connections between the families involved.

Of the first three Argents (Joseph, Stephen and John) nothing is known, except that they were born in Halstead, and when, their names appearing as mere statistics on the IGI (and therefore, from parish registers.) The wife of Joseph is unknown and the next two generations of women regrettably appear only as Hannah and Margaret, although the year of John's marriage to Margaret is given.
The next generation is more informative. Steven Argent goes to Sudbury, on the Essex-Suffolk border, to marry Mary Mash, whose parents, John Mash and Mary Pooly were from Ipswich. Anne Argent was baptized in Halstead.

At this point the Wisemans emerge from the shadows, probably originating in Sible Hedingham:

SIBLE HEDINGHAM marriages (No 112)   :
'Banns of Marriage were published between Francis Wiseman   & Anne Argent May 27, June 3, & 10 by me Alexr Cornwall Rector. The said Francis Wiseman of this Parish Batchelor   and [...] said Anne Argent Parish Spinster Married in this Church by Banns this eleventh Day of June in the Year Seventeen Hundred and Sixty-Four by me Alexr Cornwall Rector. This Marriage was solemnized between Us Francis X Wiseman
Anne X Argent In the Presence of John Lawrence   Thomas Abraham.'

In Boyd's Marriage Register they appear as 'Fran Wiseman' and 'An Argent'.
The 'Xs' indicate that neither party could sign a name.

We have two children born to Francis and Ann. There were probably others, for Anne lived until 1789 or 1798, whichever of the two given by Essex Family History Society is accepted.
James, the elder of the two known sons, married Virgin Gibson, for whose ancestry we must move back three generations.

Joseph Newton senior and Mary Purkis were married, according to Boyd, in 1685. This, however, is not confirmed by the IGI, and it is just possible that another IGI entry, Joseph Newton and Maryanne Maybee, married in 1674 at Halstead, may - with no intentional pun - be the true ancestors!
The next Joseph was probably born about 1685 but he was not baptized until he was 20. At that point, 8 Jul 1705, the parish entry specifies that this was an adult baptism, that Joseph was 20 years old and that the parents were Joseph Newton and Mary. The ceremony took place at St Andrew's, Halstead.

Joseph (junior), according to Boyd, married Mary Bowls in 1716. We know of three of their children: Mary, Joseph and Phoebe. This last child married John Gibson at Halstead in 1752, again according to Boyd and the only child we know about is called Virgin. It was she who married James Wiseman in 1785.

'James WISEMAN of this Parish [Sible Hedingham]& Virgin GIBSON of Gt Leigh by Banns 1st Aug 1785 [Neither could sign] Wits Chamberlain H[ICK?]MAN Saml. COWLAND.'

There is further information on this couple:

1841 Census: HO/107/332/8

Sible Hedingham

Swan Street
'1 inhabited :
Virgin Wiseman   78 [age]   Y   [born in county]'

The age is incorrect but such figures are unreliable in the early censuses.

SIBLE HEDINGHAM Burials: 'Virgin Wiseman of Swan Street 1848 September, 88.'

The final figure gives her age.

SIBLE HEDINGHAM Burial Register: 'James Wiseman of Swan Street 1828 May 4, 61'

Again, the final figure is his age at death.

James and Virgin Wiseman had at least three children: Francis, John and Virgin. It is the first who is Sheila's ancestor but before moving on we must again wind back to find out about the family of Francis's wife, Susanna Moss.

John Moss appears to have come from Castle Hedingham. It lies very close to Sible Hedingham. They were certainly married there. Their children included two Johns, the first of whom must have died young, Anne and James. All four were baptized at Sible Hedingham.

Mark Last and Sus(an?) Evans of Bocking, were married in 1769. Mark lived to a good age for the time - about 71 years.   Mary too had a long life:

SIBLE HEDINGHAM Burials: 'Mary Moss of Gormandey [?] 1839 Jan 3, 79.'

The location of 'Gormandey' is not at present known. It is probably a corruption. When James Moss was 24 he married Mary Last(e):

287

'SIBLE HEDINGHAM [no538] James MOSS of this parish & Mary LAST of this Parish by Banns 13 MAY 1788 [he signs; she X] Wits thomas LOCKE John DAINS.'

Only one child is known from this marriage:
29 Jun 1794 Sible Hedingham Bapt Register: 'Susan[na], of James and Mary Moss.'

Essex Ancestors in the Nineteenth Century

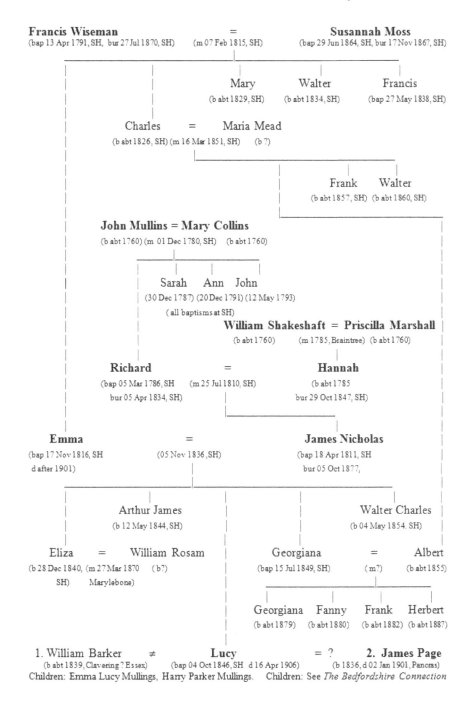

Francis Wiseman   =   **Susannah Moss**
(bap 13 Apr 1791, SH, bur 27 Jul 1870, SH)   (m 07 Feb 1815, SH)   (bap 29 Jun 1864, SH, bur 17 Nov 1867, SH)

Mary   Walter   Francis
(b abt 1829, SH)   (b abt 1834, SH)   (bap 27 May 1838, SH)

Charles   =   Maria Mead
(b abt 1826, SH) (m 16 Mar 1851, SH)   (b ?)

Frank   Walter
(b abt 1857, SH)   (b abt 1860, SH)

John Mullins = Mary Collins
(b abt 1760) (m 01 Dec 1780, SH)   (b abt 1760)

Sarah   Ann   John
(30 Dec 1787) (20 Dec 1791) (12 May 1793)
(all baptisms at SH)

William Shakeshaft = Priscilla Marshall
(b abt 1760)   (m 1785, Braintree) (b abt 1760)

Richard   =   **Hannah**
(bap 05 Mar 1786, SH   (m 25 Jul 1810, SH)   (b abt 1785
bur 05 Apr 1834, SH)   bur 29 Oct 1847, SH)

Emma   =   **James Nicholas**
(bap 17 Nov 1816, SH   (05 Nov 1836, SH)   (bap 18 Apr 1811, SH
d after 1901)   bur 05 Oct 1877,

Arthur James   Walter Charles
(b 12 May 1844, SH)   (b 04 May 1854. SH)

Eliza   =   William Rosam   Georgiana   =   Albert
(b 28 Dec 1840, (m 27 Mar 1870   (b ?)   (bap 15 Jul 1849, SH)   (m ?)   (b abt 1855)
SH)   Marylebone)

Georgiana   Fanny   Frank   Herbert
(b abt 1879)   (b abt 1880)   (b abt 1882) (b abt 1887)

1. William Barker   ≠   **Lucy**   = ?   **2. James Page**
(b abt 1839, Clavering ? Essex)   (bap 04 Oct 1846, SH d 16 Apr 1906)   (b 1836, d 02 Jan 1901, Pancras)
Children: Emma Lucy Mullings, Harry Parker Mullings.   Children: See *The Bedfordshire Connection*

This section begins with events in the second half of the eighteenth century.
In 1785 William Shakeshaft and Pris[cilla] Marshall were married at Braintree. This information comes from Boyd's Marriage Register and nothing else is known of them, except that they had a daughter, Hannah, about 1785. Hannah married Richard Mullen in 1810, by which time, according to Boyd, her name appears as Shakeshaw. This latter is almost certainly an error, because that name is not otherwise found; whereas Shakeshaft, like Shakelance and Shakespeare, are not infrequent.

Richard Mullen was one of at least four children born to John Mullins and Mary Collins:

D/P 93/1/6 (SIBLE HEDINGHAM) 'Banns of Marriage between John Mullins & *Sarah* [!?] Collins were publish'd October 29 & Novr 5 & 12...John Mullins of this Parish and Mary Collins of this Parish...Married in this Church by Banns this 1st
Day of Decr in the year 1780 [words] by me J Baldwin Pugh Rectr..This
Marriage was solemnized between us John Mullins   X
                                                        Mary Collins   X
In the presence of Phili [?] Sarjeant   John Bains [?] '

(I have found that parish registers abound in such discrepancies as in the above.)

SIBLE HEDINGHAM baptisms: 'Baptisms 1786....Richard of John and Mary Mullins March 5th.'

Hannah Shakeshaft and Richard Mullen were married in 1810 and we know of only one child, James Nicholas.

Richard died in 1834 and his age at death confirms his birth year:

   SIBLE HEDINGHAM Burials: 'Richard Mullens of Church Street 1834 Apr 5, 48.'

Hannah appears on the 1841 Census as a 'dealer'. She died six years later:

SIBLE HEDINGHAM Burials: 'Hannah Mullings of Church Street 1847 Oct 29, 59.'

We return now to Francis and Susanna Wiseman, whom we left in the last section.
In the nineteenth century parish records tend to be more informative: not only because there is now an increase in literacy but because parish priests have designated books in which they keep more accurate details. In addition, from 1837 Statutory Registration of Births, Marriages and Deaths provides more reliable information. Finally, from 1841 there are the decennial Censuses to draw upon.

First, the marriage between Francis and Susannah:

'Marriage solemnised in the parish of Sible Hedingham in the county of Essex
in the year 1815   Francis Wiseman of this Parish and Susan Moss of this Parish

were married in this Church by Banns this seventh day of February in the year 1815 [words] by me James Filewood, Rector. This marriage was solemnised between us Francis Wiseman [mark] Susan Moss [mark] In the presence of Elizabeth Smith' Clearly neither Francis nor Susan could write their names.

Next the relevant Censuses.

1851 Census Return for SIBLE HEADINGHAM   HO 107/1784 Folio 427
'Swan Street

Francis Wiseman	H	Mar	60	Gardener	Essex	Sible Headingham
Susannah Wiseman	Wife	Mar	56			"
Mary Wiseman	Daur		22	Platter [sic]		"
Walter Wiseman	Son		17	Boot & Shoe Maker		"
Francis Wiseman	Son		13			"

Note that 'Hedingham' is misspelt, as is 'Plaiter'. Mary was probably a straw-hat maker. The two eldest children, Emma and Charles, have left home.

Census Return for 1861:

Schedule 228
Swan St   1

Francis Wiseman	Head	Mar	71	Greengroce	Essex	Sible Hedingham
Susannah Wiseman	Wife	Mar	63		do	Sible Hedingham
Eliza Mullings	GrandDaur	Un	20	General Servant	do	Sible Hedingham
Georgiana Mullings	GrandDaur		11	Scholar	do	Sible Hedingham'

In the 1861 Census Susanna is incorrectly shown as aged 63. The figure should be 66. Francis now has had a change of occupation. He is a greengrocer. Perhaps he was still also a gardener. The three remaining children in the 1851 Census - Mary, Walter and Francis - have now also moved on. Instead, we have two grandchildren, both daughters of Emma: Eliza and Georgiana. Eliza is shown as a servant; it is not clear whether she is looking after her grandparents or whether she is a living-out servant of another family.

Emma had been shown elsewhere on the 1851 Census:

1851 Census:

Sible Headingham Folio 463,   pp7&8

'Schedule 31
Cobbs

James Mullings	Head	Mar	40	Ag Lab	Essex	Sible Hedingham
Emma	do	Wife	Mar	36	Dress Maker	do	do
Eliza	do	Daur	Unm	10	Scholar	do	do
Arthur	do	Son		6	do	do	do
Lucy	do	Daur		4		Essex	Sible Hedingham
Georgiana	do	Daur		1	do	do	do'

Emma had married James Mullings in 1836:

'Marriage solemnised in the parish of Sible Hedingham in the county of Essex in the year 1836

> *James Mullings of this Parish, Bachelor and*
> *Emma Wiseman of this Parish, Spinster*

were married in this Church by Banns
this Fifth day of November in the year one thousand eight hundred and thirty-six by me,
Henry Warburton, Rect'r

> *This marriage was (James Mellens [sic] [signed] [cf childrens' birth certificates]*
> *solemnised between us (Emma Wiseman [mark]*
> *In the presence of   (Thomas Mullings [mark] (Mary Palmer [mark]'*

The couple are shown on the 1841 Census with their first child:

1841 Census:HO 107/332/8

Sible Hedingham, Cobbs

1 inhabited house

James Mullings	30		Ag lab	Y [born in County]
Emma Mullings		22		Y
Eliza Mullings		6 mths		Y

Here is modern photograph of Cobbs, a farm south of Sible Hedingham, showing a cottage which the Mullings family may have shared with other families in 1841.

By 1881 Georgiana, Emma's youngest daughter, has married Albert Wiseman (presumably a cousin) and has 2 children:

1881 Census (Indexed Return) for Marylebone:

0133 121 27

'London St Marylebone, 19 Castle St E[ast]

Wiseman Albert   Head M   26   M Printers Labo   Essex   Sible Hedingham
Wiseman Georgina   Wife   M   31 F Formly [sic] Genera[l Servan] [sic]   Essex   Sible Hedingham
Wiseman Georgina   Daur   -   2   F -   Middlesex Marylebone
Wiseman Fanny   Daur   -   1   F   -   Middlesex Marylebone'

and in 1901the family is again found:

 1901 Census RG13/137 Folio? p18

'St Pancras (part of) Ecclesiastical Parish of All Saints (part of)

11 Mortimer Market

Albert Wiseman Head M 46 Railway Cab....'? [Worker] Essex Little [sic] Hedingham
Georgina do Wife M 49 Essex do
Fanny do Daur S 21 Military [Milinery?]
Embroidery do at home London, Marylebone
Frank do Son S 19 Blacksmith do do St Pancras
Herbert do Son S 14 ....? Worker do do'

6 others in the house

But to return to James Mullings and Emma Wiseman.
James probably died in Halstead and was buried at Sible Hedingham on 5 October 1877.
His place of death seems to confirm the implication of the 1861 Census that he and Emma
had parted:

1861 Census Sible Hedingham p34

'Schedule 224 Swan St
Emma Mullings Head Mar 43 Dressmaker Essex Sible Hedingham
Arthur Mullings Son Un 17 Agricultural Labourer do Sible Hedingham
Walter Mullings Son 6 Scholar do Sible Hedingham

Emma, shown as married and head of household, is now living very close to her parents.

Ten years later she has moved with her sons to London:

1871 Census:

Marylebone Folio 31, p55

'Schedule 322

30 Castle S[treet] E[ast]

Frederick Osborne Head Mar 50 Coachman Essex Gosfield
Emma do Wife Mar 54 do Sible Hedingham
Walter do Son Unm 16 Groom do do
Arthur Mullings Son in law Unm 27 Carman do do
Lucy do Dau in law Unm 24 do do
William Barker Boarder Unm 22 Carman do Clearlandling[??]'

(NB 'Son/Daughter-in-law' commonly meant 'step-son/daughter.')
There are some interesting pointers in this Census. We do not know who Frederick
Osborne was but Gosfield is only a few miles from Sible Hedingham, so he probably met
Emma in Essex and they moved to London from there. In 1871 James Mullings was still
alive so Frederick and Emma could not have been married.

The status of Emma's two sons is interesting. Frederick seems to have 'adopted' Walter, perhaps because he was still legally a minor. Arthur, on the other hand, has shown his independence by retaining his father's name, Mullings. As has Lucy.

Lastly, the lodger, also from Essex. William Barker claims to have been born in what appears to be 'Clearhandling.' But there is no such place. I suggest 'Clavering', which is well to the west, less than mile from the Hertfordshire border. William is to figure large in Lucy's life.

The exact occupations of the males are not certain, but it seems they might all have been involved in a haulage business.

The 1881 Census has more curiosities:

1881 Census   (from Indexed Version 0133 124 33 1341030)

'Ldn, St Marylebone
30 Castle St E[ast]

| Osborne Thomas | Head | M | 56 | M | Coachman | Essex Hedingham |
| Osborne Emma | Wife | M | 59 | F | - | Essex Hedingham |

Different household at same address

Mullings Charles	Lodger	M	25	M	Labourer	Essex Hedingham
Mullings Harry	Son	-	5	M	Scholar	Middlesex Marylebone
Barkes [sic] William	Lodger	U	30	M	Coachman	Essex	-	'

The address is the same but the husband seems different! Other oddities, however, suggest that this is an error of transcription: some of the ages are incorrect; Barker has become Barkes.

Walter (Charles) Mullings is now known as Charles. Harry Mullings *appears* to be Charles's son but we shall see that that is not so.

When Emma died is not known but she is found on the 1901 Census. Living with her are her widowed daughter Eliza (in fact aged 61) and her granddaughter, Emma, (daughter of Lucy Mullings)

Judging from the number of families in 22 Warren St it was well named!

As we shall see later, Lucy herself was at this time (ie 1901) living a few doors away in no12.

1901 Census: RG13/137 Folio 36 p 17

'London, St Pancras part of Ecclesiatical Parish of St John the Evangelist

22 Warren St [other occupants: mother and two daughters, all ballet dancers]

Emma Mullins	Head	Widow	84		Essex,	Sible Hedingham
Eliza Rosam +	Daur	Widow	52		do	do
Emma Mullins	Niece *	S	25		London,	Marylebone
Thomas Baily	Boarder	S	47	Porter (Corn) Worker	Middlesex,	Pinner

+ Eliza Mullings had married a William Rosam in 1870.
* meaning granddaughter.

Two other households, one including a music stamper (printer) '

We now turn to Emma's daughter, Lucy Mullings.
She was born at Cobbs, a settlement just south of Sible Hedingham. A few years ago, Sheila, David, the twins and I visited the area and found a substantial dwelling-house, dating from the early nineteenth century. According to the present owners, this building originally housed several families and it is thought that it may have been the home of the Mullings.
We have already seen above that Lucy is found, aged 4, with her family on the 1851 Census, but ten years later she appears to have moved on, possibly to London. By 1871 she is back with her mother and the new family, now in Marylebone. (See p 294 above.) We have already noticed the appearance of the lodger, William Barker.

We shall now revisit the 1881 Census.
First of all Emma (Mullings/Osborne):

1881 Census   (from Indexed Version 0133 124 33 1341030)

'Ldn, St Marylebone
30 Castle St E[ast]

Osborne Thomas	Head	M	56	M	Coachman	Essex Hedingham
Osborne Emma	Wife	M	59	F	-	Essex Hedingham

Different household at same address

Mullings Charles	Lodger	M	25	M	Labourer	Essex Hedingham
Mullings Harry	Son	-	5	M	Scholar	Middlesex Marylebone
Barkes [sic] William	Lodger	U	30	M	Coachman	Essex - '

Now her daughter Lucy:

1881 Census Return Fiche 0136   66   34:   [3/4 APR 1881]
'London St Marylebone

296

12 Clipstone St [part of the house, which lay very close to 30 Castle St E]
Mullings Lucy Head U 34 F   Dressmaker   Essex Headingham
   do   Emma Daur - 9 F   Mid   Marylebone

It took me some time to sort out the relationships between the persons shown.
I shall start with Emma Mullings, aged 9 and daughter of Lucy. Here are the details of her
birth certificate:

No	When and where born	Name, if any	Sex	Name and surname of father	Name, surname and maiden surname of mother	Occupation of father	Signature, description and residence of informant	When registered	Signature of Registrar
237	Twentieth August 1871 51 Castle Street East	Emma Lucy	Girl	-	Lucy Mullings	-	x the mark of Lucy Mullings 51, Castle Street East, Marylebone	Eighteenth September 1871	John H Hickson Deputy Registrar

No father's name is given and Lucy is clearly a single woman. Was William Barker the
father, as it seems he was of Harry a few years later? We cannot be sure, but it seems likely:
in 1871 but they were living in the same house.

Three and a half years later 'Harry Parker's' birth is registered:

'Registration District St Marylebone
1875. Birth in the Sub-district of All Souls in the County of Middlesex

No	When and where born	Name, if any	Sex	Name and surname of father	Name, surname and maiden surname of mother	Occupation of father	Signature, description of informant	When registered	Signature of registrar
309	Third March 1875 30 Castle Street East	Harry Parker	Boy	James MULLINGS	Lucy MULLINGS formerly WISEMAN	Carman Piano-forte Makers	Lucy Mullings Mother 30 Castle Street East Marylebone'	Twelfth April 1875	J Cawston

This really is an alarming document.
In the first place, the boy's name 'Harry Parker' (sc Barker?)   would suggest that William
Barker was his father. But James Mullings was Lucy's own father! This entry is most
disturbing until we see that in the next column Lucy has given her own mother's maiden
name as her own. To understand all this, picture the scene at Mr Cawston's office. Lucy,
who could not write, wearing her best hat and speaking with a strong Essex accent, is
confronted by an imposing official:

'What is the child's name?'
'Harry Barker, sir.' [Thereby revealing the father's name as a Harry's second forename.]
'Father's name?'
[Thinking he means her own father] 'James Mullings.'
'Mother's maiden name?'
[Similar thought process] 'Wiseman.'

297

Thus the registrar thinks Mrs Mullings is registering the birth of a child named Harry Parker and that Mrs Mullings used to be called Wiseman. She (unwittingly?) avoids the stigma of having no father's name for her child (for at that time on the birth certificates of illegitimate children no father's name was given.) Total confusion for the family historian 150 years later!

Moving on to the 1891 Census we find, still in the Marylebone/St Pancras area:

Census Return 1891. 20 St Pancras Fiche no 3
Schedule 479

'27 Warren St 1 inh house

James Page	Head M	36 [sic]	Blacksmith	Employed	Bedfordshire
Harry Page	Son	15	Grinder's boy	Employed	London City
Lucy Page	Wife U [sic]	43			Headingham....?
[Absolom] John Page	Son	8	Scholar		Marylebone
[Hephzibah] Clara Page	Daur	6			do
Elizabeth [Ann] Page	Daur	4			do
James Page	Son	1			St Pancras'

This is the Census first shown on p 283 of this document. As we saw earlier, there are some anomalies.

Lucy Mullings is now living with James Page but paradoxically she is shown both as 'wife' and 'unmarried'! James has given his year of birth instead of his age. Harry has been placed before Lucy as if he were James's son but we now know that this is almost certainly not the case. The other entries are recognisable.

How do we know this Lucy Page is the Lucy Mullings we have been dealing with?
First, there is the evidence of Sheila's mother, who remembered all the children as uncles and aunts, except for Harry, who is alleged to have died young. Hephzibah Clara, Louie Parish's own mother, told her that Lucy came from Sible Hedingham.
Secondly, we have the evidence of three birth certificates: those of Absolom John, Hephzibah Clara and James. On all three the mother is shown as 'Lucy Page, late Barker[!], formerly Mullings.'

There are two more anomalies:
Absolom John was born on 14 June 1882. His father is shown as James Page. If he really was James's son, and conceived in September 1881, this is only six months after Lucy was living alone with her nine-year old daughter, Emma, in Clipstone Street. Where and when did she meet James Page? The 1891 Census states that he was born in Bedfordshire and Louie Parish long affirmed that this was so. But she also had another story that James came from Marks Tey, in Essex. Is that where he met Lucy in late 1881? Or is 'Marks Tey' a corruption of a place-name as yet unidentified?

Secondly, one more mystery: Elizabeth Ann Page's death certificate in 1971 gives a precise date of birth: 4 July 1886, in Marylebone. No birth certificate for her has yet been found. Is she registered under another name - perhaps Mullings?

Ten years later what remains of the family is still in Warren St, but at number 12.

1901 Census   1379/46

12 Warren St

N/K Page	Head	Wid	49	Charwoman	Worker	Essex	N/K
Harry do	Son	S	26	Timber Porter	do	London St Pancras	
Clara do	Daur		17	Envelope Packer	do	do	do
Elizabeth do	Daur		14	do	do	do	do
James do	Son		11			do	do

We know that Absolom John was in the Army.

The 'N/Ks' ('not known') in line 1 are very peculiar.   The entry must certainly refer to Lucy Mullings, the late James Page's wife. But who gave the answers? Surely everyone in the household knew her first name, even if they did not know where in Essex she was born.

James Page (senior) had died in 1901.

Death Cert: RD Pancras. SD Kentish Town.County of London
'127/Second   /James/Male/Blacksmith   /Cystisis   /R.E.Lloyd
    /January   /Page /64 /(Journeyman)   /Haematuria /Assistant Resident
    /1901   /   of   /Exhaustion /medical
    /St Pancras/   /   /12 Warren Street /Certified by /officer
    /Infirmary /   /   /   St Pancras   /R.E.Lloyd /Highgate Infirmary

Lucy lived on until 16 April 1906, dying of breast cancer:

Death cert:

'119   /Sixteenth April/Female/ Widow of / Carcinoma / E.A.Page /Seventeenth
        /1906 /   /James Page / (Mammary)/ Daughter /April
        / 69 Stanhope /   /a Blacksmith /Exhaustion / Present /1906
         Street   /   /(Journeyman) /Certified   /at the death /
        /69 StanhopeSt/ 59 years/   by M.J.Corbet'

Poor Lucy: she must have had a hard, stressful yet eventful life; perhaps she was typical of the women who came to London in the second half of the nineteenth century, seeking a better existence than she had had in the country, where agricultural depression was hitting rural living.

As regards the children of James and Lucy, we have limited information, partly because of family disagreements, accounts of which were passed on to us by Sheila's mother.

Absolom married some time after Lucy died and had at least five children. It is not known how long he stayed in the army.

Hephzibah Clara was of course Sheila's grandmother. We have a poor quality snap of her holding a goldfish bowl.

Elizabeth Ann was a source of strife in the family. She married and had at least one daughter. She died in hospital on the Isle of Wight in 1970.

James was in the army (before 1914?) and was badly wounded at Gallipoli. He stayed at the home of William Charles Parish and was the cause of many rows because he found it difficult to hold down jobs and would stay at home in bed. He expected Louie Parish to get his meals when she came home from work. He was finally evicted when William came home unexpectedly at midday and found him still in bed. He never married.

Finally, let us return to the question of the Christian names given to children in the Page family. We saw there a use of unusual biblical names (shown below in *italics*):

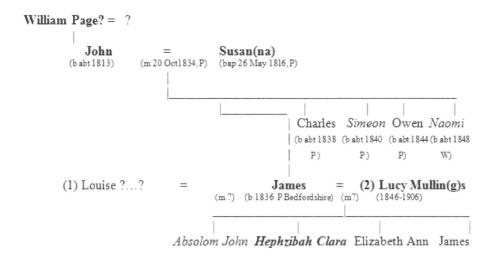

Unfortunately evidence is lacking from earlier Pages. Louie Parish was convinced that there were Quakers in the family and that that accounted for some lack of evidence for conventional marriages. On p 277 of the chapter *The Parishes* I described how I visited the Headquarters of the Quakers in Euston road and the negative result of this enquiry indicates that a Quaker source may be discounted. My judgement now is that as there were many non-conformist establishments both in Bedfordshire and in Essex, the use of these biblical names may be attributed to attendance at these churches.

We have come to the end.

Lightning Source UK Ltd.
Milton Keynes UK
UKOW07f1130310715

256090UK00012B/15/P